HIGH ALTITUDE

HIGH ALTITUDE

by

MIKE ALLSOP

ALLEN&UNWIN
SYDNEY • MELBOURNE • AUCKLAND • LONDON

This edition published in 2014

First published in 2013
Copyright © Mike Allsop 2013

Allen & Unwin
Level 3, 228 Queen Street
Auckland 1010, New Zealand
Phone: (64 9) 377 3800
83 Alexander Street
Crows Nest NSW 2065, Australia
Phone: (61 2) 8425 0100
Email: info@allenandunwin.com
Web: www.allenandunwin.com

A catalogue record for this book is available
from the National Library of New Zealand

ISBN 978 1 87750 545 4

Set in Adobe Caslon by Midland Typesetters, Australia
Printed and bound in Australia by McPherson's Printing Group, Maryborough Victoria

10 9 8 7 6 5 4 3 2 1

This book is dedicated to beautiful Wendy.

CONTENTS

PROLOGUE

I clicked the transmit button on the control column to tell the Coast Guard pilot, 'This is it, we're going in!' The words never came out. Instead what emerged was a sound I had never heard before – a scream, a spine-chilling scream of death. I remember being shocked when I realised the noise was coming from me as the aircraft I was flying nose-dived into the sea.

My seat snapped off its rails and I was pinned against the instrument panel with the control column smashing into my right ribs. My head was pinned back against the head rest and my jaw was locked open by the force of the deacceleration I had been practising for my focus point before we ditched but as I tried to find it nothing made sense. I scratched at the metal pillar of the aircraft trying to get out, all the time swallowing and swallowing sea water.

Everything was so dark and the noise of the impact didn't seem to stop. I couldn't hold my breath any longer when a thought came into my head. 'Take a breath of water and you'll be relaxed.' Then another thought followed: 'This is what it's like to die. Just take a breath of water and you will be so relaxed!' The muscles in my chest cavity relaxed and I inhaled …

It had always been my dream to be an Air New Zealand pilot and I managed to get a foot in the door in the industry when I purchased a type rating (training course) on Great Barrier Airlines' Britten Norman Islander aircraft. At the time the company's owner, Jim Bergman, was losing money flying people to Great Barrier Island and was trying to generate a little more income by providing type rating training.

Jim was a very charismatic aviator. We first met at Auckland domestic airport. There I was, eager to start my training when he walked into the terminal, shirt half unbuttoned exposing his chest. He walked over to me and put one foot up on the chair beside me and began laying down the rules. 'Five hours' flying you pay for and I'll give you another five co-pilot time for free.' I was in awe, as Jim had quite a reputation as a great aviator. I couldn't quite believe I was going to be flying with him.

Together we walked out to the Islander aircraft. With 10 seats and a 2994-kilogram maximum take-off weight, it was huge compared to what I had been flying. I climbed into the captain's seat with Jim next to me and off we went. It all seemed very complicated as it was the first twin-engine aircraft I had ever flown. We lined up on the runway at Auckland International Airport and were cleared for take-off. I pushed the throttles slowly up and we took off and then started a turn to the right. As we were passing about 800 feet Jim failed an engine on me. The aircraft yawed wildly and I had no idea what to do. I'd heard other pilots at the aero club talking about using the rudder to control an engine failure in a twin-engine aircraft. So I pushed on the rudder, any rudder … Jim laughed and quickly took control, saying, 'Ha ha! Wrong rudder. I just wanted to see what you were going to do.' It was a bit of a mean trick to play on a total beginner, but I loved it. I felt so at ease with Jim, he was an amazing instructor.

I had soon flown three of the five hours required to complete my initial twin rating and had a lesson with Jim booked the following Saturday. That Friday night I went out on the town and blew off a bit of steam with some friends. I had been working two jobs for four years and I didn't get the chance to have a big night out very often. My lesson with Jim wasn't until 3pm the next day so I had a great night and ended up crashing at a mate's house.

In the meantime, though, an early morning freight run to Great Barrier Island had come up. Jim was going to fly it and thought he could save me some money on lessons by letting me co-pilot the run with him. Jim rang my house at 5am waking my flatmates. He apologised for the early call and explained that he wanted to save me hundreds of dollars. When one of my flatmates came to wake me, he found my bed empty, so told Jim I must be at my girlfriend's house and gave him her number.

Jim rang her house asking if I was there. She wasn't happy to hear I hadn't made it home last night. When she finally tracked me down she was irate and wanted to know exactly where I had been. When I showed up at the airfield that afternoon for my lesson, Jim came out and sheepishly said, 'I rang your house this morning at 5am trying to save you some money. When you weren't there I rang your girlfriend. You weren't there either. I know what I was doing at your age so I hope I didn't drop you in the shit!'

I had completed my five hours, and another five as a co-pilot as promised, when Jim came into the office and said, 'I like you. There's a job here for you this summer but you have to get an instrument rating.' (An instrument rating enables you to fly on instruments in cloud.) I was stoked, but I didn't have any money as I had spent it all on the type rating. I went straight to the bank and got a $5000 Visa card and a $5000 Mastercard, which I maxed out to pay for my multi-engine instrument rating. I rang Jim six weeks later and told him I had an instrument rating. All he said was, 'That's great!' Nothing else – no mention of the job he'd promised me. I asked him if I could come and work in the Great Barrier Airlines office for free. So began my aviation career. What followed was four years of hard work and exciting flying, in fact the best flying of my life.

Great Barrier Island is 54 nautical miles north-east of Auckland. It has very rugged terrain, beautiful beaches and is a place that seems untouched by time. There is no mains power, sewerage system or town water supply. The runway is a basic grass strip with no lights. It is surrounded not only by very high terrain but also by small mound-like hills of about 100 feet. Rumour has it that the airfield was named after a man who crashed into one of these mounds and was killed. At night, the hills and terrain are impossible to see as they all blend into the darkness.

One night, Jim rang me at about 9.30pm. 'Hi, Mike, have you been drinking?' I said, 'No, not yet.' Jim then explained that a little girl on the island had fallen off a mezzanine floor onto a concrete slab below and was bleeding from both ears. The island's doctor didn't think she would make it through the night unless she got to the hospital on the mainland. The Westpac helicopter had already tried to make the run out to Great Barrier but had turned around because of a raging storm out in the Hauraki Gulf.

I arrived at the airport and went outside to pre-flight the Britten Norman Islander. As I was doing my pre-flight I saw the Westpac chopper land. I went over and asked the pilot about the weather out in the gulf. He said, 'We were on the deck most of the way before we turned around. There is no way in hell you will ever get out there in an Islander.' He wasn't very friendly and his manner pissed me off a bit, and I went back to preparing the aircraft. Another pilot, Gary, arrived and he would be my co-pilot.

Just before we departed, at about 11pm, I rang the police officer on the island and asked him what the weather was like over there. His exact words were, 'It's blacker than the inside of a cow's belly, and there is a massive storm.'

The level of concentration in the cockpit was very intense as we got airborne. It was dark, raining and very windy. The Islander aircraft had no weather radar so we were taking our chances if we flew into a thunderstorm. Once airborne, we spoke to the departure air traffic controller whose voice I recognised. It was Richard, who flatted with one of my best mates Pinky (aka Brendon).

'Richard, it's Mike. We have a little girl out on the Barrier who is really ill. There are massive thunderstorms around so could you call the radar controller at Whenuapai [an air force base, where they have a radar that can see storms].' Richard agreed to get in touch with the air force in order to help us get to Barrier safely.

Between the air force controller and Richard, I was given radar vectors around most of the big thunderstorms. As we were approaching the island, Richard's voice came through: 'Mike, there is a clear patch of weather over the island now but a huge line of storms hitting soon. You've got about twenty minutes.' That was enough for us. We made a quick approach in the dark. When emergency night flights have to be made the locals would line their cars up along the runway so their headlights would help guide the pilot in to land.

With the car headlights as a reference, I managed to line the Islander up on the runway centre line and, at about 50 feet, as I came over the sand dunes the aircraft's landing lights picked up the ground. We landed, taxied in and shut down. The doctor, the injured girl and her parents were at the airfield. Needless to say they were all very happy to see both of us. I told them about the storms that were due to hit and that we only had minutes to get back in the air. There was no mucking around as the girl was loaded into the aircraft. With minutes to spare, we were airborne for a bumpy but uneventful ride home. The chopper pilot was wrong. Not only did we get out there in the Islander, we got home again safely with the little girl. I finally crawled into bed at 4.30am, very satisfied with what we had done. The little girl survived.

It wasn't long before I was called out again for another night evacuation. This time, I used up one of my nine lives. It was a Saturday night and the local storekeeper had managed to reverse his car off a 30-foot cliff, flipping it end over end into the ocean. The car sank immediately, but luckily for the storekeeper, a man was sitting on his boat in the bay eating dinner and saw what happened. He then swam over to the submerged car and dived down, freeing the badly injured occupant.

I was called out at about 10pm to do the night evacuation. The flight over to the island was pretty much standard for a night flight – a bit dark and unnerving. But when we flew over the airfield, something was different. I could only see four cars and one of them only had red tail lights on. Normally there are half a dozen cars all with working headlights.

Once we established ourselves on approach I could see that there was one car at the end of the airfield with its headlights facing us and two cars were halfway along the runway. There was one at the closest end of the runway facing the wrong way so all we could see were his tail lights. The crude runway lights did their job and landing was eventually uneventful.

As we loaded the patient into the aircraft, he was looking very ill. The local police officer came over and apologised for the lack of cars providing runway lights. He said he'd had trouble finding people who were sober enough to drive. As a last resort, he finally agreed to use the car with no headlights, just tail lights.

There was a hive of activity loading the patient, the ambulance officer who'd flown over with us getting the handover from the Island doctor and all the cars turning around to face the opposite way as it was a one-way strip at night. Because there was no electricity on Great Barrier Island, there were very few house lights visible and no street lights. Everything was just pitch black so you couldn't take off toward the hills, instead we had to fly out the exact way we'd come in to land.

Once we were loaded and ready to go, I started both engines and taxied out to the start of the runway. I paused for a moment to allow my eyes to adjust and to work out what the deal was with the car lights. Sure enough, there was a set of red tail lights at the far end, two sets of headlights halfway down the runway, and closest to us was another car marking the start of the runway.

As we bounced along the runway gaining speed, some- thing outside didn't seem quite right. The car lights did not match where I thought the runway was going. Everything was happening so quickly that my brain didn't register what was going on.

Out of the dark, I saw the police car right in front of me. Then I saw the policeman dive out of the way. As a reflex,

I pulled back on the control column and closed my eyes. How I didn't hit the car I will never know. I radioed the policeman once we were at a safe altitude. He said, 'Oh my God, Mike! You were within an inch of taking the red and blue lights off the top of my car!' What had happened was the two cars had parked on either side of the runway but had staggered themselves, creating an optical illusion of the runway going off in a different direction. When it's pitch black and I mean totally black it is very easy to get disorientated. The poor policeman had been using his car to transport the patient and had parked off to the side of the runway.

ONE LIFE DOWN, EIGHT LEFT

Great Barrier Airlines was growing and it was time for them to buy a larger aircraft. After leasing a Twin Otter from Air Fiji for a summer, the company decided it was the perfect aircraft to expand their fleet. The Twin Otter is a 21-seat aircraft made by de Havilland in Canada. It is especially designed for rugged strip type operations. The company directors searched all over the world for a good Twin Otter, finally finding one in the French Caribbean.

All the pilots at Great Barrier Airlines were excited at the thought of getting a twin turboprop. As a pilot you are always hungry not only for hours but to fly bigger and bigger aircraft, and turbine time is what the major airlines like to see in your logbook.

Two of Great Barrier Airlines' company directors, Murray Pope and Gerard Rea, purchased the Twin Otter.

Murray had a rather large reputation, one of being a good man but if you crossed him or he simply didn't like you then look out. My relationship with Murray was a little cool. I think he felt a bit uneasy about my loyalty to Jim Bergman.

Gerard Rea was a Boeing 767 captain for Air New Zealand. He was very well liked by all the young pilots as he went out of his way to help them progress their careers into the bigger airlines.

Having bought the Twin Otter, it had to be brought back to New Zealand – it couldn't be dismantled and shipped, it had to be flown. Flying a small plane a long distance like this is called a ferry flight. The aircraft is stripped and ferry fuel tanks are installed inside the cabin so it can fly further than it is designed to fly normally. As part of the purchase arrangement for the Twin Otter, the French pilots flew it to the United States and delivered it to a sleepy little town called Mena in Arkansas. Why Mena? Because the largest aircraft paint shop in the world was there and getting the plane painted in the US was a lot cheaper than in New Zealand.

Following a bit of internal company politics, Alister McEwan and I were asked to travel up to Los Angeles then on to Texas where we would meet Murray Pope before driving to Mena to fly the Twin Otter home. Alister McEwan's father was Hunter McEwan, a Boeing 747 captain with Air New Zealand who is one of the legends you hear about when you are learning to fly. Captain McEwan had been flying a B747-200 out of Christchurch in the 1980s when it struck birds on take-off, sucking them into three of the plane's four engines. So severe was the damage that there was no emergency checklist to work through and one had to be improvised. Many people believe the aircraft only landed safely due to the outstanding skills of Captain McEwan and his crew.

Alister would captain the Twin Otter for the flight home and I would be the co-pilot. At the time I was the senior pilot at Great Barrier Airlines but Alister had a lot more hours flying Twin Otters than I did so it made sense to crew the flight this way. There was also a third pilot with us by the name of Mark Roberts. Mark was an accountant by trade but he wanted to buy shares in Great Barrier Airlines and do some flying as well.

In late February 1995, Alister and I flew to Dallas, Texas to meet Murray Pope. Before we left New Zealand, Pope asked us to buy five sector passes each. These passes could be used to fly anywhere in the US. You could use one pass to fly from Los Angeles to Las Vegas or Los Angeles to New York, the sector length didn't matter. We used one each to fly from Los Angeles to Dallas Fort Worth.

Arriving in Dallas was a new experience for both Al and me. Neither of us had been to Texas before. Everyone was so polite, it was unbelievable. We spent three days there arranging our United States commercial pilot's licences before meeting Pope. Getting the US licence was just a formality – we met a Federal Aviation Administration (FAA) inspector who assessed our logbooks. In my logbook, I had photos of all the different types of aircraft that I had flown, and the friendly FAA inspector spent more time looking at the photos than checking my hours. It only took a few hours and we were both issued with US commercial licences.

That night we went out to celebrate and have a few beers at the world's tallest bar. It was a bustling, busy bar with really friendly staff. We soon started talking to the people at the table next to us and joined them for dinner. They seemed fascinated with our accents. We had a great time and drank far too much American beer. Our new friends offered us a ride back to our hotel, which we accepted. They had a pick-up truck with an extra cab at the back that we squeezed into – behind our heads was a gun rack with two shotguns on it. As we were driving along I leaned forward and asked if there were any alligators in the swamps on the side of the motorway that we were passing. With that our new Texan friend pulled the truck onto the motorway shoulder and leaped out. He handed me a shotgun and a torch and we started looking for 'gators ... Luckily, we didn't see any.

The next morning, we slept in and Pope was downstairs waiting for us. As I came into the hotel lobby he started yelling at me about how unacceptable it was to be so late and so hungover. He was right, but I was too young to appreciate how rude and unprofessional it was of me. The yelling didn't stop when we got into the car and started driving. He seemed to rant and rave for ages before pausing for a second and pointing out the window: 'That's where Kennedy was shot.' Then he went straight back to berating us.

Eventually I fell asleep, and woke to an Arkansas state trooper leaning in the driver's window saying to Pope, 'Where the hell is Neew Zee Land? Don't they have speed limits there?' Pope proved that he could be charming when he wanted to and spoke very politely to the trooper who let us off with a warning and a 'Welcome to the state of Arkansas.'

We arrived in Mena, a sleepy town of about 5000, and were greeted by the owner of the paint store, his wife and their 17-year-old daughter, Kelly. They were extremely friendly and the daughter offered to show us around. Mena is in a dry county where there is absolutely no alcohol sold – not even in cough mixture. Not long after dropping us in Mena, Pope took all eight of our remaining flight sector vouchers off Al and me and vanished, leaving the pair of us in Mena for a week while the Twin Otter was painted. A week is a long time in Mena.

That night we took a taxi to a club we had been invited to by the paint store owner. The cab dropped us off and didn't wait around. The place looked all deserted and closed. I knocked on the door and a little peephole opened. A voice from behind the door said, 'What do you want?'

I explained who I was and that we were meeting the paint store owner. 'He is not here,' came the reply and the peephole door slammed shut. We could hear a heated conversation going on behind the door before it flew open. There was the paint store owner's wife arguing with a man. He was saying no women were allowed to sign guests into the club, and she was saying they are from New Zealand so don't worry. Eventually he decided to bend the rules and we were allowed inside.

It was unlike anything I had ever seen, full bar, huge dance floor, and everyone had a cowboy hat on. It was very obvious that we were outsiders and within minutes we were taken by the hand by some pretty young girls and led onto the dance floor. Everyone arranged themselves in a long line and began line dancing. Al and I didn't have a clue; both of us had two left feet and kept bumping into anyone near us. Every time a song finished we thanked our partner and tried to go back to our beer but someone would grab our hands and drag us back on the dance floor. We both had a great time and eventually called it a night with two sore (left) feet.

The next day at about 7am there was a knock on our motel room door. Kelly had come to take us out for the day and show us the sights of Mena. Kelly was only 17 years old, but seemed a lot older. We all got on really well and the conversation and jokes flowed naturally amongst the three of us. Over the next few days we spent a lot of time with Kelly. One night she came and collected the two of us and said she would be taking us to a bar across the border in Oklahoma. Kelly asked me to drive, so I jumped into the driver's seat and off we went. Crossing the border Kelly announced, 'You two guys have just committed a state felony.' We were shocked. Kelly explained, 'Well, here if you transport a minor across the state line it is a felony! I'm only 17 years old so I'm officially a minor.' Scared of getting in trouble, I wanted to turn the car around. Kelly started laughing and said, 'Don't worry, they never enforce the law.' As we were heading to a bar, Al then asked Kelly what the legal drinking age was. Kelly replied, 'Yeah, it's 21 years old, but don't worry, I have my fake ID and I come to this bar every week, it's all cool.'

We turned up at this bar that looked like something out of a western movie. As we walked across the car park, Kelly pointed at a patch on the ground and said, 'Last Friday night two guys got in a fight just here and one guy pulled out a .45 and killed the other guy ... right here!' I was stunned. Going into the bar, I was very apprehensive. Once we were inside and bought a round of drinks we relaxed just a little. It was so obvious we were strangers to everyone in the bar as we were the only people not wearing cowboy hats. There were a few strange looks, but these gave way to huge smiles and friendly introductions as people found out we were from Nooooo Zeeland!

We played pool and line danced until the wee hours of the morning.

All this time our Twin Otter had been getting its new paint job. When we saw it roll out of the paint shop it looked like a new aircraft. She was perfect, all shiny and smart. Murray Pope had returned from a week at some mystery location and Mark Roberts had arrived to join us. Pope and Al took the aircraft for a test flight while Mark and I sat in the back. Al carried out a few circuits then Mark and I flew one each. It wasn't the ideal preparation for a ferry flight but we were on a tight budget.

After a long week in Mena, it was finally time to depart. The first leg would be approximately 300 nautical miles to Tucumcari in New Mexico. We did all the flight planning, filled the aircraft up with Jet A-1 fuel and launched.

Climbing out over Arkansas and Oklahoma the scenery was spectacular; beautiful rolling hills that eventually gave way to barren desert as we flew into New Mexico. With about 30 minutes to go to Tucumcari, a low-fuel light started flickering even though there was plenty of fuel showing on the gauge. We continued flying to the nearest airport, with some concern but soon landed safely in Tucumcari.

Once we landed I tried to call Pope but he was out of contact again. Being resourceful, I decided to call Jim Bergman back at Great Barrier Airlines and told him about our low-fuel light. Jim checked out an aircraft flight manual and also rang another airline that operated Twin Otters. He got back to me with the news that a boost pump had failed. There are two of these pumps and they help boost the pressure from the fuel in the tank in the belly of the Twin Otter up to the engines high on the wings. If these pumps fail, you can't pump all of the fuel out of the tanks to the engines. This means you have a higher amount of unuseable fuel. To avoid waiting for a week for a new boost pump in Tucumcari, we consulted with an engineer and worked out the amount of fuel we would need to make the rest of the journey safely and added an extra stop into the flight plan.

We checked into a local motel where Al and I were sharing a room. Mark came in and said he had Pope on the phone and he wanted to talk to me. I picked up the phone expecting him to ask how it was going and to thank me for my hard work with the issues we had experienced. I was wrong.

Pope started off in a low tone. He was deeply unhappy that I'd called Jim. I apologised, saying I thought I'd done the right thing. He then went on to accuse me of making him look like a fool. I apologised profusely but to no avail.

Once Pope had hung up, I looked at Mark and asked him what he had said to Pope. I was angry at Mark as I thought he had been telling tales to Pope. But he assured me that he had just outlined the facts of the situation.

Before we left Tucumcari for the Grand Canyon airfield, we spoke to another engineer who agreed operating with only one boost pump would affect our range and would mean an extra refuelling stop before San Francisco, where Pope had arranged to have a new pump waiting for us.

The flight to the Grand Canyon airfield was unreal. I had never seen anything like it before. At the altitude we were flying all these different canyons seemed to go on forever. The Canyons were a deep red colour and everything looked so hot and inhospitable. We landed at the airfield and a lot of pilots who worked on the airfield came over to say hello. One older pilot with years of experience gave us the inside knowledge for the airfield: 'Ya get airborne and look for the titties, these two big rocks that look like big titties and then away ya go ...' He was a classic.

We fuelled up and taxied out among the huge line-up of all sorts of aircraft waiting to take off. The air traffic controller was talking so fast we couldn't understand him clearly. We were told to 'N37Stlineupbehindthelandingaircraftandcommence ahighspeedtaxidonottakeoffuntilisay.' Or something like that. Al and I looked at each other confused. Too late. The controller shouted, 'Hold position, aircraft behind that Twin Otter pass him and line up!' We had lost our place as a punishment for not moving fast enough. Then we got the same instruction again, this time a little slower. 'N37ST, line up behind the landing aircraft and commence a high speed taxi. Do not take off until I say.' The airspace was so busy that this is how they fitted so many aircraft into the sky. We lined up and started taxiing at high speed. The controller then cleared us for take-off and off we went looking for those two big titties! At first, we couldn't see any rocks that looked like titties, but soon every rock looked like a titty. We laughed and laughed but stuck to flying on instruments and our primary navigation.

After a quick extra fuel stop in Las Vegas, we finally made it to Hayward airfield in San Francisco. Hayward was where the Twin Otter's ferry tanks would be installed. This was going to take about a week.

When we arrived at the tanking company Pope was there waiting for us. Thankfully, he had calmed down substantially since that phone call in Tucumcari. He even gave us some expense money, which made me wonder if he'd had a big win in Vegas or something.

Mark, Al and I checked into a motel before I called my friend Eric. A few years back, my mum Joan had been on holiday in Hawaii. On the way home she overheard four American guys talking about where to stay in Auckland. Typical of Mum, she started chatting with them. It turned out they were on a surfing tour celebrating their university graduation. Mum liked them so invited them to stay at her house – with me thrown in as a tour guide.

When I met Mum and my brother Bob at the airport, she introduced me to these four surfer dudes and told me that they would be staying at her house, or my flat, and that she'd told them I'd show them around. I was 21 at the time and not impressed. It must have shown on my face because later, after we all became friends, the guys would do an imitation of me, usually after a few beers.

I spent the next couple of weeks showing these guys around the country and getting up to all sorts of antics. One night in Raglan, me, my best mate Matthew and Eric, one of the American guys, decided to steal (well, borrow, really) a sheep, put it in the back of the car, bring it over to the camping ground and put it in the others guys' tent. Great plan. It took us hours to finally get a sheep (they are fast), and when we got it in the back of the car, it ripped my seat. We then drove it back to the camping ground and quietly unzipped the tent and slipped the sheep in. Next thing one of the guys starts shouting, 'There's a lamb in the tent, there's a lamb in the tent!' The sheep freaked out and starting baaing really loudly before running around in circles shitting itself absolutely everywhere.

The other three American surfer dudes panicked and all tried to pile out of the tent at the same time, resulting in the door zip getting jammed. There was sheep shit everywhere – all through their gear, their sleeping bags and all over them. Eric, Mat and I laughed so hard our ribs ached for days. We then loaded the sheep back into the car and drove it home. The sheep had the last laugh as it shit itself again in the back of my car and spun around while it was doing it. The entire car was covered in sheep poo. I didn't realise one little sheep could produce so much poo.

During our week in San Francisco, Al and I spent heaps of time with Eric and his fiancée Meredith. It had been five years since we'd seen each other but it was like no time had passed. We went to some really cool bars and restaurants, and biked over the Golden Gate Bridge and into the forest.

In the days leading up to the ferry flight, I couldn't help thinking about what a huge undertaking it was. We had done a lot of preparation for the flight and studied everything we could think of. We had even got permission from Air New Zealand to do some of our airport briefings on their computers. This way we knew exactly what all the airfields looked like for the entire journey. From my point of view, nothing was left to chance, but there was still a little voice niggling in the back of my head. In all honesty, I was scared.

When the day of our departure finally arrived, the weather was looking really good all the way across the Pacific to Hawaii. At the airport we met the owner of the tanking company and started flight planning. The idea was to take the Twin Otter for a test flight from Hayward to San Francisco's larger Oakland airport to ensure the ferry system was working as it should, then we'd refuel at Oakland and use their extra-long runway to take off for Honolulu.

Twin Otters are difficult to ferry between the United States mainland and Hawaii as the distance between them is over 2000 nautical miles (NM). The Twin Otter is slow, at around 120 knots, so the flight time is over 16 hours. We had to carry enough fuel to not only get to our destination but also extra fuel for contingencies like changing winds or incorrect weather forecasts. We calculated we needed 20 hours of fuel. The aircraft is only designed to carry fuel for two to three hours' flying, so the ferry tanks that had been fitted carried the rest of the fuel.

Mike Allsop

Murray Pope and Colin, our engineer from New Zealand, were out on the tarmac looking at the ferry system. Colin was not allowed to actually work on the aircraft as he was not licensed to work in the US. But that didn't stop him doing his own inspection of the work. He was a little shocked when he saw that 3/8-inch pipe had been fitted throughout the ferry tank system. When Colin had put ferry tanks in a Twin Otter in Auckland, he'd installed 1/2-inch pipe. Colin queried this with the American engineer and was told that 3/8-inch was fine and there'd be no problem with the fuel flow rates. All the seats had been taken out of the aircraft and five huge aluminium fuel tanks covered almost the entire cabin. There was a gap of only 18 inches across the top of the fuel tanks, through which we would have to crawl in order to swap pilots in flight.

Al and I did the pre-flight and started preparing the aircraft for the test flight. We studied the instructions that had been given to us by the tanking company that installed the fuel system. The system was a gravity feed, meaning there were no additional pumps to get the fuel from the ferry tanks into the aircraft tanks. These pumps were not needed as the aircraft tanks were in the belly of the Twin Otter and the ferry tanks would simply gravity feed into each of the two tanks depending on which one we selected. Once the fuel was in the aircraft tanks, boost pumps would pump it up to the engines on the wings.

I lifted two or three fuel caps off the ferry tanks and shone a flashlight inside. There was about an inch or two of fuel in each tank. Al and I got into the cockpit and switched all the tanks on and watched the aircraft tank fuel gauges to see if they increased. The tanking company had told us that this was how it would be in the final stages of the flight – getting all the small final amounts of fuel out of the ferry tanks. However, when we tested it, we didn't see the gauge move at all on the aircraft tanks. This really concerned us and I told Colin of our concerns. He opened the filler cap on the outside of the aircraft, where you normally fuel it, and we then selected a ferry tank. The fuel started flowing and we could see it feeding in down the filler throat … well, trickling in. I was a bit concerned about the fuel flow keeping up with the demand of the engines. Colin wasn't impressed. He snapped at me. 'How do you know if that is one gallon a minute or ten gallons a minute … You don't! It's a dumb question. The ferry tanking engineers have flow checked it and it's fine. Now go and test-fly it and see if it feeds!' I felt very told off and watched Colin check all five ferry tanks individually, making sure each one flowed. We would have to trust that the ferry tanking engineers had done their jobs properly.

During the final stages of the actual ferry flight all the ferry tanks would be open, all draining into the main tanks. We decided that we would configure the fuel system this way for the entire test flight as we had already established that each and every ferry tank flowed and delivered fuel. We had to trust that the American engineers had flow checked them. This was our big mistake! When we landed some 45 minutes later we had more fuel in the aircraft tanks than when we started, so we thought the ferry system was doing its job. In hindsight it was feeding from the front two ferry tanks and the other three were not keeping up. But we would not find this out until later.

On landing at Oakland International Airport, I still had a nagging feeling about the ferry system. We called Pope and he came over to the airport. He looked at the feeds from the ferry tanks and rang the tanking company to query the flow. They assured him that the tanks had all been checked at low level and they would definitely keep up with the engines.

They also said if we wanted electric boost pumps installed it would take another week and another $5000. The time and cost were out of the question so all five ferry tanks and the two aircraft tanks were filled to the brim with Jet A-1. The extra weight meant we had to pump up the aircraft's tyres as they were sitting very low.

We then rechecked the flows from the ferry tanks visually and they looked great as there was a large head of pressure. Pope, Mark, Al and I stood outside the aircraft and strategised the best way to tackle fuel management for the flight.

Our doubts remained so we came up with a plan to burn fuel from each and every ferry tank over the first few hours of the flight to ensure they were all working as they should. That way, if we encountered any problems, we could easily turn back to the mainland.

The Twin Otter looked so heavy sitting low down on its suspension. Pope had insisted that all the seats and some spare parts were loaded into the nose locker and the rear locker. I had understood that these would be shipped back to New Zealand separately. Al and I were not impressed at having to carry the extra weight when we were already over the allowed maximum weight but there was little we could do about it.

As the refueller was finishing topping up the last tank, Al noticed a really cool tool he was using. It was a Leatherman multi-tool, kind of like a more grunty version of a Swiss Army knife. Al was so impressed with it, he bought it off the guy for $50. It turned out to be the best $50 he ever spent.

There wasn't much left to do except get in and get going. The three of us loaded up and taxied out. Al was in the captain's seat, I was in the first officer's seat and Mark was way down the back, behind the ferry tanks, sitting in the last row of seats. We taxied very, very slowly, trying not to stress the aircraft in any way. I felt like I was flying a very heavy fuel bomb. We lined up and started trundling down the runway; it seemed to take forever to get airborne. As we climbed out, Al skilfully milked the Twin Otter higher and higher. I can still remember the figures – at 117 knots, we were climbing at about 100–200 feet per minute. If Al pulled back even a little the stall warning would sound at 115 knots … We were that heavy.

I looked ahead at some of the bridges across San Francisco Bay and wondered how we would clear them. There was actually an instrument departure especially designed for overweight aircraft departures like this so we were not the first or the last to do this.

We flew through the centre span of the Golden Gate Bridge and as I looked out I could see we were just a few hundred metres above each bridge tower. Having cleared the bridge, there was now just pure ocean in front of us … 2100 nautical miles of it … 16 hours' flying, all going well.

Mike Allsop

We were trying to get to 8000 feet initially and at 100 feet per minute it took over an hour. It was our first time using a high frequency (HF) radio, which is used for communicating over long distances. We had a bit of trouble using the HF radio and the San Francisco air traffic controller got a bit annoyed with us. He said, 'November 37 Sierra Tango, if you can't establish contact with me on your HF radio, you will have to turn around at the 200 NM boundary and return to San Fran.' We tried again and this time established very scratchy comms with him. At that point, we thought it would have been a disaster if we had to turn around.

As we flew out across the Pacific, we transferred fuel from each of the ferry tanks into the main aircraft tanks. We used about an hour of fuel from each ferry tank and all five tanks worked well. Then we decided to burn one ferry tank completely dry. We chose the biggest tank, tank number 1, which ran lengthwise along the cabin for about 6 feet and was 3 feet wide. I made an estimate of the fuel we had already used and then did a calculation of how many miles we could get out of that tank. I then plotted this on our chart.

When the number one tank was completely empty, we talked about which tank we were going to use next. Al wanted to use the number two tank at the front as it was smaller than the rest. I wanted to use tank five down the back. Al explained that if we used tank two it would move the centre of gravity (C of G) of the aircraft aft, which would increase the lift produced from the tail of the plane thus reducing the lift required off the main wings slightly. This would increase our range and our fuel efficiency. His suggestion sounded reasonable so I pulled out the flight manual and calculated a centre of gravity with the number two tank empty. The proposed C of G was still well inside the operating envelope of the Twin Otter.

We had already proved that all the ferry tanks worked perfectly well so I could see no reason not to use tank two next. We started transferring fuel and the entire tank drained normally, exactly as the first one had.

I went down the back and rested for a little while and managed to get some sleep. When I came back up the front, Mark and Al were looking very worried.

'Tank five is feeding really slowly. We're not sure why but it's hardly keeping up with the engines.' In fact, it was only just keeping up with the engines even with the fuel valve left fully open all the time. Luckily we hadn't been running the main tanks below 900 pounds each, so we had some options. Time ticked by and then we started getting below the 900 pounds comfort figure in the main tanks. Tank five was not feeding at all so we selected the next tank. Switching to tank four fixed the problem and quickly filled up the main tanks back to 1200 pounds. But after a few hours tank four started running slowly as well. We had the fuel transfer times written down from the first two tanks so we could compare them. It was very alarming.

I thought, 'Well, this is a small problem, but we can work it out – after all, we are good pilots.' This feeling didn't last long once tank four stopped draining as well. We selected tank three and filled up the main tanks. We could see that it was feeding very slowly too. I did some fuel calculations and I worked out that we would only have a one-hour reserve when we got to Honolulu. It was tight but still ok. We were well past halfway at this stage and there was no option but to continue.

We did everything we could to keep the fuel flowing from the ferry tanks into the main tanks, knowing that if we couldn't keep up with the engine we were in serious trouble. Keeping the main tanks at 900 pounds each had bought some valuable time.

I went down the back and tried to come up with ideas on how to get the back tanks working better. Our options were very limited. I made a mental note that if we started burning below 900 pounds in each tank, it would be because the ferry system had completely stopped working. If this happened it would be time for drastic action.

I had just got my head around the reality of this when Al shouted from the cockpit, 'WE ARE BURNING OUR 900!' I crawled up the front, stuck my head into the cockpit. 'What? Really? Shit!' We were at least four or five hours away from Honolulu with only three hours of useable fuel. We had plenty of fuel in the ferry tanks but we couldn't get it to feed into the main tanks. My heart just sank.

'We need to cut the fuel lines and transfer the fuel by hand,' I said. The thought horrified all of us. I grabbed Al's Leatherman and went down the back, Mark following. It was now pitch black outside, but we had the cabin lights on. We needed something to transfer the fuel with. We had brought a couple of five-gallon water bottles to use as pee bottles since there was no toilet on board. Unfortunately, we had been using them and they each had a few litres of urine in them.

Without hesitation, I forced open the back left emergency door and shoved the pee bottle out in an attempt to tip the contents out. Unfortunately, it just blew back in and I got pee all over my arm. It didn't matter. In fact, I didn't even react to it. I just grabbed the other one and did the same thing.

I then opened the Leatherman and picked up the fuel line to the number five tank. I bent it in half and looked up the front to Al. I then heard a strange noise of the right engine stopping and winding down. Al had shut down one engine to save fuel and keep us in the air longer. I looked out the window at the right engine and the propeller had completely stopped. This was serious now. I looked down at the fuel line, took a deep breath, and cut it. There was no going back now.

I filled one of the urine bottles with jet fuel and handed it to Mark, who was lying on top of the fuel tanks. He spun around on his tummy and shimmied back up to the number two tank. He then poured it into the tank and came back to where I had the second container of fuel waiting. We continued doing this for a while then swapped places. The smell of fuel was so powerful it instantly gave me a headache and started stinging my eyes. Mark and I were both covered in fuel and we stank. After a short time, spilt fuel had soaked right down to my underpants and it wasn't just my eyes that were stinging but the flesh on my legs, tummy and forearms. I remember thinking how much it hurt and how little I could do about it.

Mark and I were frantically filling bottles and transferring fuel. As I was a little bit quicker than Mark, I did most of the crawling over the tanks, pouring in a gallon at a time. Every time I came forward, I would stick my head in the cockpit and ask Al how it was going. 'They can't understand me, Mike! I can't get them to understand what is going on.'

'Don't stuff around, just put out a pan call,' I told him. A pan is the second highest emergency call, just one level down from a full blown Mayday.

I transferred a few more gallons of fuel before talking to Al again. 'Mike, it's still no good. Bloody hell, it is so hard. They can't understand me.' Once again, I told him to put out a pan call. Surely they'd understand that.

I crawled down the back again and next thing I heard the stall warning horn going off. This is a warning that the aircraft was about to stall. As we were only on one engine we were flying a lot slower and closer to stalling. Every time one of us would move back down the cabin the nose would pitch up a little and the airspeed would reduce. Al was working very hard – he was flying on one engine, and trying to co-ordinate our rescue. Every time the stall warning went off, we would feel the aircraft pitching down gently and regaining speed. Al was doing a fantastic job.

The next time I stuck my head into the cockpit, Al said, 'I just put out a Mayday call. "Mayday, mayday, mayday, November Three Seven Sierra Tango, we are running out of useable fuel, we can not make Honolulu." That got their attention. They have shut down the HF frequency and dedicated it to us. A navy ship is relaying comms, two F-15 fighter jets are coming to find us and they are sending out a C-130 Hercules to help.' Holy shit!

I scrambled back down the rear and we continued transferring fuel. Sometime later Al shouted, 'It's not working, it's not working!' I did some quick sums in my head. We were transferring about 60 gallons per hour and the aircraft was using 75 gallons per hour. We couldn't keep up.

I went down the back and got one of the fuel pipes and looked around for something to secure the open end of it. I grabbed a pen and shoved it down the end of the fuel line then slid a jubilee clip (a steel band you can tighten with a screwdriver) over the pen and tightened it. I used this to plug the fuel line. I shouted at Mark to do the other line as I jumped over to start jacking up tank number three.

Tank three had a small gap beside it; I hoped I'd be able to get my hand down it then lift up one side of the tank, stick a chock underneath it then do the other side of the tank too. I thought this might increase the static head pressure of the tank and make the fuel flow better. Mark turned up really quickly and the smell of fuel seemed to be getting stronger. I went down the back and there was the fuel line lying on the floor pumping fuel out all over the place. I grabbed it and managed to stem the flow with another jubilee clip and pen combo.

As I came back, Al shouted, 'It's no use, guys, we're running on fumes. We're going to have to ditch!' I couldn't believe it. But once I saw the look on his face I knew he was serious.

I squeezed into the cockpit and strapped myself in. Al looked at me and said, 'Mike, only one of us needs to be in here for the ditching. Go down the back!' It was one of the most defining moments of my life.

Al was my mate. I couldn't leave him to ditch the aircraft on his own. I knew that it was more than likely anyone in the cockpit would be killed but I simply couldn't go down the back and leave him. If anyone was going to die, then we would die together. 'No, mate, we do this together.'

Al protested a bit but gave up when he could see I wasn't going anywhere. He looked at me and just said, 'Thanks, mate.' Nothing more.

I grabbed a pen and paper and wrote a quick note to my girlfriend. I then stuck it down my underpants so if they ever found my body they would find the note. Al looked at me and asked what I'd done.

'Nothing,' I said. 'No, tell me what did you do!' he insisted. 'I wrote a note to my girlfriend and put it down my undies so if they find my body she will get the note.' 'Good idea,' he said, and handed control over to me. Al started to write, and then paused. 'What did you write?' I laughed and said, 'I just told her I loved her.' Al started writing again and then folded the paper and put it down his pants.

Both of us knew we would soon be dead. There was no hope, really. I turned to Al and put my hand out and looked at him and simply said, 'Good luck, buddy.' His reply came: 'Yeah, you too.'

Then a clear thought came into my head – if I was going to die then I would die being the best, most professional pilot I could be. That clicked me into action.

'Right, let's do this. I think we are stuffed because we have no shoulder harnesses.' Al agreed with me. 'I think we should open the doors and jam our boots in them to keep them open. One little ding on the aluminium will jam them closed and we'll never get out.' I also suggested opening the windows so the water in the cockpit might stop us from hitting our heads on the dash and drowning. Al agreed.

Just then on the emergency frequency, the United States Coast Guard C-130 was asking us for our position. I read it off the GPS. Just then I saw two lights screaming past us on our left-hand side. It was the two F-15 fighters they had sent to find us. I tried to call them but they wouldn't answer. The C-130 captain said that the F-15s could hear us but not reply.

Next thing, this huge F-15 flew past our right wing really slowly and, only about a hundred feet away, I could see the pilot waving. I waved back. Next another one did an even slower pass with all his flaps and gear out. They had found us! Then the cold harsh reality sank in … we were still going to die – they couldn't save us.

Just then there was a startling roar and a blur out the front followed by flames everywhere. One of the F-15s had pulled up right in front of us with its afterburners going. We flew straight through his wake and the Twin Otter almost went out of control. I could see Al struggling to regain control as we were still operating on only one engine.

After a few tense seconds, Al managed to regain control but had lost a little altitude. I shouted down the radio, 'Don't fly in front of us – we are on one engine and almost lost control!' We never saw the F-15s again after that.

A short time later, the huge C-130 Hercules turned up flying very slowly off our right wing. We now had very clear communication with the C-130. The first thing the captain of the Hercules said was, 'N37ST – retract your undercarriage.

It is imperative that you retract your undercarriage. You have minimum chances of survival with your undercarriage down.'

The fact was that the Twin Otter had a fixed undercarriage that was permanently locked down. I replied, 'We can't! The undercarriage is locked down. We are a fixed undercarriage aircraft.' 'What type of aircraft are you?' 'A de Havilland Twin Otter.' There was no reply.

The next voice on the radio said, 'Sir, my name is Dave. We're going to try and help you. What is your name?' I told him.

'Ok, Mike. Are your crew preparing to ditch?' I confirmed that we were and that there were three of us on board.

'Ok, Mike. Listen up. What is your stall speed? Give us your stall speed and we will work out a speed that we want you to hit the water at, with no flare at the end, ok? ' (No flare means you don't flare out at the end to make it a smooth land, you simply drive it on hard.)

'Ok, Dave. Our stall speed is 70 knots [140 kilometres per hour].'

'Roger, stand by … Mike, we want you to hit the water at 90 knots, no flare, just drive it down. Ok?'

Al and I just looked at each other. Like hell were we doing that.

Captain Dave then said something that was really useful. 'Mike, we want you to get yourself a focus point, some point that you know, close your eyes and aim for that point. Once you hit the water it will go dark really quickly and you must go for your focus point … ok?'

This was a fantastic piece of advice. Over and over in my head, I told myself, 'You've got to look for Al, you've got to look for Al.' I said it about 20 times, trying to get it into my sub-conscious so that when we crashed, I would automatically look for Al.

The next thing Dave said was, 'We want you to hold on to a first aid kit, just hold on to one.'

I couldn't help thinking this was a bit strange. How was I supposed to fly and ditch the aircraft while holding on to a first aid kit? I just replied, 'Aaaahh, ok ... '

There was a brief moment when I seemed to get lost in my thoughts. I was so scared. It's difficult to describe the feeling of knowing I was going to be dead in a few minutes. I thought about how to be brave. What was brave? What did bravery mean? I thought about the bravest men I knew of – World War Two Spitfire pilots. Then I remembered reading that a few of those brave pilots wet themselves in battle. If men that brave had wet themselves what hope was there for me? I didn't want the last thing I remembered to be wetting myself. Oh my god, I was so scared!

Then I remembered something my mum had told me. She'd once talked about how some athletes would convince themselves that a bear or a tiger was chasing them. Apparently, this had the effect of tricking their sub-conscious minds into thinking they were in a life or death situation and they'd get an extra boost in performance. I decided I would do something similar.

Al and I decided to start the right engine so that we could ditch under control. I told the C-130 what we were doing. With both engines running off the front aircraft tank, I worked out that we had 12 minutes of useable fuel in that tank and 10 minutes in the aft one.

Dave then told me that they had some flares on board that they would drop to float on the water to help us see where to ditch. No sooner had he said that than both engines started to flame out and wind down. The front tank had run dry – there was an error in the gauge. We quickly changed over to the back tank before the engines stopped. There was even less fuel showing in this tank. There was no discussion between me and Al. There was no time.

I keyed the mic. 'Dave, we need to go in NOW! Can you get us a QNH [altimeter setting], wind direction and sea state?'

'Ok. Stand by, Mike.' With that we saw the huge C-130 pitch almost straight down and dive at the sea. We were at about 5000 feet slowly drifting down, but needed to steepen our descent before we completely ran out of fuel.

Ironically, the last thing I did was take the leather strap of the GPS bag and use it as a dipstick on the three tanks that were not feeding. I calculated that we had at least three hours of fuel inside the cabin but none of it was useable.

Within minutes, the C-130 formatted back on our right wing. Dave said, 'Mike, we went down to 50 feet and there is no wind, the sea state is calm and your altimeter setting is 1013.'

'Ok, thanks. Drop the flares on our heading of 180 degrees …'

The C-130 flew in front of us and descended to the sea. It looked so dark. I stuck my head through the internal cockpit door to the cabin and shouted back to Mark, 'This is it. We're going in!' I then slid the two cockpit doors closed.

We followed the C-130 down as it descended. We had three emergency beacons on board and we set them all off. We took off our boots and took it in turns to open the cockpit doors slightly and used our boots to jam them open. We took off out belts and removed any sharp objects like pens from our pockets. I grabbed a life jacket and put it over my head and did it up, making sure I didn't inflate it.

I looked down at my jeans and T-shirt. They were soaked with jet fuel. It was so painful and burned my skin but I couldn't think about it.

Just then the C-130 disappeared into cloud and we followed it. Al was now flying on instruments and kept descending. It seemed like ages before we popped out of the cloud at about 800 feet and there was the C-130 right in front of us in a perfect position, dropping flares out the back cargo door.

We descended down onto the flare path. It was very hard to judge our height over the black water. As we got closer, I stuck my head out the window and, with my left hand, waved Al down. I could see the water. It looked so black.

I kept waving Al down until we were about 10 feet above the water. We were so close I could actually smell the sea. I pulled my head back in and looked at Al. He was looking at my hand and scanning back to his instruments, skilfully descending as carefully as he could.

I looked up and all I could see was pitch black sea, one flare and pitch black sky. It was like looking at a black wall with one light on in the middle. There was no way we could judge our landing like this. We needed at least two flares.

I shouted, 'GO AROUND!' and grabbed the thrust levers and pushed them forward.

Al shouted, 'What are you doing?'

'No flares … we can't land!' I shouted back.

Al banked the aircraft around to the right. No sooner had we turned than his shoe flew out the door and his door slammed shut …

'You have control!' he shouted. 'My shoe has fallen out.'

I grabbed the controls and started flying. There were no instruments on my side of the aircraft so I had to look over to Al's set and turn the aircraft around 180 degrees.

The altimeter was reading between 0 and 1 which meant we were less than 100 feet above the water. We were literally skimming across the tops of the waves. All hell seemed to be breaking loose.

The radio was blaring. Dave from the C-130 was shouting, 'YOU GOTA PUT IT IN BEFORE YOU LOSE CONTROL!'

Every cockpit warning light was flashing – door lights, low fuel lights, boost pump pressure light – the emergency beacons were screaming in my ears. It felt like the world was caving in on top of me. Any second I would know what it was like to be dead … the other side.

All this noise and commotion made me really, really angry and I channelled this into flying the critical turn. My focus was intense.

I completed the turn and gave Al back control, with the words, 'You have control.'

'I have control,' he said. We would be professional pilots to the end.

After I gave control to Al, my anger welled up and I grabbed the annunciator panel with all its flashing lights and with all my might ripped it clean out of the instrument panel. It was pissing me off! There was a big red flashing propeller reset light next to it. I smashed that with my fist. The flashing lights stopped. I looked up at the fuel cut-off controls. They had a safety cover over them but I ripped it clean off the ceiling. This all took a matter of seconds but it seemed like slow motion. Not a word was said between us, but somehow I think Al knew exactly why I was doing what I was doing.

Again I stuck my head out the window and started waving Al down. One flare light passed and then another … now we could see. There was a massive sea swell and from the smoke off the flares we could see there was about a 10 knot wind blowing 90 degrees from our right. Al asked if I thought we should get the C-130 to drop more flares.

'There's no time!' I shouted and kept waving him down.

Again we got so close to the water I could smell it. It looked frighteningly cold and black … pitch black.

I pulled my head back in and looked at Al. 'We've got to do this, Al. We've got no chance otherwise!'

'I know! I know!'

'Close the thrust levers! DO IT, AL! JUST DO IT!'

Al hesitated for a split second and I screamed at the top of my lungs, 'JUST FUCKIN' DO IT, JUST DO IT, CLOSE THE THRUST LEVERS NOW …'

With that Al closed the thrust levers and you could hear both engines wind down. I reached up and feathered the propellers to stop them from spinning, pulled both fuel shut-offs and – as I reached for the engine fire extinguishers – I keyed the mic and said, 'Dave, this is it. We're going …' The last word never came out.

The Twin Otter hit the pitch black sea with huge speed and pitched straight down into the water. The aircraft flipped right up with only its tail sticking out of the water. Al and I were trapped.

Everything went into super slow motion. My seat snapped at the base forcing me to collide with the control column and hit the instrument panel, cracking my ribs on the right side. My head was forced right back and my mouth was forced wide open. I heard a scream. That scream was terrifying. It sounded like the kind of scream you'd hear from a person just before they died. Then I realised it was coming from me …

My jaw was locked open and water was getting forced into my mouth under high pressure. I had no choice but to swallow and swallow water.

The noise was horrendous. I scratched and clawed like crazy to get out. Going for my focus point, nothing made sense. I was pinned against the flight console still swallowing water until I could swallow no more … I scratched at the door, which was just twisted metal now, cutting my hands to shreds.

Then a calm clear thought came over me. 'Just take a breath. Just take a breath. You will be so relaxed once you take that first breath. Just relax. This is it …' It felt so surreal, so calm. I relaxed and took a large, deep, final breath.

At that very instant, the aircraft popped back out of the

water and settled on its belly. There was now two inches of air in the cockpit. I pushed my lips to the cockpit roof and gasped for air.

My first reaction was to look for Al and he was looking straight back at me. I screamed, 'Get out! Get out!'

My clothes had been practically blown off me and were now just torn rags. I managed to kick what was left of the door open and right there was the propeller still spinning, churning up the water. The engine sounded like it was going to blow up at any second.

I dived past the spinning propeller and swam under the wing outside of the engine. I could hear turbine blades firing off out of the engine with sparks and small pockets of flame. The wings had partially separated from the fuselage. Apparently, in cases like this both engines usually come into the cockpit and instantly kill the pilots. Twin Otters can have wing strengthening straps installed to prevent this from happening. Al knew we didn't have these but he didn't tell me before the crash because he didn't want to worry me.

I swam up to the back door and opened it. There was Mark looking very shaken up. I shouted at him, 'Do you have the life raft?'

He held it up in his arms then threw it out into the water and pulled the inflation cord. It inflated with a hiss and this little rectangular life raft popped up, exactly how it was meant to.

Mark then jumped into the water and crawled into the life raft. I asked Mark if he had all the emergency equipment and he just looked blank and said no. On board the plane, we had some serious emergency equipment – a portable VHF radio, a portable emergency beacon, and an expensive handheld GPS.

I went back into the aircraft and started looking for all the equipment. It was a mess – everything had gone flying in the impact. I grabbed two sleeping bags as I didn't know what was in the life raft. Water was pouring into the fuselage now.

I threw the sleeping bags to Mark who was now drifting away in the life raft. I screamed at him, 'Where is Al?'

Mark just shrugged his shoulders.

'Where is he? Go and find him, get out of the life raft and get him!' I was mad as hell.

'I can't,' Mark replied. 'I'm tied to the raft.'

I couldn't believe it. He'd tied himself to the raft so he wouldn't get separated from it. It was very smart on one hand but it also rendered him completely useless.

Now we needed the emergency equipment, the portable locater beacon and GPS, so I swam back into the aircraft. There were sparks coming from the lights in the roof and a huge pool of fuel sitting on the surface of the water. It looked like it was going to blow up at any second.

I scrambled around and found a cooler box that we had prepared with some food and I threw it out to Mark who was now about 30 feet from the aircraft and drifting further.

The next time I tried to get into the fuselage I had to duck under the water and come up inside. There was still a large air gap inside but it was getting scarier by the second, and I knew I was pushing my luck.

The sparks seemed to be raining down and the smell of jet fuel was almost overpowering; my eyes were stinging from swimming through it. I turned and headed for the door, which was now under water. Next thing my feet got tangled in the fuel line and I pulled hard but they were stuck. I dived down and grabbed at my ankles. Thankfully I managed to get myself free but a wave of panic came over me. I just kept saying to myself, 'Keep it together, Mike, keep it together.' I ducked under the door and came out, clear of the aircraft.

I looked for Mark and saw the life raft drifting off into the dark. There were no oars so there was not much he could do against the current. I strained to look inside the raft and there was still no Al. 'Where is Al?' I screamed.

'I don't know!' Mark shouted back.

I screamed for Al over and over again. I started swimming towards the front of the aircraft but my left arm was really sore. The area right at the top above the bicep burned like hell. I felt it with my right hand and to my horror my watch was right up, still done up, clasped above my bicep by my armpit. I pulled at the watch but couldn't get it undone. Eventually after a few really hard yanks it came free. The force of the water was such that it blew my clothes off and blasted my watch right up my arm past the elbow and above the bicep.

I could hear Mark shouting, 'Inflate your life jacket! Pull your life jacket!'

I grabbed the inflation handle on the jacket and gave it a good pull. There was a loud hiss and next thing a tightly inflated life jacket was strangling me. Shit! Now I could hardly breathe and could barely swim.

I managed to get around to the left-hand side of the aircraft and I could see a person lying face down in the water.

I couldn't believe it. I had seen Al get out of the cockpit. He was alive. He can't be dead … No, no, no. I was so confused. I grabbed at the body only to find it was the seat back cushion. I instantly looked back towards Mark and managed to just make out Al climbing into the life raft.

Sometimes in moments of chaos, a clear vision comes into your head. Mine was that I needed to get my logbook NOW! A pilot's logbook is the most important thing to him. It was in the rear luggage locker of the plane so I climbed up on the roof and as the Twin Otter started to slip under the waves, I ran down the top of the aircraft. As I was running, a slow building roar became louder and louder. It was the United States Coast Guard C-130 flying directly overhead.

I stopped and waved my arms above my head. I could feel the displaced air as the Hercules passed above me. I spun around and kept waving. They were so close I could see a row of crew strapped in and hanging off the back cargo door looking for us.

At that very moment, Mark (who had left behind the GPS, portable locater beacon and other emergency items) pulled out his camera and took a photo – the camera jammed! He reckoned it would have been a Pulitzer Prize winner – me standing on the sinking Twin Otter, in my underpants, arms waving above me as the C-130 just cleared my head.

I knew it was now or never so I ran along the top of the plane and jumped off the back. I tried to get under the water into the luggage locker to get my bag with my logbook in it but I couldn't dive down because of my life jacket.

Then I heard Al screaming at me to get into the life raft. Even I knew I was pushing my luck a little bit too much.

I started swimming toward the life raft just as the plane began to sink below the surface. As I crossed the wing I got sucked under. I could see the surface. I clawed at it and broke the water with my hand but couldn't reach it even with my life jacket fully inflated.

The aircraft drifted away and I popped up to the surface. It was probably only a few seconds of being trapped under water but it felt like a lifetime.

Al and Mark were both in the life raft and it was barely visible in the moonlight. I started swimming towards them. I could hear Al shouting to me so I tried to follow his voice. As I was swimming, I looked down and could see what I thought was sand. I was a bit confused and stopped swimming as I was convinced that we were on some sort of sand bank. I tried to stand up and touch the bottom. In fact we were in 12,000 feet of water and what I could see was shattered paint flakes off the aircraft.

I got to the raft and Al helped pull me in. I collapsed and lay on the floor. By now the Twin Otter had passed beneath the waves and was actually flying under water. I stared at the scene in disbelief – there was wreckage everywhere.

There was silence in the raft except for the creaks and groans of the aircraft descending into the water. Another strange thought came into my head. I thought of the World War Two U boats that torpedoed so many ships. Their crews must have listened to ships screaming as they sank to the bottom of the ocean. Horrific.

As I surveyed the carnage, all I could think to say was, 'Holy shit! What is Pope going to say?'

We all laughed at the relief of being alive.

Once the laughter subsided, I realised that sinking alongside the Twin Otter was probably my career as an airline pilot. This had been my dream since I was a little fella.

I didn't get to dwell on my career prospects for long as I realised that there was blood everywhere in the life raft. Al and I started looking at each other for injuries. With the amount of adrenalin flowing one of us could have been missing a finger and not even known it. We slowly and methodically checked each other, patting each other down looking for injuries. My hands and feet were all cut up but nothing major considering what we had been through.

Just then the C-130 Hercules screamed overhead again, but this time something dropped off the back. Next thing there was a huge splash and then a massive hiss about 100 feet from the lift raft. A life raft big enough for 10 people inflated right there. Then another and another all in a line. They were bright orange and had inflated ribs that formed a skeleton that you could pull a cover over.

We all started paddling over to one of these rafts, picking things out of the wreckage as we went. Someone grabbed the flight manual. It had been strapped under my seat with thick leather straps but now it was bobbing in the sea some 200 feet from where the impact had been.

We made it into one of the Coast Guard life rafts and tied the two rafts together, making it easier to spot us from the air. Mark found a flare and started undoing it, getting ready to fire it, all the while unaware that he was pointing it at my face. I reached up and put my hand on the flare and said, 'They know where we are, they are flying straight over us. We have been awake for a long time and we're really exhausted. There is a good chance we will have an accident lighting off a flare. It's my vote we don't set one off.' After everything we had been through, getting shot in the face with a flare didn't really appeal so we didn't light one off. This turned out to be a big mistake. The Coast Guard didn't know where we were and were doing a grid search for us.

Shock and exhaustion finally began to set in. I leaned over the side of the raft and vomited profusely for about five minutes. For some reason, Al decided to shine a flashlight he had found in the raft on my vomit in the sea. He started laughing. When I looked over to find out what he found so amusing, it looked like I'd puked up a big oil slick. I knew I'd swallowed a lot of fuel but I had no idea how much. I slumped back into the raft.

Next thing I started shaking uncontrollably. I was going into shock. Al found a silver emergency blanket and wrapped it around me. Then he put up the cover of the life raft and sat next to me and put his arm around me to help keep me warm. I asked Mark to sit on the other side of me as I could now hardly speak through the shivering. He refused and went over the other side of the raft, pulled the cover back and sat on the outside of the raft. I was pissed off as I was cold and it felt like I was in real trouble. I found out later he was feeling pretty ill himself and sitting under the canopy made him feel worse.

With Mark sitting on the outside of the raft and Al and me huddled together inside, we bobbed around for about an hour, each of us getting more and more seasick. It didn't seem to affect Al so much but then again he wouldn't have complained about it if it had. Complaining wasn't in Al's nature.

Mark kept muttering something to himself and I couldn't understand him. Then he said it a bit louder. 'There's a big life raft here. We should paddle to that one.'

By the time he had said it for the third time, I sat up muttering, 'What the hell are you talking about?'

I pulled back the life raft cover and there a few hundred metres away was a massive container ship. 'Holy shit! It's a ship.'

Mark had lost his glasses in the crash and everything was a blur for him.

All of a sudden there came a now familiar splash and a hiss as three more life rafts landed near us. I realised at that point that the Coast Guard had no idea where we were. Mark grabbed the flares and started trying to work out how to fire one off.

I grabbed the flashlight and started flashing it towards the ship. They had a huge searchlight scanning the waves looking for us. This was the first time I really appreciated just how big the swell of the sea was.

The ship's captain was operating the searchlight and he saw our little flashlight straight away. He put the strong spotlight on us but we would disappear in the trough of the waves only to reappear on the crest.

Very soon we saw the container ship launching a little tender to come and collect us. The tender got closer and closer and we could hear the crew talking in a foreign language. I can't remember who it was but one of us said, 'Oh no! It's a Korean fishing boat.' As if beggars could be choosers.

The tender pulled alongside and a very proper German officer asked, 'Are you injured?' I told him I didn't think so. He was then straight on the radio speaking in German to the ship.

Just then a Sikorsky Coast Guard helicopter showed up over the scene. It looked really cool with its wheels retracted. It circled a few times then departed straight away. There was still a lot of chatter on the radio. The German officer then asked again if we were sure that we were all uninjured. Obviously the helicopter was running very low on fuel.

There were other crew in the small tender and they looked like they were from the Pacific Islands. I asked one where they were from and he said they were all from Kiribati, a tiny island nation near the equator. They seemed really friendly and concerned for us.

We turned and started making our way back to the huge container ship but as we got closer Al seemed to be getting very nervous. The sea swell looked huge against the side of the ship. Just before we left New Zealand, Al had seen a documentary about a yacht race where a person had been killed trying to board a ship exactly like we were about to do.

Al said to me, 'Shit, Mike, we have to be so careful here. I'm really worried. If we miss that ladder or don't get up it we will get killed!'

No sooner had he said that than the German officer said very seriously, 'You need to grab zee rope ladder when we hit

49

zee ship and climb fast, otherwise the tender will come back and kill you.'

I didn't look at Al, I just focused on the ladder as the tender came towards the ship. We smashed into the side of the ship, I grabbed the ladder and held on. Next thing the tender disappeared from under my feet and I was left dangling there. I didn't even think, I just climbed like my life depended on it … because it did. I flew up the rope ladder and over the side.

I collapsed on the deck, my head down, and I could see a very nicely polished pair of shoes appear in front of my eyes. I looked up and there was the first mate standing to attention. He grabbed my arm and helped me up. I was a bit wobbly and he steadied me. 'Welcome to zee *Columbus Canada*, where are you from?'

I could hardly breathe, still puffed and dizzy. 'Thank you, thank you so much for rescuing us,' I gasped. 'We are from New Zealand.'

'You are a KIWI! We have rescued lots of you KIWIS!'

I was still a bit stunned and didn't realise what he meant. The *Columbus Canada* had been involved in many yacht rescues, a lot of them involving New Zealanders, as we are a very proud sailing nation and are quite well known as a people who are keen to push the limits.

'The captain wants to see you. Please go to the bridge.' As I left I saw Al collapse over the side and stand up. He had made it. I hoped Mark would be ok.

As I entered the bridge, I had almost the same conversation with the captain as I'd had with the first mate. 'Are you Kiwis …?'

The Coast Guard colonel wants to speak to you,' said the captain.

I picked up the radio and said, 'Coast Guard C-130, this is November Three Seven Serbia Tango … are you there, Dave?' My voice was cracking and I was fighting back the tears.

'Yes, Mike, we're here … you're alive. Well done!'

'Thank you, Dave. Thank you so much. You saved us. We wouldn't be alive if it wasn't for you … thank you so much!'

'Hey, Mike, that's ok, my pleasure. There have been over 300 aircraft go down off this coast, one thousand people lost and you guys are the first in history to survive. How did you do it? We really want to know.'

'We put out a Mayday early, Dave, that was the only way we survived.'

'Can I ask you why you didn't light a flare off when you were in the raft?' asked Dave.

'We thought you could see us. We didn't realise you couldn't until you dropped the next three rafts,' I said.

'No, Mike, we couldn't see you at all.'

'Dave, did you see us hit the water?'

'Oh my god, Mike. We were flying right next to you when you hit. We saw the whole thing … and you keyed the radio mic as you hit. My god, my heart was almost pumping out of my chest. I can't believe you survived the impact … Well done, my friend, well done. It's time for us to say goodbye. It's been our pleasure, Mike.'

'We owe you our lives, Dave … thank you.'

As I left the bridge, I could hear Dave asking the ship's captain to try to retrieve some of the six life rafts they had dropped as long as it didn't impact on the crew's safety. It turned out that each raft cost US$10,000.

Then I heard the words that seemed like they were out of a movie. 'This is the United States Coast Guard signing off, *Columbus Canada*, thank you for your assistance.'

I thought to myself, 'If you're going to crash anywhere in the world, then crash in the United States of America. They are the best.'

I walked down the corridors trying to find my way back to the deck where we had boarded. When I finally made it back there I found a hive of activity. Apparently the life rafts were all attached by a rope. The ship had run over the rope and it had wrapped itself around the propeller. The first officer was holding up some diving gear and running an auction for a volunteer to go over the side and cut the rope free.

As the auction went on, an officer held my arm and took me to the sick bay, as I was totally exhausted and starting to get delirious.

When I got to the sick bay there were Mark and Al. Mark was sitting in the bath washing the fuel off his skin. He got out and I took off my life jacket and underpants and got the shower head and started washing the fuel and salt water off myself. The skin on my chest and legs seemed to completely peel off revealing new pink sore skin underneath. The area around my groin was the worst.

There was only one bed and a few chairs in the sick bay. Al and Mark reckoned I had the worst injuries so gave me the bed. I collapsed gratefully on it and passed out.

I remember the captain coming in at one point and saying,

'Ok, gentlemen, it's time for breakfast.' I sat up and slurred some words along the lines of, 'Thank you for rescuing us …' and then slumped back down.

A few hours later, the captain came in again. 'You will get up now. The media are on the phone, they want to speak to you now.' The idea of speaking to the media frightened me as any publicity about this would not be good for the airline. I knew that Pope would kill me if I spoke to the media.

Officially, I was the most senior Great Barrier Airlines pilot on board. Al hadn't been there very long and Mark was really just part time, so it was decided that I would be the one to deal with it. I went up on my own and the captain took me to the radio operator's room and gave me a very new (for 1995) satellite phone.

On the line was a reporter from a Honolulu newspaper and he was just buzzing about the story. 'Wow! I've been speaking to the Coast Guard guys and they are raving about you guys. They said you are the only pilots ever in history to survive a ditching so far off the coast of Hawaii. How did you do it? How are you feeling?' The reporter just went on and on. The odd time he paused for my response, I just gave very unhelpful yes and no answers. He must've thought I was a total jerk as I didn't elaborate at all.

The Honolulu reporter finally gave up and went off to write 'his' story of the ditching as I certainly didn't give him ours. I felt a sense of relief as I thought I had got away with the media side of things. How wrong I was.

It was to be another nine days before we made landfall in

Los Angeles – a mere 1950 nautical miles back the way we had come.

The captain invited the three of us to have lunch with him. We sheepishly entered the dining area and sat at the table with all the German officers. The captain said a few words welcoming us, and then looked at us directly and said, 'You are my guests. There are two rules: first, you must have breakfast, lunch and dinner with me and second, there is a small beer fridge in the officers' club – it is your job to drink it dry every day. The mess boy will restock it every day. My favourite beer is New Zealand's Steinlager and I have a whole pallet in cold storage.'

After lunch the captain took us to where we would be staying. When we walked into the cabin it was the most luxurious quarters I had ever seen – beautiful oak-lined walls, huge beds, fresh fluffy towels … pure luxury. There were two rooms, so we quickly decided that Al and I would share one and Mark had the other one to himself.

Mark had saved his shoes from the crash and they absolutely stank of jet fuel! The odour was so strong that if any of us had lit a match, there would more than likely have been a huge poof and Mark would have gone up in a ball of flame.

The three of us were dressed in ship's overalls as we had literally lost the clothes off our backs. One of the officers brought us a large bag of clothes that had been donated by the crew – jeans, T-shirts and sweatshirts. It was nice to be in new clothes.

We all got to know the crew very well and the German hospitality was just superb. We had the run of the ship. It goes without saying that we drank a lot of Steinlager and it quickly became my favourite beer. In fact, even when I drink a Steiny now I always have a little smile.

The three of us spent a lot of time going over the flight and trying to work out just what had gone so wrong. One of the most interesting facts was that I had used Al's dad's thousand dollar GPS case strap as a dipstick. By pulling the leather strap tight and then using a flashlight to help lower it into tanks three, four and five, I could then hold the strap alongside the tank and estimate the amount of fuel we had left. For example, tank number five was half full. It was a 200-gallon tank so there were still 100 gallons in tank five.

Across the three tanks, I estimated that we had three hours' worth of fuel and we were only an hour from Hawaii. We had fuel receipts for 20 hours of fuel and we had crashed 17 hours into the flight. These figures would be critical in time to come. Most of the time, the pilots in such a crash are never alive to tell the facts so it's easy to blame the dead pilot. It sort of goes with the job and we accept that, but an alive pilot is a nightmare for an insurance company as they can't lay the blame undefended on the pilot.

I spent plenty of time on the bridge getting to know the crew during the nine days back to Los Angeles. I got to know the third mate well. He was the officer who was in the tender that plucked us out of the life raft. He was the ship's medical officer. When I asked him about his medical experience, he laughed and showed me a very thick book on medical problems. 'I simply look it up in the book.'

'So, what if we'd had internal injuries when you met us in the small tender?' I asked.

'Well,' he said, 'you would have been really sick. I looked up impact injuries and the book said a burst bladder or intestine was likely. However, you would have been really unwell if either of these had happened. Besides, I asked you if you were injured and you said no so I sent the helicopter home.'

'Holy shit!' I said. 'You sent the helicopter off because I said, "Yeah, we are fine?" Kiwis always say, "Yeah, we're fine!" It's in our nature not to make a fuss.' He just laughed.

In fact, I had wanted to urinate just before we descended onto the flares. If I had known that I was risking a burst bladder on impact, I would have just peed myself.

The captain allowed me to send one fax to Great Barrier Airlines. He told me that the shipping company had already spent US$70,000 rescuing us so they couldn't afford the US$15 per minute for us to use the satellite phone. Totally understandable. I asked him why the rescue had cost US$70,000. He showed me the budget of the exact costs – it turned out that was the cost of diverting a container ship off course.

One morning, Mark came in and said in a cheery voice, 'I've just been speaking to the *New Zealand Herald* for the last 30 minutes on the sat phone and they want to talk to one of the pilots in the front.'

I was furious as I thought we had managed to avoid the media in New Zealand. What the hell was Mark talking about for 30 minutes?

I went up to the radio officer's room and spoke to the reporter on the sat phone and said, 'You can't use any of this. Mark was never authorised to speak on behalf of us or

Great Barrier Airlines. I will not be making any statements or comments.'

The reporter said, 'Ha! I don't care. The other guy told us everything, the whole story. You guys are heroes and I don't actually need any comments from you to go to print.'

I went back into the officers' lounge and had a bit of a row with Mark. He didn't think there was anything wrong with talking to the media. Al tried to reassure me that things would be ok.

The next morning at 6am the captain came into our room and said, 'You guys had better come up and sleep in the radio room. The sat phone has been ringing non-stop with media calls.'

When I got up there the phone was ringing. I answered, '*Columbus Canada*, Mike speaking.'

'Can we speak to one of the Kiwi hero pilots, please?'

'Yes, that's me and there is absolutely no comment,' and I hung up.

With my hand still on the phone it rang again. I said exactly the same thing and hung up. It rang again … and so it went on.

Eventually, I gave up answering and went to find the captain. I asked him if I could please call our boss Jim Bergman in New Zealand. He agreed but asked me to keep the call short.

It was really early in New Zealand and I woke Jim up. 'Oh my god, Mike! How are you? We are all so worried about you. Are you ok?'

'Yes, Jim, we're fine but the media … '

'Mike. They've been ringing my phone since 3am. Quickly tell me – did you guys stuff anything up? Could you have done anything different?'

'No, Jim, we did everything we could. We didn't cut any corners, we were totally professional pilots,' I assured him.

'Well, Mike, I want you to speak openly with the media and tell them everything. Otherwise, they will think you're hiding something and if they can't find anything they will simply make stuff up.'

It was so nice to speak to Jim. He was a very good boss and a very caring person.

Once I put down the phone, it started ringing instantly. And it was a radio station in New Zealand. 'Mike, can we interview you?'

'Sure, I have just got permission from my management at Great Barrier Airlines,' I said. And I gave them a 15-minute interview with all the details, the drama, the life and almost death and exactly just how close we came.

Towards the end of the interview, they said, 'We have a surprise for you, Mike. Your mother is on the line.'

They had called my mum and asked if she wanted to speak to me live on the radio. She told them she was too upset to go on live radio. The host told her she could just listen in to the interview and she agreed.

Even though she'd said no to talking to me on air, they connected the pair of us. All I could hear was Mum sobbing uncontrollably, saying, 'Oh, Michael, oh, Michael.'

I tried to comfort her, telling her we were ok, but it wasn't any use. She was so upset.

The radio host could obviously tell his trick had backfired and Mum was really upset, so he disconnected us. There was silence on the end of the phone. The host then came back on the line and sheepishly said, 'That was great. Thanks, Mike.'

'How dare you …' I fumed and he hung up just as I was about to tell him exactly what I thought of him.

As soon as I hung the phone up, it started ringing instantly. I picked up the receiver and politely said, '*Columbus Canada*, Mike speaking.'

'Hi, can I speak to one of the pilots of the Twin Otter? It's New Zealand television here.'

'You're speaking to one of the pilots and you guys can just go and get stuffed plain and simple!' I was so mad, that was the nicest thing I could say.

The TV reporter was shocked and asked what had happened. I told her all about the radio presenter and that I was worried about Mum. The reporter said she was really close to Mum's house and offered to go and see her to make sure she was ok. She then promised to call me back.

She did go around to my mum's house and comfort Mum. But the reporter also filmed Mum sitting out on her veranda crying – without her permission. They then screened this footage on the 6pm news. I was furious when I found out. Over the next few days Al and I did heaps of interviews with different media outlets from all over the world. I didn't want to think about what Pope's reaction must have been when he heard them.

After nine days, we finally arrived in Los Angeles. Once we had berthed, Mark, Al and I remained on board and were taken to a room. Along with Customs and FAA officers, there were two other men who just stood and stared at the three of us.

After a while, one pulled back his jacket and exposed two huge guns. He then walked straight over to me and eyeballed me, leaving about an inch between our noses. Then he said, without blinking, 'I'm FBI, I'm heavily armed and I'm watching you like a hawk, sonny.' I thought, 'Yeah, good on ya, mate, what a dick.' But I just smiled and said, 'Yes, sir.'

We cleared Customs really quickly, leaving us with the FAA guys and the two heavily armed FBI agents. After about five minutes talking to the FAA inspector, he turned to the FBI agents and said, 'I'll be ok now. Thank you, gentlemen, you can go now.' With that the FBI agents turned and left, without saying a word.

'What were they for?' I asked the FAA inspector. 'Well, we weren't sure who you were. You could have been drug smugglers for all we knew so I requested two heavily armed FBI agents to accompany me.'

Once the inspections were completed the captain came in to tell us we had a few friends waiting to meet us. We went up on deck to see Gerard Rea and Murray Pope walking up the gangway. I was nervous about seeing Pope again. Gerard gave me a big hug and said, 'Thank God you're alive!'

I stuttered my reply, 'I'm so sorry about the Twin Otter, Gerard, we tried everything …'

'Mike, you guys are alive. That is all I care about.'

There were no such niceties from Pope. He just walked straight past me and didn't utter a word.

We took Gerard and Murray up to meet the captain and the crew, before going off to do an interview with a TV3 film crew that had flown up to LA especially to interview us. It was my first time on TV and I was quite nervous. The reporter asked pretty standard questions and it was painless. In hindsight, we maybe should have waited a while before giving back the clothes the crew had donated to us. Doing the TV interview wearing the ship's orange overalls made us look as if we'd just escaped from jail!

After farewelling the captain and crew, and thanking them for everything they'd done for us, we all jumped into Gerard's car. As a B767 Captain for Air New Zealand he spent a lot of time in Los Angeles so he co-owned a car with some other pilots. They kept the car at the hotel so when they were in LA they had their own car. He drove us back to the hotel where all the Air New Zealand crew stay.

When we arrived at the hotel, we noticed a few people giving us funny looks. It took a while to work out it was because of our bright orange overalls. Gerard took the three of us to the mall across the road from the hotel and said, 'Get whatever you want, guys, it's all on me.' We all bought new jeans, shirts, shoes and a few other bits and pieces. Then Gerard drove us all the way back down to the port so we could give back the ship overalls.

When we got there, we went back on board and gave the overalls to the first mate. As we were leaving, the captain came up to me and said, 'The American media are onto you. They are going nuts. CNN, KTLA and two other channels are all here with big TV trucks. It's a frenzy! I told them you are staying at the Sheraton in Long Beach … is that correct?' he asked.

I just smiled and said, 'Yep, that's right.' In fact we were at another hotel miles away and I hoped they wouldn't find us. I pulled Gerard aside and told him. He congratulated me for keeping our location quiet.

When we finally got back to our hotel, it was completely full. But rather than turn us away, they kindly organised for us to stay in one of their small conference rooms, putting five rollaway beds in it.

That night, Gerard took us down to the hotel bar to meet some of the other Air New Zealand pilots. I was a bit nervous, I didn't know what they would think of our whole event. I looked up to these guys in a big way. When we got to the bar there were about a dozen B747 pilots. I needn't have been nervous at all – they were really cool guys. They bought all our drinks and were fascinated by our story. Just as we were talking about the whole fuel transfer saga, and having to shimmy over the aluminium tanks with one-gallon urine bottles full of fuel, Mark walked in wearing the shoes he'd had on during the crash. He reeked of jet fuel – a smell very familiar to jet pilots. Someone shouted, 'Bloody hell, you, the jet fuel …' Everyone cracked up, but it instantly brought the story to life.

We stayed for an hour or so before Al and I had to leave to meet some friends of mine at Manhattan Beach. Gerard opened his wallet and pulled out two US$100 notes. He gave Al and me one each. It was the most money I'd ever had to simply go out and spend on myself. I was stoked.

The friends we went to meet were another couple of the blokes Mum had met on that flight back from Hawaii. After seeing Eric in San Francisco, it was fantastic to be able to catch up with Amondo and Jim.

Amondo was now a lawyer working in a huge law firm and was very interested in talking to us about the whole crash from a legal point of view. He listened to the story and then simply said, 'It would be good to talk about the legal side of things once everything has settled down. I think there is scope for you to sue and get some compensation for what you have been through. But tonight … let's party. You're alive, buddy!' He then gave me a great big hug.

The four of us went to a couple of really cool bars and Jim and Amondo went around telling everyone what had just happened to us. The hospitality was fantastic and we partied up a storm. People kept coming up to us and shaking our hands … and buying us drinks. One of the highlights of my night was meeting some military fast jet pilots – I thought it was pretty cool to meet guys who flew F-15s and other fighter planes.

After a few hours of partying, Jim and Amondo dropped us back at the hotel. Thankfully, Al was in much better shape than I was and he managed to find our room.

Gerard and Pope were fast asleep but Mark was still wide awake. Mark had selected the bed by the window and had turned down the cover and made the bed look nice and cosy. I staggered into the room and made a beeline for his bed. I could hear him saying, 'No, Mike, that's my bed … no, Mike … Mike, that's my bed …'

I wasn't having a bar of it. With that I flopped down on his bed and grabbed a nearby rubbish bin, hung my head over it and vomited. And vomited again. And again.

Very calmly Mark said, 'Actually, Mike, you can have that bed now…'

The next morning I woke with a rather sore head. I wasn't a big drinker, so I suffered when I pushed it a bit. Thankfully, we had the day to kill before flying back that night into the awaiting media storm in New Zealand. Pope had given us all a briefing on how he thought we should handle the media. Having given him our assurances, he cheered up a bit and was quite chatty.

We spent the day lying by the pool at the hotel before going out to the airport. Our flight home was with Qantas and we'd met a Qantas pilot at the bar in Manhattan Beach the previous night. He had told the crew on our flight all about our adventure and they took it upon themselves to keep our drinks topped up for the whole flight. I was still feeling pretty green so didn't bother them much.

To our surprise, when we landed in Auckland, there was a police escort waiting for us. We must have looked confused, as the officer said, 'You guys clearly have no idea about the media scrum waiting for you outside.'

Pope was pretty wound up at the prospect of us facing the TV cameras but he calmed down when the police guys offered to escort us out through a side door. Mark's wife and two children were waiting for him on the other side and he really didn't care about the media – he just wanted to see his family.

While Al and I slipped through the side door, Mark's emotional reunion with his family was filmed by the country's media and microphones were shoved in his face asking him questions.

Having escaped the media barrage, we headed straight over to the Great Barrier Airlines office. Jim had arranged a champagne welcome for us. Our families were there as were all the Great Barrier Airlines staff. It was just the kind of welcome I wanted. I saw exactly what I meant to my family, friends and workmates. You could see the concern on their faces and how much they really cared about us. It was quite a humbling experience.

From the Great Barrier Airlines office, we could see all the media milling around outside. We simply stayed in the office refusing all requests until everyone left. Once we thought it was safe I departed with my family and girlfriend. No sooner had I got outside than there was a TV crew poking a camera in my face asking some really inappropriate questions. They wanted to know things I couldn't answer, like, 'Why did you crash? Did you as a pilot contribute to the reason the aircraft had to ditch? Are you covering anything up?'

I politely asked the reporter to put the camera away, saying, 'I would love to answer all your questions but the flight is under investigation by the FAA. It isn't appropriate for me to comment. You are going to get me in so much trouble with my boss if he sees me talking to you on TV.'

The reporter retorted, 'Mike, you guys were on the front page of the *New Zealand Herald* and were the main story on the television news when you crashed, then again when you made it to Los Angeles. The whole nation wants to hear from you …'

When he put it like that, I realised he had a point so I agreed to a short interview with prearranged questions. Of the whole interview, the only question they screened was one about when I was going back to work. I told them that as it was Saturday and we were given Sunday off, I'd go straight back to work on Monday. No work equalled no pay – besides, I was keen to get back on the horse, so to speak.

The same reporter ambushed Al and poked the camera in his face and asked, 'So does this adventure make you a better pilot?' Al laughed and answered in a really cool, relaxed manner, 'Ahh, heck yeah!'

Just before we'd left New Zealand, Al had had a job interview with Eagle Air and he'd missed out on the job. It just so happened that Eagle Air's chief pilot saw Al's interview on the news and rang him to offer him a job. He joked that since he was now a much better pilot, Al should come and work for them!

The next few days were surreal as the media interest was unbelievable. TV vans were outside my house, reporters were knocking on the door, and magazines were calling … all wanting something. I just wanted it all to go away. I wanted to return to normal. I just wanted to go back to work and fly.

After a few days of being pretty much in hiding, a friend suggested that I choose one magazine and sign an exclusive deal for a fee. It felt a bit strange to be selling my story but I didn't own that much at that stage and a lot of it was sitting on the bottom of the Pacific Ocean. I had lost pretty much all my clothes, my camera and my watch – they needed replacing and I didn't have the money to pay for it.

One of the women's magazines was offering the best money on the condition that Al, his girlfriend Julie, and me and my girlfriend talked and had our photos taken. We all met out at a local airfield and stood next to a plane for the shoot. The magazine was particularly interested in the notes Al and I had written to our girlfriends and put down our underpants. The pressure mounted to tell them exactly what we'd written, but Al and I refused to reveal the contents of our notes. In fact, Al still had his note and gave it to Julie when he returned. A few years later Al and Julie got married and had four children. Unfortunately my note was lost in the crash.

On the day of publication the other Great Barrier Airlines pilots bought as many copies of the magazine as they could. For days afterwards, the photos from the article would turn up everywhere – in the office, in the aircraft I was flying, in my flight bag. The ribbing went on for a while but I didn't mind. Hey, life was good … I was still breathing.

A few weeks after I got home, I was talking to my mum. She was really serious and she spoke very quietly. 'Mike, you've been through a horrendous event. Even though you don't really seem to be having any issues, you need to be very careful. If or when you have another incident or emergency while you're flying I want you to pay particular attention to how you are feeling. If you are feeling invincible, not scared, or think to yourself "This is nothing, I've been in a ditching", you need to talk to me straight away and I will help you get some assistance. There is a strong possibility you could have post-traumatic stress. The first sign is, you will have no fear and that is a bad sign …' My mum is a very wise lady and these were very wise words.

After being back at work for a while I felt a bit lost, a bit sad, something wasn't right in my life. My relationship wasn't the happiest as I felt like we were on different wave lengths. We had already broken up once, but I felt so bad about the pain the break-up had caused her that I couldn't go through with it. I see now that this would hurt her more in the long run. We weren't soul mates but I didn't have the guts to end the relationship.

For a few weeks I drifted along still absolutely loving my flying job but something was missing … something I couldn't put my finger on. One night I went to my mum's house and she could see I was restless, unsettled. She told me to go and take a bath. I didn't argue with her as she had a really nice spa bath.

As I lay there I started relaxing and day-dreaming. I just let myself go. I dreamt of a life full of adventure, living to the maximum, not letting a day go by that I regretted. I day-dreamed of flying a Twin Otter in the jungle somewhere in South America; of landing on some remote hillside airstrip; of challenging flying; of living life free and fast but using my skills as a pilot. I longed for adventure in some place far off, like Indiana Jones.

I must have been in that bath for hours. I didn't want to get out as the day-dream would finish. Sometimes I really think there is some higher power up there listening to my sub-conscious mind for within days my day-dream turned into a reality that was almost exactly how I had imagined it.

Day-dreaming in that bath was where my life changed and would *never* be the same again.

FIJI DREAMING

The following week I went into work and met up with Gerard Rea. He told me that the company was planning to lease a Piper Chieftain to Air Fiji out of Suva in the Fiji Islands . He then asked if I would consider spending six months flying the Piper in Fiji. It might not have been the South American jungle but flying around the tropical islands of the Pacific sounded pretty perfect to me.

In the meantime, the Twin Otter's owners had employed an independent air crash investigator to look into what had caused the ditching. He interviewed each of us in great depth. We were all very nervous about what his conclusions would be as our professional reputations were on the line.

Finally, the day came when we were called into the office for the investigator to present his findings. The whole case revolved around the size of the feeder hose that the ferry tanking company had installed. At the time the tanks were installed, our engineer, Colin, had seen 3/8-inch hose installed throughout the ferry system. He had questioned the American aircraft engineers as he would have installed 1/2-inch hose when fitting ferry tanks. The American engineers assured him that 3/8-inch hose was fine and that they would fully flow check the fuel once it was all installed.

After the crash the tanking company quickly produced a receipt for a few hundred metres of 1/2-inch hose, but we had no doubt that they had fitted the smaller hose in the aircraft. It was hard to argue our case as the evidence lay at the bottom of the Pacific Ocean.

To our surprise, all the investigator's flow calculations confirmed what we had told him about the hose. The tanks were used up exactly where they should have been and the chilling fact that there was no way we could have got all the fuel out of the back tanks was confirmed. Despite this, the investigator said that nothing could be confirmed as we had no proof as to the size of the hose.

With that Al said, 'Wait ... Mike, you jammed a Great Barrier Airlines pen down the fuel line just before you got into the cockpit.' We quickly grabbed a Great Barrier Airlines pen – the same type I had used to plug the fuel line. The crash investigator pulled out a micrometer and measured the diameter of the pen. He looked up, took off his glasses and said with great relief, 'That's it ... it's exactly 3/8ths of an inch in diameter.'

There was now no doubt that the aircraft had been fitted with the wrong size feeder hose. I asked the crash investigator why, when we flew the test flight, we ended up with more fuel in the aircraft tanks from the ferry system than when we started.

'Well,' he said, 'as the head pressure of the fuel decreases in the tank you obviously lose pressure in the fuel line to the point where the fuel pressure is no longer able to keep up with the demand of the engine. The other thing that happens is frictional loss. The fuel line all the way back from tank five to the cockpit and then down to the belly tank has a frictional loss larger than the fuel lines from tank one. So at low fuel level in tanks one and two, the fuel flow would still be able to supply the demands of the engines, but in tanks three, four and five the friction loss was too great. That's why you had more fuel in the aircraft belly tanks when you landed than when you took off.'

It all made sense to me. We had seen the feeds from all five tanks and then selected the entire ferry system to the low fuel configuration as per the tanking company's instruction during the test flight. Our big mistake had been trusting that the tanking company engineers had flow checked all the tanks at low level. It was obvious they had not. Hindsight is a wonderful thing and I often look back and ask myself what I could have done differently. The answer is always the same – even to this day, I don't think there was anything.

With the investigation complete, it was time to focus on the future. There was much excitement around the office with the new flying happening up in Fiji. We would each do a six-month stint flying the Piper Chieftain for Air Fiji. Officially, Gerard owned the Chieftain and we would be working for him and not for Great Barrier Airlines. Jim was happy for some of his pilots to get this fantastic flying experience.

After much anticipation the day came to go to Fiji. Gerard and I were ferrying the Chieftain up to Fiji via Norfolk Island, where we'd refuel. This was my first ferry flight since the accident, so I was a little nervous.

We took off from Auckland and almost straight away flew into very bad weather, causing the aircraft to bounce around a lot. I could feel the tension inside me building. I really didn't like it but it was bearable. After about an hour we changed to long-distance HF radio communications. The HF radio has a very strange sound – it's almost haunting the way it distorts sounds and voices. This brought the memories of the ditching flooding back, and I had vivid visions of the moments before the ditching. My hands were all clammy and I was sweating. I clearly remember breathing faster, which didn't help as it made me dizzy. I talked myself through it in my head. 'You're ok, Mike. Come on, it's just the radio, it's ok, you can do this.' It worked and after a few minutes I calmed down.

The rest of the flight went without a hitch. It was fantastic to be flying with Gerard. He was a well-respected airline captain with decades of experience but the best thing about him was that he liked helping the next generation of pilots get ahead.

We landed at Nausori International Airport in Suva, cleared Customs and met the Air Fiji management. I was so excited as it was such a different place, a little rough, but everyone was really friendly. During my six months there, I was to be the main pilot to fly the Chieftain. It was a really nice plane – leather interior, state of the art instruments and it even had a built-in GPS. It had a retractable undercarriage and was very fast. Well, the fastest aircraft I had ever flown.

Accommodation in Suva was part of the deal for us going to work in Fiji, and I was to be sharing the Air Fiji house with Maurice, an older New Zealand guy who had been living in Fiji for years.

On my days off, Maurice would be flying the Piper – he had over 20,000 hours of flying time and just loved the island type of flying.

My daily schedule was usually Suva–Nadi–Lambasa–Nadi–Matei–Savusavu–Nadi (three-hour lunch break)–Lambasa–Nadi–Suva. It averaged nine hours' flying and 12 hours' duty each day, which was right up to the maximum you were allowed to do. I certainly wasn't in Fiji for a tropical holiday.

Gerard flew with me to check out all the airstrips I would be flying in to. Each one had its own unique issues. Matei and Savusavu were both very short. The problem with flying a high performance twin engine aircraft into a short strip is that if you have an engine failure before you reach a certain speed you can have difficulty maintaining control of the aircraft. When one engine fails, the aircraft will yaw towards the failed engine. If that happens, we use the rudder to keep the aircraft straight. But the rudder is only effective when there is air flowing over it. We use a speed called 'blue line speed' (there is literally a little blue line on the air speed indicator). Below this speed there is not enough air flow over the rudder to keep the aircraft straight if one engine fails. Because the airstrips were so short we would have to get airborne quickly and level off to get the aircraft accelerating past the blue line. With any engine failure once airborne and below blue line speed the procedure was to close both thrust levers and land straight ahead. Well actually, crash straight ahead – either into the sea or into the coconut trees. Coconut trees might look soft from the air but they are rock hard!

The most difficult strip was Savusavu as it had a big hill right at the end, and most of the time we landed one way but we could only take so much tail wind. There was no tower controller to give you a wind direction so you had to estimate it yourself. I got very good at looking at coconut trees and estimating the wind on the ground. If there was too much wind to land towards the hill there was another very scary approach from the other end. This involved skimming the tops of the coconut trees and then pushing hard over on the controls and flying at tree top level down a very narrow valley. The problem was, the valley was on a 30-degree angle to the runway so you were literally linking up with the runway 10 feet above the ground. The strip was so short there was no other option. This approach was nicknamed the Cambodian approach, after some secret CIA airstrip in Cambodia during the Vietnam War.

After a few weeks Gerard left and I was on my own. The flying was hard but so very rewarding. I loved it.

At Air Fiji there was a stream of local guys who spoke no English. They had never seen a Piper Chieftain before and were confused by all its luggage lockers – one in the nose, one on each wing behind the engine and one in the rear of the fuselage. It was critical that it was loaded correctly especially as, most of the time, I was flying at maximum all-up weight so how the weight was distributed was very important. There have been many accidents over the years caused by the aircraft being loaded incorrectly. Everything goes fine until you have an engine failure and then the whole dynamics of the aircraft change and if it's outside the centre of gravity limits, it's a really bad time to find out.

To ensure correct loading, I would get all the luggage delivered to the aircraft and put the bags outside the aircraft lockers where I wanted them loaded, then the local Fijian loaders would load the aircraft.

One morning, I got to work just as the sun was rising and there were these drums playing in the distance. It made me realise just how much my dream had become a reality. I hopped in the plane and taxied over to the terminal. The luggage was weighed and organised by each luggage locker. I then went inside to sign off the load sheet and the fuel dockets.

Once that was done, I briefed the passengers and waved goodbye to the loader. The plane was totally full and easily at maximum all-up weight. I taxied out and took off and as soon as I got airborne things started to go wrong. To keep the wings level I needed almost full aileron control; the control wheel was almost full left and this was barely keeping the wings level.

I declared an emergency – from my previous experience I wasn't shy about doing this. I asked the control tower for clearances so I could make mostly right hand turns to get in to land. Then I lined the plane up on a long final approach and landed. It wasn't that stressful as I still had control, but what worried me was what had caused the controls to be so out of the norm.

The landing was uneventful and I taxied in and shut down. I got all the passengers into the terminal and then, with an engineer, started looking at the controls. We checked everything – he even unscrewed some inspection panels and looked at all the control cables. We were both scratching our heads in confusion. Then I opened the wing locker and to my horror it was overloaded, absolutely jam-packed with gear. There were two dive weight belts, and a bag which must have weighed 25 kilograms on its own. I opened it and it was full of jars of preserved fruit. When I was sorting the luggage, I hadn't even seen the dive belts. It turned out the passengers had carried them on to the plane themselves and a loader thought he was being helpful by putting the belts in a luggage locker!

The maximum weight allowed in a wing locker was 15 kilos but there must have been 50–60 kilograms in there! I was furious, as I had left a couple of light bags by that wing locker expecting the loaders to put those bags and only those bags into that particular locker. But at the end of the day, no matter what happens, the captain is the person ultimately responsible for the safety of the aircraft and this was a very valuable lesson for me.

I went in and saw the Air Fiji manager and told him that from now on, I was going to be loading the plane myself even if it meant I'd need a little extra time to depart. He said, 'Mike, these guys are from the local village. If you load the plane, I'll have to let some of them go … and this is their only income. Why don't we have a meeting about it later?'

I agreed, then loaded the plane myself and took off for the day's flying.

When I arrived back at the airport at Nausori, there were about 10 loaders and the manager waiting for me. The manager pulled me aside and suggested I get the loaders to teach me to speak Fijian as a way of engaging with them. He pointed out that it would have the added bonus of me being able to instruct them exactly where to load the luggage. Brilliant idea.

So I sat down and started my Fijian language lessons. The baggage handlers set a couple of rules – firstly, no naughty words, we want you to take this seriously, and secondly, we will give you six words per day and then test you at the end of the day. I was up for the challenge.

From then on, the loaders were really friendly. I not only got the plane loaded correctly but I also provided them with great entertainment with my faltering Fijian. I would depart every day with six words on my sun visor and say them over and over again, most of the time taking the opportunity to try them out with any locals on the aircraft.

Word travelled so that when I arrived in Nadi, the loaders there would test me on my day's words but they would also give me six naughty and funny words to learn. On arrival back at home base in Suva, the loaders sat around a big bowl of kava (a local root drink that has a mild intoxicating effect). I would be invited to join them and practise my words while drinking kava. Well, bloody hell, after three or four bowls of kava, I was very merry and could hardly walk. I quickly learned to limit myself to only two bowls.

Not long after my lessons had begun, I landed on one of the strips and all the passengers were on Fiji time – by which I mean moving very slowly. Even in those days, on-time performance was very important so I took a big deep breath and loudly said, 'Tolomai, tolomai! Wan mi waqavuka lili.' ('Quickly, quickly! Hop on board my little aeroplane.') All of the passengers just cracked up laughing. One lady even had to sit down, she was laughing so much. I asked what was so funny, a little bit worried I'd said something wrong. One guy said, 'You – just you! This skinny white man with skinny white legs sticking out of your shorts shouting at us in fluent Fijian – it's not a sight we see every day my friend!'

One morning Maurice was coming flying with me so I could train him on the Chieftain – not that a man with 20,000 hours under his belt needed any training. We taxied out, took off and just as we were climbing away there was a huge bang and a violent swing to the right followed by more bangs and misfires. One of the passengers shouted that there was a ball of fire coming from the right engine. I looked back and saw black smoke. Maurice was flying and I put my hand on the right thrust lever and suggested we throttle it back. He agreed. We had to completely close the thrust lever for it to stop misfiring and settle down.

We made it back to Nausori, declared an emergency and landed on one engine. My heart was pounding though I tried to look as calm and professional as possible to the passengers. But I was glad to finally be on the ground.

Once we landed, I remembered what my mum had said about my next big emergency. I knew I was fine because when the engine was failing and misfiring, and the passengers were shouting about flames, I was scared. Despite my fear, I still felt very confident with flying the aircraft and dealing with the emergency. This meant that I didn't have any signs of post-traumatic stress from the Twin Otter crash but I was certainly ready for my bowl of kava that night.

Unfortunately, it was going to take three weeks to fix the engine and instead of sitting in Fiji doing nothing, I headed back to New Zealand to work at Great Barrier Airlines. When word arrived that the plane was fixed, I hopped on the next flight back to Fiji.

As soon as I landed in Nausori, I couldn't wait to get back into the cockpit of the Chieftain for a test flight. The plane was sitting in the middle of the hangar all polished up and looking like a million dollars. I walked into the engineering hangar and asked for the foreman or supervisor who had worked on the plane. A very nice guy came out and said he was the boss.

'Great,' I said, 'you're coming flying with me on the test flight.' He looked horrified and said, 'No way!'

I asked him why not and he said that he never went on test flights.

'Well, if you don't have confidence in your work, do you honestly expect me to fly it?' I asked. There was a lot of talking in Fijian and Hindi among the Fijian-Indian engineers. I had no idea what they were saying. Eventually a little Fijian-Indian man sort of got pushed towards me. 'He's the supervisor, he'll fly with you!'

'Ok, let's go,' I said.

I pre-flighted the plane, logged a flight plan for a 45-minute local flight and off we went. I talked a little to the engineer as he was sitting next to me in the cockpit. He had been the engineer who rebuilt the engine so I was happy that I had the right man with me.

We taxied out, did all the pre-take-off checks then started the take-off roll. I applied a little power, everything looked good, and then I gave it full power ... all good ... the Chieftain was humming! I pulled back on the controls gently and we rotated into the sky. I reached over and grabbed the landing gear lever to put the gear up.

With this, there was an awful noise – a really sick hydraulic sound – and the gear wouldn't completely come up to lock in the correct position. I looked at the engineer, who had turned a few shades paler than his normal colour. He started rocking back and forward, banging his head with his left hand, and shouting in a strong Indian accent, 'No no no no no no no ...'

'What?' I shouted. 'I forgot to pressurise the hydraulic system and ...' I couldn't understand him as he was rambling on and banging his head at the same time. He was very upset.

I said, 'But I checked the hydraulics!'

He responded, 'No, no, no, your pre-flight check only checks you have pressure in the ... no, no, no.'

He immediately started hitting his head again. I thought about the checks I had done on the ground and I was sure I hadn't missed anything as I had followed a checklist. I pulled out the flight manual and handed it to the engineer and told him to look up how to use the alternative system to manually lower the landing gear.

'We will never get it down; there is no hydraulic pressure in the line … '

Oh great. Here I am and in the last two months, I've ditched in the Pacific, had an engine failure and now I had to deal with a bloody wheels-up landing. I told him to carry out the procedure anyway, so he read it out loud and I confirmed everything he was doing. He then extended this long lever and started pumping the undercarriage down. Either there was no fluid in the system or it hadn't been pressurised correctly so we would never get it down. There was no hydraulic gauge in this particular plane.

The engineer pumped away at the gear for ages, all the while sweating profusely. Still there was no green light showing the undercarriage was locked into place … just three red lights telling me it was unlocked.

Yet again, I declared an emergency, then got a clearance to climb a bit higher to 6000 feet. I wanted to put the plane into some steep turns or shallow dives to gently pull some Gs (g-force). I hoped that this would lock the undercarriage into place. We climbed up and did a few steep turns and shallow dives, all the while making sure I didn't overstress the aircraft. The poor engineer had now gone a sort of ash colour, and he looked like he was going to throw up any second. Unfortunately we still had no green lights.

We spoke with the tower and arranged for the fire service to be on full alert, as we would more than likely end up with our undercarriage collapsing on the landing roll. I made a low pass past the tower and they said it looked like the wheels were locked. Well, they said they were hanging straight down, which provided the engineer and me with little comfort.

The Fijian crash rescue service was very keen to lay down a blanket of foam for us to land on – the idea being that the foam would stop any sparks and perhaps prevent an explosion. I had seen a video of two aircraft landing with a foam pad waiting for them. The first one missed the foam pad completely and landed just fine with the landing gear up. The second one hit the foam way too fast, with the consensus after the fact being that the pilot was so fixated on landing on the foam pad that he missed the fact he was flying too fast.

I declined the offer of a foam pad, as I would be landing with the wheels partly down and I hoped that they might not collapse. I needed to make as smooth a landing as I could and the foam would block my view of the runway.

I burnt as much fuel as possible so if the undercarriage collapsed and the fuel tanks burst there would only be a little fire … but I knew that if there was any fire at all, I would be toast. I asked the engineer to go down to the rear of the plane by the emergency exit. I knew this wasn't necessary but I thought it would make him feel better.

I lined up for the final approach and made sure I was flying at exactly the correct speed. As we flew across the fence of the airport, I could see all the firemen sitting in their trucks. I flared the plane and as gently as possible touched the main wheels on the runway and slowly lowered the nose. I quickly feathered the engines, pulled the fuel shut-offs and gently coasted to a halt without using the brakes. We were down and the undercarriage hadn't collapsed.

Mike Allsop

I shouted to the engineer to get out and go under the aircraft to see if the undercarriage locks were in place. He wasn't very keen on doing it but I told him firmly that he had to and off he went. He quickly came back out and said the locks were all in place. With that I waved the fire trucks off, started the Chieftain back up and taxied over to the engineering hangar. The engineer wasn't taking any more chances and chose to walk back.

It didn't take long before my friends had heard about my little incident and came around to the Air Fiji house. Talking to other pilots about your incidents or events really helped especially over a few beers.

A few nights later I arranged a barbecue at the house and decided to have a competition to see who could bring the biggest firework. We are talking bangers, ones that simply go bang really loud. I searched all of Suva looking for the biggest one I could find and eventually befriended an Indian storekeeper who took me down into his cellar and showed me this huge pile of fireworks.

He said, 'Help yourself, but no smoking, eh?' He had a cheeky little smile on his face. I rummaged around and kept finding bigger and bigger fireworks, and then I spotted this huge stick. I pulled it out of the pile. It was about eight inches long, red, with a fuse out of the top. When I rolled it over it had the letters TNT written down the side. This had to be Suva's biggest firework.

I took it up to the storekeeper and he laughed. 'That one not loud,' he said. 'But still good. Trust me these are the best.' He showed me this box of firecrackers called 'Daddy's Single

84

Voice'. They were only about three inches long and three-quarters of an inch wide. I took 10 boxes.

The night of the barbecue came around and everyone turned up with beers, sausages and firecrackers. I had these 10 boxes of Daddy's Single Voices just sitting on the dining table and no one took any notice of them as they didn't look that impressive.

Everyone took it in turns bringing out their most impressive firework and lighting it on the veranda before throwing it onto the lawn. The fireworks got bigger and bigger until it was finally my turn. I had been saving the big one. I pulled out this stick of TNT, and everyone cracked up. I knew it wasn't really TNT (well, according to the storekeeper) but no one else did. As quick as a flash, I lit the fuse and chucked it on the lawn before anyone was ready. There was a mad scramble with guys taking cover all over the place. It was like someone had thrown a hand grenade. We all blocked our ears and braced for the explosion. It went off with a loud bang but nothing spectacular.

A little disappointed I went inside and got a Daddy's Single Voice. I lit it and threw it a few feet off the veranda. No one was expecting much but it just went ka-boom! I could feel the explosion in my chest and everyone's ears were ringing. We were in total disbelief that something so small had such a huge punch. And we had almost 10 boxes of these suckers.

Next thing, someone got one, lit it and dropped it into a mongoose hole on our front lawn. We had been having big issues with mongooses digging holes in our lawn. The cracker went off with a bang and blew a huge hole in the lawn. Next thing, the mongoose came flying out of another hole and took off. We never saw him again.

As the night progressed it became clear that if you give a bunch of young pilots in the tropics a few beers and a heap of fireworks there is bound to be trouble. We all filled our pockets with crackers and headed into town. We piled into the local pub and started planning. Someone came up with the idea that we should tie a few of these Daddy's Single Voices together and stick them inside a rubbish tin … that would make a huge noise.

We left the pub and started looking for a good rubbish bin, somewhere safe away from any crowds but close enough to the main street to cause a bit of drama and excitement. We found the perfect bin, twisted about 10 crackers together and one of the guys lit the fuse and plopped them into the bin.

As we walked off down the street quite quickly, two Fijian police officers came out of a doorway in front of us. I looked up and there was a big sign saying 'Suva Police Head-quarters'. Shit!

We managed to walk past the police officers before an almighty explosion let rip. They would have been about 30 feet away from the bin when it went off. It must have given them one hell of a fright. They shouted for the three of us to stop and they lifted their skirt-like uniform sulus up really high and started sprinting after us with their batons drawn. We knew we were in for a hiding.

Instinctively the three of us split up and took off. I ran down to the beach and one officer followed me. Now I was running from the police – not usually a smart thing to do but even stupider in Fiji. I flew around one corner and then immediately turned left again as the policeman carried on straight ahead. I doubled back and then calmly walked across the road as even more police officers came out of the police headquarters. A few of them saw me but had no idea I was one of the culprits.

The next day I caught up with the other two and they had managed to lose their pursuing policemen. We decided it would be best to put the fireworks away for a while after that.

The exciting flying continued and I loved it even though it was sometimes a real challenge. Along with the tricky airstrips and the changeable weather, the local passengers could also be very interesting.

One morning when I was on my way to work in the Air Fiji shuttle van, the driver accidentally ran over a dog as we were passing through a reasonably remote village on the way to the airport. We all got out to see if there was anything we could do for the poor dog. We knew it was still alive because it was howling its lungs out. The next thing we knew there was a heap of local people running out of their homes. They were not happy and they made sure the driver knew about it. They were absolutely screaming at him. It was all getting a bit serious so me and two other pilots climbed back into the van just as the first rock was thrown at us. The driver then ran back, hopped in and sped off amid a barrage of flying rocks … not the best way to start a day's work.

My first flight that day was pretty normal and I landed in Nadi, refuelled then taxied out and took off. Flying out I realised the air traffic controller was the same one who had cleared me to land an hour earlier. I asked him if he was doing overtime. He told me that the next controller had not shown up for work so he had no choice but to do a double shift, after he had just done a night shift. He sounded very tired.

As we climbed out past about 1500 feet I could see a large line of thunderstorms ahead. The Chieftain had a really good weather radar and the thunderstorms looked very ugly! I requested a deviation of my usual course by 20 miles so I could go around the storms. This was approved. The clearance from the controller was, 'Fiji 122 you are cleared around weather up to 20 miles left of track, requirement to be back on the 055 radial by 70 miles from Nadi.' The 055 radial is basically the track from Nadi to Labasa.

I was in cloud most of the way but as I returned to the prescribed track, I reported to the controller, 'Fiji 122 is on track 055 radial at 70 miles maintaining 10,000 feet.' Just then I popped out of cloud into clear skies.

A little voice came over the radio. 'I'm at 70 miles on the 055 radial and I'm at 10,000 feet.'

'Are you in cloud?' I asked.

'Yes, I'm in cloud … No, wait, I've just come out of the cloud.'

I looked over and 100 feet off my right wing was a Twin Otter, so close I could see the expression on the pilot's face. I broke left to get away from him. 'Holy smoke!' I said on the radio. 'You can say that again,' came the reply.

The air traffic controller had forgotten that he had given me clearance to be off track and when the Twin Otter departed, the pilot flew straight through the storms as he didn't have weather radar. Thus we caught each other up with

Mark Roberts and me in the cockpit of the Twin Otter a few hours before the emergency began.

Our Twin Otter N37ST at Grand Canyon airport.

just 10 seconds between us. We were so close to having a mid-air collision. The controller was obviously tired from working a double shift and had made a potentially fatal mistake. Neither the Twin Otter pilot nor I had any confidence in the controller so we simply arranged separation ourselves. Once on the ground we both filed formal incident reports.

Thankfully, all of the odd things I experienced while flying in Fiji weren't as serious as that. On one flight to Matei on the island of Taveuni, I was commencing my approach and I could see something on the runway. The aircraft was fully configured ready to land and at about 100 feet I still couldn't work out what was in the middle of the runway. The closer I got the more puzzled I was – it looked like some sort of animal lying right in the middle of the runway about halfway along.

I had no choice but to go around – I couldn't risk running into it. I put the gear and flaps up and then decided to buzz this animal to scare it off the runway. I flew along the start of the runway very low and the animal jumped up and ran off into the coconut trees. Only it wasn't an animal at all – it was a person wearing a brightly coloured sarong.

Once I'd landed and unloaded all the bags and passengers, sleeping beauty wandered out of the coconut trees carrying a large cane knife and eating peanuts. He looked a bit scary and as he walked up to me, I started to worry that I'd pissed him off with my low pass over his head.

I needn't have worried. He apologised in English for making me go around. He then offered me some peanuts. I asked him why on earth he'd been sleeping on the runway. He said, 'I was tired because I have been working and wanted

to have a sleep. The coral runway was nice and cool so I lay down thinking your plane would wake me up when it was coming in to land … I never thought I would make you go around. I'm really sorry.'

'Hey, no problem … did I scare you?' I asked.

'Holy smoke,' he said. 'I thought you were going to land on me …'

We laughed, then shook hands and said goodbye. I watched him disappear back into the coconut grove.

The very next day I flew back up to Matei and saw the same person. I had to look twice as he walked towards my plane. He was dressed in a full pilot's uniform. I smiled and greeted him with a handshake and said, 'No cane knife? You didn't tell me yesterday that you are a pilot!'

'I was a little embarrassed about making you go around,' he replied. I put him in the front seat and we chatted all the way to Nadi.

Sadly my time in Fiji was coming to an end. I had done my six months and now it was someone else's turn. This time had been a bit of an escape, really. I was away from New Zealand and I hardly ever thought about the Twin Otter crash, which was a relief.

I had so much fun in Fiji – the flying was fantastic and the Fijian people were so friendly and welcoming. I left with about a two hundred word vocabulary – enough to know when the old women at the markets were talking about me marrying their granddaughters. You should have seen their faces when I answered them back in Fijian!

STEPPING UP

Arriving home was a bit of a reality check. I loved flying for Great Barrier Airlines, but I knew that at some stage I would have to move on. The normal progression for a pilot in New Zealand is to work for a small airline or as a flying instructor before getting a job with one of the two commuter airlines, Eagle Air or Air Nelson. From there, it was on up to flying for Air New Zealand.

I had enough flying experience to apply to both airlines but I enjoyed working at Great Barrier Airlines so much that I decided to stay there and try to make the step straight up to Air New Zealand. It was a risky decision.

My friend Gary Spicer was a Boeing 747 Captain for Air New Zealand. On my behalf, he had asked Air New Zealand management if it was feasible to make the transition from Great Barrier Airlines to the international airline. I was

stoked to hear they'd told him that is was possible as they were looking for experienced pilots from outside their usual sources of Eagle Air, Air Nelson and the air force. Gary managed to get them to look at my file and they liked my experience but said I was a little short on hours. I only had 2500 hours and they wanted 3000.

Gary Spicer has always had a big influence on my life. In fact, it was he who had taught me to fly. In 1985, I was friends with Gary's son. Gary told me one day that he had heard I wanted to learn to fly. He told me that if I rented the plane, he'd teach me for free. To rent a Cessna 152 at the time cost $70 per hour with an extra $15 an hour for an instructor. It was a big saving for me.

I worked after school on Tuesdays and Thursdays then all day Saturday in the supermarket, earning $33 over the three days. I also had a paper round one day a week adding $3 to my earnings. I could afford half an hour's flying each week. But I didn't rush in. I saved a few hundred dollars so I could get regular lessons until I had my solo licence. Gary taught me for the first few hours then his best friend, David Morgan, who was also an Air New Zealand pilot, took over for the final few hours until I could fly solo.

I have fond memories of flying with David. One day, I flew a circuit at Ardmore and at the end of the circuit I landed and taxied back around to the holding point where David let me have it.

'That's a shocking display of flying. You didn't trim the aircraft once and your checks were sloppy. I'm not wasting my time on a Saturday morning teaching you to fly if you're

going to fly like that. We'll do another one and if it's no better I'm going home!'

I sheepishly taxied out, flew the circuit then landed. David was silent. Finally, he said, 'Pull over, I'm getting out!'

'Oh no!' I thought. 'I've stuffed it up again and he's going home.' Once I stopped, David looked at me, smiled and said, 'That was a lot better. It's now time for you to do your first solo.'

Your first solo flight is a huge deal for every pilot. I taxied out, took off, flew a circuit and landed all on my own. I was 16 years old and still at high school. The freedom of it was incredible.

I taxied over to collect David, who was standing on the taxiway nervously watching me. He congratulated me and we taxied back to the flying club.

I grew up without a father and to have a person like Gary Spicer look after me all through my flying training helped shape me into the person I am now. Both David and Gary simply gave their time to help young keen aviators and I will always be grateful to them for that. David went on to become the Chief of Flight Operations and Safety Officer and Chief Pilot of Air New Zealand. Gary retired from Air New Zealand in 2000.

With thoughts of working for Air New Zealand, I slipped back into life at Great Barrier Airlines and enjoyed the summer. That was until one day Jim called me into the office and sat me down. I knew it must be serious. He told me that

he had sold the airline. I was a bit shocked to find that Pope was now the major shareholder. I loved working for Jim, but Pope … ? It was time for me to leave.

About that same time, a rumour had been circulating around a few pilots that a senior Air New Zealand manager had said none of us who had been involved in the Twin Otter crash would ever get a job with the airline because it was our fault we'd run dry of fuel.

This worried me as I knew it could affect my plans to work for the airline. I rang Gary Spicer and he went straight into fleet management and spoke to the person who was rumoured to have said this. His response was heartening. 'Even if I thought that, which I don't, I would never say it.' He then told Gary that I was getting close to having enough hours to make the step up to working for the national airline. I guess it just proves the old aviation saying, 'Believe none of what you hear and only half of what you see.'

A few days later I got a letter from Air New Zealand inviting me for an interview. I was over the moon. Finally, the chance that I had wanted for the last 15 years.

I immediately took three weeks' leave and started studying, researching and talking to other pilots who had been through the interview process. There were a few stages to get through, including a simulator test flight in a Boeing 737, a three-person panel interview, a group/team dynamic session, an interview with a physiologist, some psychometric testing and finally a full medical. I studied my butt off for those three weeks.

lips. She looked like a supermodel. Within a few minutes I was introduced to her – her name was Wendy – and we started chatting. She asked about the Leatherman tool that I had on my belt. It was the same one I had used during the Twin Otter crash, so I told her all about the crash. She was fascinated.

Then we danced and spent the entire evening talking and laughing. Before long, she had to leave to go back to where she was staying with her friends. There was another party the next night and I knew she would be going.

I worked the next day and turned up at the party a little late. It was rocking. I looked for Wendy and saw her on the dance floor. She looked even more beautiful than she had the night before. I ended up dancing a little with another girl but all the time I just wanted to talk with Wendy. I finally excused myself and went over to the bar to speak to Wendy. She was a little tipsy but really friendly and we just clicked.

She grabbed my hand and dragged me onto the dance floor. Unfortunately we were dancing next to the girl I had just been dancing with and she grabbed my hand and pulled me towards her. Wendy grabbed my other hand and pulled me back.

I gently eased my way back towards Wendy, trying not to make a fuss. Wendy then positioned herself between me and the other girl. This didn't go down well and the other girl pulled Wendy's hair ... Well, Wendy wasn't having any of this and turned around and gave her a huge shove.

All hell broke loose. I disappeared back to the bar and could see a bit of shouting going on, nothing too major. But it was time for me to get out of there. I gathered up the Great

Barrier Airlines guys and we piled into the car. I had never had two girls fighting over me before. The guys gave me a really hard time.

The next day I turned up for work in the afternoon only to find that Wendy was on my flight. She was mad as hell and wouldn't speak to me. I put her in the front of the plane and asked her to hold my open can of drink as I taxied out and took off.

She slowly came around and started talking to me as we flew back towards Auckland. By the time we got back, we said an awkward farewell but I didn't get her phone number as things were still very messy with my relationship break-up. Wendy walked into the terminal and I wondered if I would ever see her again.

Later that day one of the other pilots came to see me. He had found a jacket on the aircraft that belonged to Wendy's sister. He could tell what was going on and said to me, 'This could be an opening for you, Mike. Call Wendy and drop off the jacket at her house.'

Am I glad I did. I went around to her house and dropped off the jacket. We started talking and I told her I couldn't really date her as things were not right after my break-up. But then I asked her to come over to the island with me and have lunch.

I flew Wendy over to the island a week later. We walked down the beach, had lunch and talked and talked. I wasn't ready for another relationship so we agreed to just be friends … but not long after that we went to the movies together and, well, broke our agreement.

There was a huge farewell party for me on the island. Jim put on all the alcohol and paid for a band. Some of the locals decorated the hall and put on a big feast.

Before I headed out to the party, I had a pretty good idea that some of the pilots (actually all of the pilots) would try to strip me naked at some point in the evening… a strange New Zealand tradition. Determined not to let them get the better of me, I drilled a little hole in my belt and wired the two ends of my belt together. As the night hit full swing, about 10 pilots grabbed me and my shirt, shoes and socks vanished in a flash. But no one could get my belt off. My dignity and my pants were left fully intact!

I had a fair bit to drink and I decided I needed some fresh air so I went for a walk down the beach on my own. Sad to be leaving all my friends, the island, and Great Barrier Airlines, I sat down on a rock feeling sorry for myself. And a little bit sick – perhaps the combination of oysters, crayfish, curry and the home brew beer wasn't such a great idea.

I hadn't been sitting there long when Wendy came down the beach. She sat down next to me and we talked for a while before walking back to the party. As we walked back, my stomach finally rebelled and I threw up all over Wendy's boots. Oh god. I really liked this woman and I'd just chundered on her footwear. A few years later Wendy told me this was the exact moment she fell in love with me. Go figure!

I left Great Barrier Airlines with very fond memories, even of Pope. He wasn't a bad guy – just a larger than life character. He gave aviation some colour and kept things interesting. We need people like him.

The person I knew I'd miss the most from my time at GBA was Jim. He always went out of his way to help young keen aviators, gave brand new pilots their first jobs and championed them through to the larger airlines. It was a pleasure to have worked for him.

THE DREAM JOB

On my first day at the Boeing 747 training course, Air New Zealand's personnel manager greeted our group then went on to say, 'Before I begin, I have had two phone calls regarding Mike Allsop. Both of them were from people asking me NOT to employ him.' I was a bit confused.

He went on, 'They both said he is a fantastic pilot and they would prefer it if he kept working for Great Barrier Airlines.' I just sat there bright red not knowing what to do or say.

'We really like that, welcome to Air New Zealand.'

Even though I was going from a six-seater Cherokee to a 396-ton, 395-seater Boeing, the training was pretty straightforward, largely due to the very well structured three-month training course and simulator training. And before I knew it I was off on my line training flights in the B747. One of the first flights was to Frankfurt in Germany.

I was so excited to finally be doing an international flight but by the time I arrived in Frankfurt I had a terrible head cold and just wanted to stay in bed. But my crew members had different ideas. One of the flight attendants, a beautiful Polish girl called Wandzia, who was dating another pilot, came to my room at the hotel. I told her I wasn't well and I just wanted to stay in. She told me that she'd take me to the doctor's before we went out for dinner. I reluctantly agreed, hoping that the doctor might be able to give me something for my cold.

Wandzia knew Frankfurt well so I followed her to the train station below the hotel and she guided me to Dr Muller's. I naively walked in expecting a doctor's surgery. I got a huge shock ... instead of being a medical clinic, Dr Muller's was a full-on German sex shop!

I went bright red; I had never been in a shop like it before. In fact, I was pretty sure that nothing like it even existed in little old New Zealand. My eyes were as wide as saucers. The old lady that owned the store saw how uncomfortable I was and grabbed a huge ribbed dildo and chased me around the store.

When I finally managed to escape the store and its dildo-wielding owner, Wandzia turned to me and said, 'I bet you feel better now!' She was right. The shock and hilarity of it all made me completely forget my cold. When we finally met up with the rest of the crew, Wandzia entertained them at my expense over a fantastic traditional German dinner.

This was my first experience of the camaraderie among Air New Zealand crew. I was really well looked after and

Crossing the finish line after 7 marathons in 7 days on 7 continents.

My beautiful family. Me, Ethan, Dylan, Wendy and Maya.

On the summit of Everest with no one there but Lhakpa and me.

Me, Dr Anna Shekhdar, Dr Rob Casserley, Prof Pat Hickey.

Heading for the summit of Everest. I'm halfway up the ridge in the middle, just below the Hillary step. (Photo by Mike Davey)

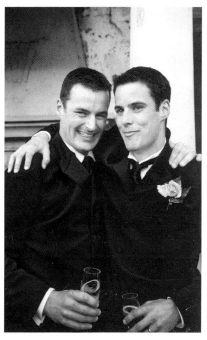

Me and my brother Bob on my wedding day.

Wendy and me with Ethan on our wedding day.

On the summit of Aoraki Mt Cook.

Climbing Mt Aspiring.

My mentor Paul Scaife.

Baby Ethan.

there seemed to be an unwritten rule that staff went out of their way to help out the new crew. I knew that I was going to love working here.

For the first few years as an international airline pilot everything was very exciting, with new cities to explore and lots of things to do on the stopovers. But after a while every trip seemed to blend into one – Los Angeles, London, Sydney and Frankfurt … I loved my job, I loved Air New Zealand, but I felt like I was getting lost. I was going away on long duties and I didn't have any focus. I felt like a ship without a rudder just drifting along but I couldn't quite work out what was wrong or how to change it.

On a layover in Los Angeles one night, I went out for dinner with my friend Herwin. We were talking about what we wanted to do with our lives when Herwin casually mentioned that he wanted to climb Mt Everest. The idea sounded so ludicrous, it seemed like a fantasy. But he said, 'Just imagine what it's like. How amazing would it be?'

That night, I dreamed of climbing Everest, standing on the summit, the cold, the danger, Nepal and the Himalayas. A seed had been planted in my mind.

The next morning, I sprang out of bed and went down to the computer room in the hotel and started researching how to climb Everest. It all seemed so difficult. There were guided expeditions but I would have needed a heap of climbing experience and US$60,000. I had neither of those things.

It was a bit like when I decided to become a pilot. I decided I just had to get started. I went down to a sports store in Los Angeles to check out climbing gear. Everything was so expensive – $400 for an ice axe, $600 for a down jacket, $900 for high altitude climbing boots … this wasn't going to be easy. Feeling a bit disheartened, I bought an aluminium drink bottle for $12. It was a start.

This was my first piece of climbing gear and it gave me an idea. If I was going to reach my goal of climbing Everest, I had to break it into small parts, small stages – starting with learning to climb!

I had heard of another Air New Zealand pilot who was doing an advanced climbing course with a South Island company called Aspiring Guides, who were based in Wanaka. I gave them a call and booked myself in for their next advanced climbing course. The only problem was I wasn't by any means an advanced climber, but I guess by the time they found that out, it would be too late.

In preparation for the course, I headed down to my local indoor climbing wall in Auckland. They were running courses that taught the basics of rock climbing and rope skills. I had a few lessons and felt pretty confident, but they were very small walls – only 10–20 metres high.

At the same time as I was acquiring some basic climbing skills, I set about slowly buying all the gear I needed according to the required gear list that Aspiring Guides had sent me. Before long I had a good set of gear – a harness, karabiners, climbing jacket, alpine sleeping bag and heaps of other stuff. It turned out to be a bit cheaper in Los Angeles than in New Zealand, so I would bring a little gear home each duty.

When the week of the course finally came around, I had only been climbing for three months. I flew down to

Queenstown and caught the bus over to Wanaka. I checked in to a backpackers' and spent the night a bit worried about what I would have to face the next day.

In the morning, I turned up at Aspiring Guides and the rest of the students were there. We met our two guides. Paul Scaife was the head guide and one of the owners of the company. Paul was an interesting character, a little quiet but I'd soon come to learn that he had a great sense of humour. Simon Howells was a new trainee guide and this was one of his first courses. Both he and Paul had an aura of the mountain man about them. You could just tell they were extremely tough and had probably seen and experienced many amazing things in the mountains.

We drove over to the spectacular Franz Josef glacier on the South Island's west coast. At Franz Josef, we loaded all our climbing gear into the helicopter and took off. I had never seen a glacier before – it was so impressive with huge blocks of ice just hanging ready to topple over at any stage and massive crevasses that could swallow an entire building.

We landed high on the glacier, at Centennial Hut, our home for the next 10 days. This was very much a climbers' hut. It had one big room with a table, a bench and a few bunks. The hut was perched precariously on a cliff, the only place safe from avalanche. But the long-drop toilet was stuck on top of a little rock some 15 metres from the main hut. There was a huge drop off either side of the walkway out to the toilet, and a handrail only on one side of the track. In the icy conditions, my first challenge was going to be surviving getting out to the toilet.

There were only five students on the course, and over the next 10 days we learnt the basics of climbing – self arrest, crevasse rescue, mountain navigation, avalanche awareness and emergency shelters. Oh, and also actual climbing techniques. We were all pretty much thrown in the deep end, although I suspect I was a bit more of a novice than the others.

While we were up on the glacier, we experienced a typical mountain storm with wild winds and blizzarding snow that saw us stuck in the hut for three days. One morning during the storm, I woke up and started chatting to Paul. After a few minutes, I realised someone was missing. I asked everyone if they had seen the missing member of our party and someone said he had gone to the toilet.

Looking outside, I could just see the toilet hut through the raging storm. To close the toilet door from the outside, you had to turn a six-inch block of wood that was screwed onto the door. I could see the block of wood was locked from the outside, so I knew no one was in the toilet. I told Paul. Neither of us said anything but I could tell that we both thought the missing guy had fallen off the walkway to the toilet.

While Paul got ready to start a search, I opened the door of the hut and the wind chill just hit me. It was absolutely freezing. I grabbed the handrail and inched my way out to the toilet, all the while looking over the sides to see if I could see anyone. I spun the wood lock and sitting on the toilet in his long johns was our missing climber, covered in spindrift snow that had blown through the gaps of the toilet walls.

'You bloody bastards. I've been out here for ages!'

I helped our frosty friend back into the main hut where we reheated him with blankets and hot drinks, all desperate to find out what had happened. Apparently, he had nipped out to the toilet and the wind was so strong that it had blown the wooden latch across, locking him in the toilet. Thank goodness I woke up when I did as no one had noticed him missing. What a way to go … frozen to death on a long-drop toilet.

During that course I fell in love with the mountains, the environment, the risks and the sport of climbing itself. It was so peaceful up there, it was just me and the mountains. All my senses seemed to be heightened when I was in the mountains. I felt so alive and free.

Taking up climbing meant that I got my mojo back. I had a spring in my step. I was motivated. Life had a purpose again. I had fantastic dreams of climbing mountains all over the world. And, of course, there was always the big end goal – Everest.

During our 10 days climbing on Franz Josef, I got to know Paul and Simon really well. Once the course had finished I booked in with Paul to do a guided climb of Mt Aspiring, the Matterhorn of the southern hemisphere. But first I wanted to get some high altitude experience and started planning a climb of Mount Kilimanjaro in Tanzania.

I knew Kilimanjaro would be a steep learning curve for me. It's a very high mountain – 5600 metres – and it is also one of the most dangerous mountains in the world because people don't take it seriously enough and trek up it too quickly. I was determined to do everything right and nothing was going to stop me.

Wendy had always wanted to do the traditional Kiwi OE, travelling around the world, but meeting me had put a spanner in the works and she never managed to go. After we had been together for a few years, we talked it over and decided that if she wanted to travel then she should go and live and work in London for a year. Being an international pilot meant that I could fly up every month on a duty and see her. The theory sounded good but when it came to putting the plan into practice, the separation put a huge strain on our relationship.

With six weeks' leave booked to climb Mount Kilimanjaro, then meet Wendy in Egypt for a long-awaited holiday together, I departed Auckland on my final duty to Los Angeles on 10 September 2001.

After getting to LA, I went out for dinner with a few friends. The next morning I awoke to a ringing phone. The hotel receptionist rang to inform me that my next flight had been cancelled indefinitely. I was a bit confused. Air New Zealand was in crisis at the time with the whole Ansett collapse, and my first thought was that the Australian airline's demise had somehow led to the whole operation being shut down.

I asked her why.

'We're at war! Buy some food and lock yourself in your room. Tanks will be coming down the streets!' she shouted and then promptly hung up.

That didn't help to clear up my confusion so I turned on the television to see the first World Trade Center building collapse. It was horrifying.

I rang the captain and he told me to go up to his room. Most of the crew were there and we all watched the events of that day unfold. The world would never be the same again.

All flights in United States airspace were cancelled and we were completely stuck in Los Angeles until it was reopened. It was to be nine days before I could fly out of the States back to Sydney and then on to Auckland. In order to make the departure date for my climb at Kilimanjaro I had to fly non-stop all in one go. I flew Los Angeles–Sydney–Auckland–Los Angeles–London–Nairobi, and then hopped on a bus for nine hours to Moshi. Some 72 hours after I left Los Angeles the first time, I finally arrived at the base of Kilimanjaro.

Arriving in the small town of Moshi, the bus dropped me off at my hotel. I checked in and went to the bar, where I met some other people doing the same climb as me. Three of them were young women from the United States who had been working for the Peace Corps in Africa for a year.

Before long, one of the climb organisers arrived to give us a pep talk. A young African woman began speaking to us, in a very slow monotone. While she was talking, she moved her head back and forth like she was talking to two hundred people … but there were only six of us! Her main message was that it would be our mental attitude that would get us to the summit; that we should focus on the summit and never give up. These were very wise words.

After the talk I wanted to leave the hotel compound and have a look around Moshi. As I approached the gate the security guard stopped me and told me that it wouldn't be safe for me to leave. I asked him if I could just walk up the street a little. He thought about it and decided it would be ok but that he would keep an eye on me.

As I walked out the gate, I saw the three young American girls sitting having a cigarette. I went over to talk to them. Next thing all these kids turned up and started asking us for coins.

Among them was one beautiful little African girl, who would have been about eight years old. She spoke very good English and I chatted away with her for a few minutes. She asked me if I could give her a coin. I said yes, but that I would like to take a photo of her. She agreed and I went to hand the coin over, when one of the American girls shouted, 'Get the photo first!'

After taking her photo, I gave her the promised coin. She smiled, said thank you and ran off. All of a sudden, about 30 kids chased her down, pushed her to the ground and started kicking her. I ran over and grabbed the bigger kids off her and pulled her up. A boy who was as tall as me had stolen her coin and then started to walk off. I grabbed his hand and prised the coin free. I then handed it to the little girl. She wiped her tears, said thank you again and ran off.

I couldn't believe it. There was an instant replay. She got chased and beaten up again by the same kids and the same boy stole the coin. But this time they all took off as they could see me running after them. I walked back to the gate a little pissed off, and the little girl came walking over again, this time bleeding from her nose.

She was crying and said, 'They took it again! Can you bring some sweets back when you finish your climb?' I agreed and promised I would.

One of the American girls said, 'I bet you feel awful. We could see you were going to get that little girl beaten up, but you managed to get her beaten up twice. Well done!' I felt so bad. I thought the American peace corps girls could have warned me instead of watching me. But this was Africa, life is different here.

After that little interlude, I was looking forward to starting my climb the next day. Due to the time I'd lost because of the September 11 attacks I had had to change my plans. There are five possible routes up Mt Kilimanjaro and as my time was now limited, I had no choice but to climb the Marangu route – also known as the Coca Cola route as there are tea huts all along the way – if I was going to meet Wendy in London in time for our planned holiday the following week.

Marangu is the cheapest and shortest of all of the routes up the mountain and I had booked directly with a guiding company at the bottom of the mountain to make it a bit cheaper than going with a big guiding company. They provided me with a guide and a porter, and booked me into huts all the way up the mountain. The climb would take five days, but it is insane to climb that high and that quickly. Which is why Kilimanjaro is such a dangerous mountain. But I had no choice.

The initial climb is through tropical jungle before turning into an alpine landscape with no vegetation. The views over the African plains are just spectacular.

At the second hut, which was at a height of around 3700 metres, a German climber and I were sharing with an Australian guy who had just descended from the summit. He looked a little sick, nothing major but just unwell.

I pulled out my book on altitude sickness, which at this stage I knew nothing about – unbelievable, I know – and started reading out the symptoms of serious altitude sickness.

The Australian chap nodded his head and answered yes to pretty much all of them. Then he freaked out a bit, packed all his bags and disappeared down the mountain with his guide.

My German roommate laughed and said, 'Great work, Kiwi! If anyone else turns up, just pull out that little altitude book of yours and start reading. That will scare them off and we can have the room to ourselves.'

A few days later I dragged myself up to the summit of Kilimanjaro. I only just made it and it was the hardest thing I had ever done. The biggest lesson I learned was about the determination it takes to climb big mountains. I learned never to give up. I had to just keep putting one foot in front of the other until I made the summit. As I descended I felt very proud of myself, but it was such a long way and such a big thing to do on your own, I felt very emotional. I was so happy to have summited.

Then I flew to England to meet Wendy. We had planned to go to Egypt but because of the heightened security alerts about travelling to the Middle East, we decided to go to Greece instead.

We spent three glorious weeks together in the Greek islands before I had to go back to work. Leaving Wendy in London was very hard and I knew being apart would be tough.

SNOW AND ICE

A few months later, I flew down to Wanaka and met up with Paul Scaife to climb Mt Aspiring. At a height of 3027 metres, Aspiring provided me with plenty of challenge.

We helicoptered in to the Colin Todd Hut, a classic climbers' hut at about 1800 metres, from which the ascent to the top of Aspiring via the mountain's south-west ridge would take us somewhere between 10 and 12 hours. Two nights in a row we tried to climb Aspiring but each time turned around after a few hours on account of rapidly deteriorating weather. Even though we had turned around twice I felt confident we would get there, after all I had one of the best guides in the world.

On the third night we left at 2am and started trekking across the crevasse field to the start of the climb. We crossed the bergschrund, which is a large crevasse always present at the bottom of a steep face, and then started climbing. It was still dark and there were a few more hours to go before dawn.

I had two ice axes and crampons and started edging my way up the 70-degree slope looking a little like an awkward insect. Whacking my ice axes into the ice and kicking the front points of my crampons in hard, I soon found a rhythm. I just loved climbing on the ice, it was strangely peaceful.

That was until I looked down between my legs and realised just how exposed I was to the drop beneath my feet. The exposure felt frightening but, in reality, we were very safe. We were roped together and Paul was ahead of me putting screws into the hard ice for us to attach our ropes to.

At one point during the climb, Paul pointed and said, 'Look at that. Best bit about my job.' I looked up and saw the dawn breaking and the sun rising. It was indescribably beautiful. And I thought *I* had a great job.

We kept climbing up the ridge and then came to the crux of the climb. It was a six-metre high frozen waterfall – a vertical frozen waterfall with a few hundred metres of air below it. I belayed Paul as he seemed to effortlessly climb up the ice. (Belaying is when you adjust the length of your climbing partner's rope, applying friction when they are not climbing, and removing friction when they need more rope to continue climbing.) Then it was my turn. All my good technique went out the window and I just grunted my way up with brute strength. My heart was pounding; I didn't look down as I was scared I might freeze. When I finally popped over the top there was Paul smiling at me.

Then I heard him say, 'Ok, this is the serious bit. Do not

slip or fall. Make every placement with your ice axe count.' And I'd thought the frozen waterfall was the serious bit. Ahead lay some very steep ice on a very exposed ridge leading to the summit.

With Paul's warning ringing in my ears, I concentrated as hard as I could. Every time I whacked my ice axes into the ice, I'd make sure they were hard into the ice.

We climbed like this for about 30 minutes before the summit opened up before us. It was spectacular. On one side I could see the South Island's west coast and the Tasman Sea and, on the other, the east coast and the Pacific Ocean way in the distance.

Once we were at the summit, Paul opened his pack and set up a beautiful lunch for us both – sardines, cheese and crackers. I had a huge smile on my face. Moments like this made me realise what it was I loved about mountaineering.

We descended along the north-east ridge, mainly on rock. All the way Paul was teaching me how to move efficiently and safely in the mountains. We arrived back at the hut totally stuffed as we had been climbing for almost 18 hours.

Paul had brought a bottle of red wine with him and we drank it sitting on the deck of the hut staring up at Aspiring's summit. In that moment I felt so alive. The risks we had taken were calculated and reasonably safe but all the same, I knew mountaineering was a dangerous sport. Sometimes to really appreciate life you have to risk it just a little.

The next day we walked down into the Matukituki Valley and back to Wanaka.

At this stage, Wendy had returned home from England after eight months. She met me in Wanaka and I introduced

Paul. They got on really well, which was a relief as mountaineering was in my blood now and it was important to me that Wendy understood the people and places that attracted me to it.

As soon as I'd climbed Aspiring, I started thinking about my next expedition. On Mt Aspiring, I had met a Swiss guide called John Falkiner. While we were on the mountain, John had given me a few tips and tricks. He didn't have to as I wasn't his client, it was just the code of mountaineers – helping each other regardless of experience.

While I was chatting with John, he told me that he guided expeditions to Mt Elbrus in Russia – the highest peak in Europe. I'd already climbed Africa's highest mountain so I decided that attempting Europe's would be my next adventure.

As I got into planning my trip to Russia, Wendy and I were also spending a lot of time renovating our first home. Before Wendy had gone overseas, we begged and borrowed to get the money for a mortgage together and bought a house in Ponsonby. We rented it out straight away intending to keep it rented until we could afford the mortgage repayments and move in.

When Wendy returned from London, she walked straight back into a nursing job at Starship children's hospital. Her salary combined with me being on good money as a pilot meant we could afford to move into our house. It might have been in a nice area but it was a complete do-up. Pretty much everything had to be fixed but, hey, I love a challenge.

Now that we were in the same country and in our own

home, there was quite a lot of pressure on us to get married. Wendy and I were getting on well but I just didn't want to get married. My parents had split up when I was eight years old and I never saw my father after the age of 10. One of the cruellest things in the world is to be abandoned by your father – no matter what the reason. My mum was amazing and really looked after me and my brother but I grew up thinking I had done something wrong for my dad not to love me. I used to lie in my bed at night thinking about my dad and crying. When I achieved something, like a certificate or a prize, I would wish my dad was there to see me. But he never was and this would just crush me inside and take away anything good.

I think he thought we were better off without him in our lives as he and my mum would fight and argue after the divorce. The truth is I just wanted a dad, I didn't care if he and Mum fought. To any dads out there – never, never, never give up on your children regardless of what your relationship with their mother is like. Kids need their dads.

Despite my hang-ups when it came to marriage, the pressure all around me was mounting. I went to a wedding with Wendy and it seemed to be the only topic of conversation: 'When are you getting married?' 'When are you going to ask Wendy?' 'Don't leave it too long …' People just went on and on about it. Every time someone asked me when I was going to marry Wendy, I got more and more irritated.

While everyone else was hassling me about marrying Wendy, the one person who didn't seem to be worried about it was Wendy. She could see that my past had a lot to do with my hesitancy and she was happy with things the way they were.

One weekend not long after the wedding, I was busy cutting down trees and tidying up the yard at our house. Wendy had been working in the morning and went to a travel agent with her friend to book a holiday to Thailand with her girlfriends. But when she got there she was feeling sick so she came home. I don't know why but I asked her if she was pregnant. She laughed and reckoned it was impossible as she was on the pill. But I wanted to be sure so I went down the road and bought a pregnancy test kit.

Even though Wendy was convinced she wasn't pregnant, she agreed to take the test to shut me up. I waited outside the bathroom and it took a long time, a really long time. Much longer than the time it takes to pee on a stick. Finally, I knocked on the door and went into the bathroom. Wendy was just sitting on the bath staring at these two little blue lines. 'I'm pregnant!'

I was stunned – our lives were about to change in a huge way. As we walked out of the bathroom, Wendy's mum Lorraine was there. 'She's pregnant,' I said, still not really believing it. Lorraine let out a squeal of joy and gave me a big hug.

I walked outside and saw Wendy's dad, Brian. He is a very traditional man and was not really impressed that his daughter was living with me without being married.

'There's no easy way to say it but Wendy's pregnant.'

He wasn't very impressed but he is a very wise man and there was no point in saying so after the fact, so he shook my hand and looked me straight in the eye and said, 'I know you will make a great dad.'

Over the next few months, I spent a lot of time trying to come to terms with the fact that I was going to be a dad. I was all over the place and couldn't really understand what was going on with Wendy. Eventually, I bought a book on pregnancy that explained the changes that happen when a woman gets pregnant. I sat in a park and read the book cover to cover. It all made sense – perfect sense.

Suddenly, I understood what had been going wrong in our relationship. Wendy rocked, she was everything I wanted in a partner. It was me being a complete dick, being non-committal and not making my mind up. That day changed me forever. I was going to marry Wendy. Maybe not right now, but when the time was right.

I thought Wendy would want to change me now she was pregnant but my fears were completely unfounded. She knew who I was, she knew what drove me, and how much I loved mountaineering and adventure. Despite her pregnancy and everything that was going on in our lives, Wendy supported my need to climb and refused to entertain the thought of me cancelling my trip to Russia.

I left Wendy at home five months pregnant and I flew to Moscow. I went to my hotel and had to wait a few hours until my room was ready so I sat in the hotel bar. This gave me the perfect spot to suss out a scam that the hotels had going with Russian working girls and their pimps. A guest would arrive, check in and then go to their room. The pimp would go and pay the hotel receptionist a bribe and he would hand him a slip of paper with the room number on it. The pimp would then give this to the girl who would ring the room. She would then give the thumbs-up or the thumbs-down.

I sat in the bar for hours watching this going on and about one in four would be thumbs-up. When it was finally time for me to check in, I got my key and went to my room. Within two minutes of getting into the room, sure enough, the phone started ringing. I waited a few seconds and then answered it.

'Hello,' said a woman in a thick Russian accent. 'Would you like a sensual sexual massage for $50?'

'No, thank you,' I replied.

'How about $30? … Ok, then how about $20?' My reply was unchanged. I simply said, 'No, thank you,' and put down the phone. Thumbs-down.

The next morning I met the climbers who I would be attempting Mt Elbrus with. There were two Japanese, one American and two Irish climbers. The minute the Irish guys opened their mouths I knew we would get on like a house on fire. They were really hard cases.

With introductions done, we all hopped on a bus and headed to one of Moscow's domestic airports. If we thought the airport was rough, it had nothing on the jet that we were going to be flying on. As soon as the plane took off, everyone on board seemed to stand up to go to the toilet. The big Russian flight attendant screamed at everyone to sit down. They didn't listen so she screamed even louder. She was rough. The whole experience was … rough. It was a far cry from life as an Air New Zealand pilot, that's for sure!

A couple of hours later, we landed in a town called Mineralnye Vody. While this city was the gateway to the Caucasus Mountains, which is where we would be climbing, it was also near the Russian border with Georgia and also near the highly volatile Russian region of Chechnya. This was going to be no walk in the park.

Our guide met us off the plane. She spoke great English and seemed very nice. She escorted us to a van in the car park from which I could see a barbecue stall about 100 metres away. I asked if it was ok to go over and buy some food. The guide looked worried and said, 'Ok, but go straight there and come straight back.' She then left to go and collect our luggage.

I walked over and no sooner had I got there than this policeman appeared pointing his AK-47 at me. I had never had a gun pointed at me before but I knew what to do. I put my hands high in the air as he screamed, 'Passport!'

'It's in the auto bus,' I said and pointed.

He waved the gun in the direction of the bus. It didn't take a rocket scientist to work out he wanted me to go towards the van … and NOW.

When we got to the bus he angrily took everyone's passports. The two Japanese women started shouting at him that they wanted to call their embassy. As soon as he pointed the gun at them, they shut up pretty quickly. The policeman then disappeared with all our passports.

When the guide returned with our luggage, she was not happy to say the least. She went off to find the policeman. On returning she leant into the van, opened the glove compartment and grabbed a huge wad of money before walking off again. Another 45 minutes passed. She returned and did the same thing, this time with even more money.

She came back about 10 minutes later and handed us back our passports with a smile. I asked what all the money was for and she said it was to pay for visas. I looked in my passport and couldn't see a new stamp.

'Ummm, there's no visa in here,' I said.

'It is electronic one,' came the reply. Then I saw her writing the cost of the bribe in her book. It was about US$60 each.

We drove out the main gate of the airport and there was the same policeman standing at the gate. He had his AK-47 slung around his neck and a cigarette hanging out of the corner of his mouth. Our van driver waved nicely at him. In reply, he sneered back and slowly raised his middle finger. Then one of the Irish guys said in a Russian accent, 'Welcome to Mineralnye Vody, everyone.' We all cracked up laughing.

Over the previous few weeks, there had been major flooding in the Caucasus region and as a result the most direct route to Mt Elbrus was closed. This meant that instead of approaching it from the Russian side, we had to drive very close to Chechnya and over the border into Georgia to approach it from the other side. The Chechen Republic is part of Russia but has been the scene of a protracted fight for independence since the dissolution of the Soviet Union. The area was incredibly dangerous and we were heading pretty much right for it.

The minivan ride was about 10 hours long, and the only English words the driver knew were, 'Please sit back and pull the curtains.' He would say this every time we came to an army or police checkpoint, which was often. We were stopped at least twenty times. Most of the time we were waved through but on the odd occasion we were stopped. Each time, the van door would slide open and the barrel of an AK-47 would appear followed by a police officer or an army guard. This would inevitably be followed by a look of delight on discovering a van full of westerners. They would then go around to the driver's side and demand a wad of roubles.

We arrived in the town of Tyrnyauz. The place we were staying, which was like a big house, had a tank parked outside. It looked so out of place. There were a few guys beavering away on it trying to get it to work. I hate to think what they were planning to do with it if they succeeded.

The following day, we planned to cross over into Georgia. Formerly a part of the Soviet Union, Georgia declared its independence in 1991 but had been the scene of considerable unrest since then. The current tension was largely based around rumours that Osama Bin Laden was hiding there.

Political stresses aside, as a group of climbers we got on well. Conforming to national stereotypes, the two Japanese were very quiet, the American was loud and the Irish guys were very funny. I'm not quite sure where the Kiwi fitted in.

We met our Russian guides that evening . They spoke no English and seemed extremely grumpy. Clearly, this was a case of getting what you pay for.

As Mt Elbrus is 5430 metres high, you can't just head straight up it. Acclimatisation is important so we packed our gear into the van the next morning and headed up to a ski field on a mountain adjacent to Mt Elbrus. The guides paid an operator to turn on a chairlift for us. Huge belches of smoke poured out of the generator room and the lift sprang into life. We all hopped on and moved a few hundred metres up the mountain. Then there was another huge puff of smoke and the chairlift stopped, leaving us all swinging in the breeze.

After what I can only imagine was a lot of swearing and cursing in Russian, the operator grabbed a big sledgehammer and started pounding away. His method was crude but effective. All of a sudden the chairlift started up again and managed to transport us all the way to the top.

Having survived that adventure, we put on our packs and started walking up the mountain. After about 45 minutes, our guide gathered us all around and said, 'Georgia,' before motioning us to keep quiet and follow him. We were approaching the border between Russia and Georgia.

As we walked over a nearby ridge an alarm sounded. It was just like something out of World War Two. Ahead of us was a Russian machine gun post with all these Russian soldiers running around on full alert because of the ringing alarm. Three of the soldiers jumped onto this great big gun and I could hear them cocking it ready to fire. I was scared.

Our Russian guide put his hands in the air and we did the same. He shouted out to the soldiers and they beckoned us towards them, all the while pointing this huge gun at us. As usual, some money was exchanged and we were on our way.

We trekked up to about 4000 metres and then sat down, had lunch and soaked up the views until, eventually, it was time to head back.

When we neared the border, the alarm sounded and the troops swung into full battle stations again. This amused me as they had seen us only a few hours earlier and there was absolutely no one else around. But they had to go through the motions. We all raised our hands again, and I whispered to the two Irish guys, 'Lads, do you dare me to take a photo?'

Their reply came through gritted teeth. 'Don't you dare! You'll get us all shot.'

'Aw, come on, I've got the flash turned off,' I replied.

'Fuckin' hell, Kiwi, you will get us all killed!'

They were panicking a bit more than I expected so I finally let on that I was kidding. Then the money was paid over and we were back on our way. Once we were out of sight, the Irish guys came over and both punched me. 'We almost wet our pants because of you. Bloody hell, Kiwi!'

We rode the chairlift back down to the ski resort and went into the only restaurant there for a restorative beer. While we were sitting outside on the deck, a large Russian army truck and what looked like an officer's jeep drove up. A very grumpy looking Russian army officer walked onto the deck, then barked what I assume was his drink order to a junior officer and just stared at us. I mean fully stared at us, not even blinking. It was very unnerving to say the least.

By this time we were all onto our second beers and I was feeling pretty brave. 'I'm going to go over and say hello.' The Irish guys were quick to reply, 'Don't you dare! You can't ...' but their efforts were wasted, I was gone.

I walked straight up to the army officer and in my politest Russian I said, 'Hello, sir. My name is Mike. I am from New

Zealand.' Apart from 'please', 'thank you', 'yes' and 'no', that was my Russian vocabulary exhausted.

He looked back at me with no expression and said, 'Novozeelandchi, da?'

'Da!' I replied, using 'yes' from my list of untried Russian words.

With that he smiled and slapped me on the back. Then he shouted at his junior again and a bottle of vodka turned up. The junior officer spoke English and said, 'The general would like to drink with you.'

He poured two glasses and we toasted Russia and New Zealand. Then I thanked him very much and gestured that I should now return to my friends.

He wasn't having a bar of it. 'No, you must finish the bottle with the general, this is Russian tradition.'

There was no escaping, so another glass was poured for me and we toasted again. This time I sipped the vodka and went to put it down.

'No, you must drink all in one go to be polite.' So down it went.

After a few more vodkas, we finished the bottle and the general invited us all in to have dinner with him. There was only lamb – well, old sheep, really – but after all that vodka, it tasted good.

I asked for a glass of water and the waiter simply said, 'Nyet!' so I asked for a beer. The beer arrived and as soon as it was put down in front of me, the junior officer jumped up and took it off me before I had even had a drink.

'Drinking beer in front of the general is showing him no

respect.' I apologised again and looked over at the general. He didn't seem bothered.

Soon we were all up dancing Russian style with a little added Kiwi flair – arms folded, squatting down and flinging your legs out. The general was getting into it, laughing away. After a few hours of this, the bar finally closed. Our guides had long since gone home but the lodge owner had come down to keep an eye on us.

As we went outside there were many Russian soldiers around. The smile quickly vanished from the general's face. He shouted a few orders and two soldiers grabbed me and started marching me towards the waiting army truck. The lodge owner shouted in a very concerned tone, 'No, Mikey! Come here, come here now!' It was no use, I couldn't get away. Things had suddenly turned very serious.

The soldiers threw me into the back of a large truck and I landed face down. As I got up, all I could see was Russian soldiers, about 12 of them, all carrying AK-47s, and they didn't look happy to see me. The general hopped in the front of the truck and I leant forward to say something but he and the junior officer completely ignored me. Even in my state I knew I was in trouble.

As the truck drove off, I started to sing loudly. I had sobered up very quickly but I didn't want them to know that, so I played the drunk. I sang, swayed a little and spoke all of my Russian words – all the while keeping a note of where we were going. It was no use, I didn't recognise anything. I started singing again and seeing a corner coming up, I decided that I was going to jump out and make a run for it as the truck slowed down. Just as I was getting ready to jump, I recognised a building ahead of us – my lodge. What a relief.

Two soldiers escorted me to my bed, providing me with water and a bucket. Then the general came in to say goodbye, leaving me his card. The last thing I remember him saying was, 'Keep this card. If any Russian troops give you trouble, show it to them.'

I missed the next acclimatisation trek and just stayed in bed all the next morning. Around midday, the lodge owner came in and he said, 'Well, the general must like you. Normally Mt Elbrus permits take three to seven days to be issued. Yours was done in five minutes.' This was good news indeed. But then he continued, 'He wants me to call him when you return from the summit so he can have dinner with you again.'

Oh god. Even though it would have been a great honour to have dinner with the general again, the thought of vodka made me dry retch.

I sat around all day waiting for the team to come back. The best entertainment was watching a bunch of guys trying to get a tank working. I watched for a while before heading back inside. After a few hours there was this absolutely deafening noise. I rushed outside and the tank was belching thick black smoke and slowly moving forward with the lodge owner at the controls. It was completely tearing up the nice concrete driveway, leaving huge chunks of concrete behind it. The lodge owner's wife was going berserk. Then, with a comical puff of black smoke, the tank stopped dead. There was silence for a few seconds as everyone looked at the damage to the driveway. Then the owner's wife started up again – she was almost as loud as the tank.

The next day saw the real beginning of our ascent of Mt Elbrus. We woke early and piled into the van, drove around the broken-down tank in the middle of the destroyed driveway, and headed towards an all but abandoned ski area.

While we were unloading our gear, the familiar sound of the Russian sledgehammer rang out. I looked at the chairlift and realised the sound was coming from the generator room. 'Better take some warm clothes, chances are we are going to break down again.'

Each of us got on a double chair with our own packs. The lift started and continued all the way to the top, surprisingly with no issues. We unloaded and then had to walk a few hundred metres to what looked like a cluster of red and white barrels. They turned out to be very large barrels that contained bunks enough for us all. This was to be our accommodation for the next few nights.

The Barrels Refuge was at 3750 metres and the next day we did another acclimatisation hike up another 1000 metres to the Pastukhov Rocks. The terrain was a bit boring, like walking up a huge ski field. I reached the rocks with the Irish guys, Richard and Andrew, but they wanted to climb a little higher so I descended back to the Barrels by myself.

A few hours later, at around 5pm, the Irish boys returned and they were in a mess. Richard had got very badly sunburnt and dehydrated. He lay down, insisting that he would be ok.

Over the next few hours, his condition deteriorated and I decided it was time to get some help. There was a team of

Korean climbers on the mountain so I stopped one of their members and asked if they had a doctor. Thankfully, this guy, whose name was Park Young-Seok, spoke English. He sent another guy off to get the doctor. A few minutes later, the message came back that the doctor would be with us in 10 minutes. I was very relieved.

As I waited for the doctor, I got chatting with Park and it turned out that he was a professional climber. I then asked the most obvious question ever. 'Have you climbed Everest?'

'Yes. Twice,' came his reply.

The other climber then chimed in, 'Park has climbed all 14 of the 8000-metre peaks.'

I gasped. 'No! But there are only nine climbers in the world that have done that.' I was impressed.

Park quietly responded, 'No, there are only eight, and I'm number seven.' He was so humble.

His friend then said, 'He is the only man in the world to have climbed all 8000-metre peaks, all of the highest peaks on each continent and also been to both poles.' I was clearly in the company of greatness. Sadly some years later Park went missing on Annapuna, never to be seen again. It was a great loss to the climbing community and Korea.

The Korean doctor arrived soon after and examined Richard. He diagnosed my Irish mate as having high altitude cerebral oedema, a swelling of brain tissue that is often fatal. The doctor put Richard on an intravenous drip of dexamethasone, a powerful anti-inflammatory steroid, and ordered him off the mountain as soon as possible. Given it was already getting dark, that was clearly going to be first thing in the morning.

By this stage, our not-so-friendly Russian guides had seen all the commotion and realised that I had got a doctor without asking them first. They were pissed off.

One of them pushed past a few people, tapped the doctor on the shoulder and rudely said, 'He ok. Just drink. Be fine tomorrow. No problem.'

The Korean doctor replied sternly, 'I am Korea's leading brain surgeon, I am a high altitude medicine specialist, and I am telling you this man has a cerebral oedema. Who are you to question me? Please tell me?'

The Russian guide backed out of the hut. And I stood there, unable to believe Richard's luck at having such a qualified medic on the mountain. The doctor asked me to come and wake him immediately if Richard's condition worsened.

The next morning Richard woke up feeling like a million dollars. The Russian guide told him this was good news and that he could keep climbing. When Richard came and told me this, I was glad that I'd spent some time talking to the doctor. I explained that the steroid would only last 24 hours and if he went any further up the mountain, not only would he need to be rescued, he could die. Thankfully, he saw sense and set off back down to the lodge to wait for us.

Following a rest day, the remaining five of us were ready to set off for our climb at 2am. Our Russian guide announced that we would be catching a snow plough to the top of the Pastukhov Rocks. The snow plough was owned by his brother and we must pay US$100 each. The two Japanese guys kicked up a fuss because they wanted to climb all the way. Just quietly, I was happy as it was a long way up to the rocks and I had already been there so technically I would still have climbed the whole mountain. This would just help me out by a few hours. There wasn't any choice in the end so we all paid and piled onto the back of the snow plough.

Eventually, the snow plough stopped and we began climbing. It was bitterly cold – I guessed around –30°C. After a few hours of climbing I noticed a young guy sitting on his own off to one side, obviously in distress. I went over to see what was wrong. It turned out he was 18 years old and from Poland. He and his mates had come to climb Elbrus together but his friends had turned back because of the cold. He had kept climbing but now his toes were frozen.

He spoke good English so it was very easy to communicate. I took off his boot, making sure to secure it so it didn't slide down the mountain. I then pulled off his sock and shoved his foot up my jacket and into my armpit. It felt like a block of ice.

As his foot thawed out, it was clear he was in a lot of pain. Once his first foot was warm I repeated the process with the other foot and only then did I notice the smell. His feet stank to hell. And that smell was going to stay with me for the next hour. It was hideous.

Eventually, his feet were thawed enough to put on some fresh woollen socks. He thanked me for saving his toes and turned back down the mountain.

From there, the climbing was steep but ok. After a few hours I reached The Saddle at 5300 metres. The real summit climb started from here. By this point everyone had thinned out and the only people ahead of me were a Spanish military team, who I passed a few hours later not far from the summit.

The final summit pyramid was about 10 metres high. I staggered up it and proudly stood on the summit of Europe. Then I sat down and just looked at the view. Tears started welling up in my eyes. They were not tears of joy though – I was feeling homesick. I was such a long way from home and I was alone.

Before long, the Spanish military guys turned up. They asked me where I was from and why I was up there without a guide.

'I'm from New Zealand and my guide is Russian and he is useless!' I replied.

They laughed and said, 'You're a long way from home …' Tell me about it, I thought.

Then I saw Andrew staggering towards us. He got all the way to the summit pyramid and collapsed at the bottom. I watched him for a bit, expecting him to get up, but he just lay there motionless, his chest heaving, gasping for air.

I climbed down from the summit and picked him up. Then I pushed him up the steep snow slope. As we reached the top I shouted, 'Do you want to take the last few steps to the top of Europe yourself?'

'No! Stuff that, keep pushing,' came his reply.

I gave him one last heave and he collapsed on the summit. All the Spanish military guys were clapping and cheering.

Once the Spanish guys had gone, I realised that Andrew was in trouble. We both started descending together and I could see he was seriously tired. He had given everything he had just getting to the top and had nothing in the tank for the trip back down.

As I was weighing up my options, Andrew started to stagger badly. I knew the most important thing was to look after myself, because I was getting tired too. If I got into trouble, I knew it could be fatal for both of us.

I could make out The Saddle in the distance and I knew there were supplies there that I could use to replenish my energy. It was a tough call but I decided to leave Andrew and go ahead to The Saddle as fast as I could.

Once there, I ate some sandwiches, put on more sunscreen and picked up some safety equipment. As I was preparing to go back to find him, Andrew arrived at The Saddle.

I sat him down, pulled out his food and gave it to him. I was shocked at the stuff he was carrying. He had a GPS, two cameras and a pair of binoculars. His bag was so heavy – it probably weighed about 20 kilograms. I went to throw out all the stuff to make his descent easier but he said it was his friend's gear and he couldn't afford to lose it. There was only one thing for it. I put it in my backpack.

It really was time to get going. We were the last on the mountain and we faced a long traverse across a steep slope to get back down. I watched Andrew walk along the small track that had been cut in the snow by previous climbers. He was staggering very badly and looked like he was going to fall over at any moment. I realised that if he slipped, it would probably be to his death.

Back in New Zealand, Paul Scaife had short roped me while we were climbing Mt Aspiring. He had attached a rope to my harness, looped a few coils in his hand and held his arm up. The idea was that if I slipped, his arm would act like a big spring, providing tension and hopefully helping me to regain my footing. If it didn't, he could then have dropped the coils giving him a split second to dive into the snow with his axe and arrest us both.

I had a small rope, about 10 metres long, and I decided to short rope myself to Andrew. I attached it to the back of Andrew's harness, held a few coils and got my axe (and myself) ready to arrest at any second – Andrew was that wobbly.

Off we went traversing along the ridge. Andrew slipped a few times but fell inwards towards the slope. Even so, my heart would skip a beat every time he staggered.

After a few hours, Andrew started getting slower and slower. To make things worse, I could see a huge thunderstorm building away in the distance. As an airline pilot you pay attention to thunderstorms and how they develop as they are a big threat. This storm was huge, and sure enough it was coming towards us. Soon it started snowing lightly and visibility started to drop. The scariest thing was that my axe started to hum. I was convinced we were going to get hit by lightning.

At this stage, I got really firm with Andrew. 'Mate, I have a wife who is pregnant at home. This is getting serious. That is a huge thunderstorm. We are in danger of getting hit by lightning so if you don't walk I'm going to leave you here on your own. Now get up!' I would never have left him but I needed him to start moving faster. It had little effect.

In desperation, I asked him if he wanted to lie down and I would drag him by his feet. He slumped into the snow and I picked up his feet and started dragging him down the mountain. At first we made great progress but then snow built up under the back of his jacket and we had to stop.

I sat in the snow, wracking my brain about how to get him to move. Then I remembered that I had an orange in my bag. I pulled it out, peeled it and made him eat it. Within moments, Andrew stood up and started moving quite fast. It was like some sort of miracle, just that tiny orange had such an effect on his energy levels. A few hours later Andrew staggered into the Barrels camp, with me staggering along behind him. We both slept well that night.

The next day we descended off the mountain. I kept my fingers crossed that the chairlift wouldn't break down. Finally, something went right. It carried us smoothly back to base. We arrived back at the lodge where a now healthy Richard was waiting. We planned to go to the local pub that night and meet the Spanish climbers.

I told the lodge owner our plans and he looked very concerned and pointed to his mouth to reveal a full set of gold teeth.

'Don't go to that bar, Mikey. It is where I got these. There are Russian soldiers and farm boys who like going to that bar to fight with westerners. It's really dangerous, Mikey.'

I explained we would be meeting with members of the Spanish military but it didn't change his mind. He sighed and said, 'At least, let me drop you off.'

Perhaps heeding his warning, Andrew and Richard decided not to come out so the lodge owner dropped me off at the bar. When I walked in you could feel the tension in the place. I saw the Spanish guys and they called me over.

I chatted to them and found out that they were all the ex- and current members of the Special Forces and that they acted as security guards for the King of Spain. Apparently, the King was sponsoring them to climb the highest peaks on each of the seven continents and just loved hearing their adventure tales.

The senior officer said he had told the King about meeting a lone Kiwi guy on the summit of Mt Elbrus. He then gave me an insignia that looked a bit like a police badge out of the movies and told me that the King would like to meet me one day. He said he couldn't make any promises but that if I was ever in Madrid, I should show the insignia to any of the King's guards and they would contact him and he would try to arrange for the King to see me. Wow! What an honour. I still don't know if it's true as I haven't been to Madrid since. Maybe it's better not to know.

We all had a few beers and the Spanish soldiers gave me a lift back to my lodge. I didn't get any gold teeth that night.

The next day, Andrew and Richard took me out for lunch to thank me for helping them. The pub I'd been at the night before was the only place open. We went in cautiously and were relieved to find nothing more than a few families having lunch.

We had a magnificent feast and possibly a few beers too many. As we left the pub, we could see two huge artillery guns perched up a hill with no one guarding them. Apparently, they were used to trigger potential avalanches, thereby protecting the village. I suspect they had some military value as well.

Seeing a chance for some fun, the three of us jumped the barbed wire fence and started playing on the artillery guns. They were positioned so close together that if you swung the barrels toward each other you could 'clash' the barrels together, letting off a huge noise. Needless to say, the three of us got a bit carried away with this boyish fun …

Our fun didn't last long. An army truck pulled up and half a dozen or so Russian troops piled out of it with their AK-47s pointed squarely at us. The three of us froze and put up our hands. An officer started screaming at us. Even with my limited Russian, I knew he was mad as hell. We got off the guns and kept our hands raised high.

He shouted at us in Russian and I gestured to my jeans pocket. Slowly and carefully I put my hand into my pocket, only too aware that any rapid movement could result in a barrage of automatic weapon fire. Then I pulled out a small piece of paper and handed it to the Russian commander.

He looked at it, then looked back at me. It was the general's business card. The officer then said in English, 'Your friend?'

'Da! Good friend. Good friend,' I replied.

He leaned forward, gave me the card back and said, 'Don't play on guns.' Then he shouted a few orders to the soldiers, who stopped pointing their guns at us and hopped back into the truck.

The three of us laughed all the way back to the lodge … nervously.

CLIMBING COOK

On my return to Auckland, my entire focus was on Wendy and preparing for the birth of our first child. When our son, Ethan, finally arrived it was just magic, the emotion I felt was indescribable. I was so happy to be a dad, and I was sure I was the proudest dad in the world.

Wendy was a totally natural mum and I couldn't have been happier with our little family. While we both adjusted to having three of us in the house, I continued working my butt off to make sure that house was as perfect as it could be for the two most important people in my life.

It was fantastic to be a new dad, but I was a little worried that I wouldn't be able to spend as much time in the mountains as before. Thankfully, Wendy knew how important adventuring was to me and she had no intention of trying to change me. I like to think that no one can change anyone else but that we all need to change and evolve to make life as good as it can be.

Three months later, with Wendy and Ethan completely thriving and the house looking pretty good, I set off on another adventure. This time my mission was to climb New Zealand's highest mountain, Mt Cook, with my friend and mentor Paul Scaife.

Before I left for Wanaka, Wendy and I went to our lawyers and I filled out a form giving her full power of attorney. I also made sure that I had a decent life insurance policy so Wendy and Ethan would be provided for in case anything happened to me. With every climb comes risk but I knew I was climbing with the one of the best and most experienced guides in the world. Confident that nothing much would go wrong, I promised Wendy that I would be off the mountain in nine days' time to meet her for a family holiday at Wanaka in the South Island.

When I got down to Wanaka, Paul asked me if I would be ok with him bringing a trainee guide along on our climb. The guy's name was Milo and he was a very experienced climber who had climbed all over the world. Even knowing how experienced he was, I wasn't that keen as I wanted to climb one on one with Paul. Looking back it was pretty arrogant of me but thankfully I had my mind changed after I spoke to one of the other owners of Aspiring Guides, Nick Craddock. I told Nick that I wanted to climb Cook with Paul alone.

He told me straight up, 'Mike, Cook is totally different to Aspiring. Mt Cook is a very serious climb. It is huge. The vertical rise on the mountain is one of the largest in the world. Do not underestimate it. Take two guides and you'll be safer. Even with three of you together this climb will push you to your limits.'

So it was that our duo became a trio. The night before our climb began, we stayed at Unwin Lodge near Mt Cook village. Here we met another of the owners from Aspiring Guides, David Hiddleston. David told us that the weather forecast was looking 'a little stink' for the next few days, but that he didn't think it would be too bad. Little did we know.

We woke at 3.30 the next morning and went into the hut lounge to pack our gear. There were four people asleep on the floor. We woke them up and offered them our recently vacated beds, which they gratefully accepted. They looked totally wrecked as they had just been rescued off Mt Cook. And we were just setting off.

Light snow was falling in the car park, and we had about a nine-hour walk to Gardiner Hut, the first hut up the Hooker Valley on the lower reaches of the mountain. Mt Cook National Park has a no-fly zone in place up the Hooker Valley, so climbers and trampers can enjoy peace and quiet with no helicopters buzzing around. The downside of that is that the only way to get up the valley is on foot.

The first few hours hiking were fine. Paul kept commenting on the amount of water coming down the streams, but I was none the wiser. Progress was slow as our packs weighed about 35 kilograms each as we had to carry all our food and gear for as many as nine days in the mountains.

As the day wore on, the weather continued to deteriorate. In order to reach the hut, we had to cross the Hooker Glacier.

As we got onto the glacier, the wind had reached at least 60 knots with gusts hitting over 80 knots. The gusts were so strong that you could see them coming down the glacier. They were impossible to stand up in so as a gust approached, all three of us would lie down and dig our axes in and wait for it to pass before continuing on.

I was by far the weakest and slowest of the three of us. At one stage, Paul and Milo grabbed my pack and moved as much gear as they could into their own packs in an attempt to help me move faster.

We were all roped together, with Paul in the lead, me in the middle and Milo at the rear. The glacier surface was scarred with huge crevasses. At one stage, the ground cracked beneath my feet and a huge crevasse opened up and I fell in. Paul and Milo dug their axes in and their expertise and the ropes were all that saved me from certain death. As I looked down, all I could see was a huge expanse that disappeared into darkness.

My feet were kicking away in free air. Only my head and two arms were above ground level. I could see Paul shouting at me but the howling wind meant I couldn't hear him. Eventually I worked out he was asking me whether I could get myself out. I nodded and gestured towards the rope, indicating that I was going to pull on the rope and try to drag myself out. As I grabbed the rope, Paul dug his axe further into the surface of the glacier, giving me the security I needed to heave myself out of the crevasse. Once out, I lay on my stomach and edged my way towards Paul, all the while fearing another collapse.

I was relieved to be out but my fall had delayed us further. The weather was closing in and we huddled together as Paul shouted his plan above the fury of the wind. I could barely hear him even though he was yelling directly in my ear. The three of us walked down into the lee of a huge bergschrund (like a crevasse). Here we were out of the wind and could hear Paul's plan.

'We need to climb this frozen waterfall, Mike. It will take us another two or three hours to go around the glacier and it's getting serious. Milo and I will go first. We will have you roped to us but we will not be putting in protection.'

I asked Paul what would happen if I fell. 'Don't worry. Milo and I will have eight points on the ice, two axes each and two sets of crampons.'

He then looked up at the slope of snow leading to the start of the ice waterfall and said, 'I think that could avalanche. Let's put on our avalanche transceivers and go one at a time.'

We each crossed and climbed up the snow slope without triggering an avalanche. Paul and Milo went ahead side by side and I clipped into the rope at the bottom, sort of like a V formation.

Unfortunately, as we started climbing tons of snow fell on me from Paul and Milo climbing above me. It was freezing and I was completely blinded as my goggles had a thick coating of snow all over them.

We all had our huge backpacks on and at this stage we had been on the move for nearly 13 hours. I closed my eyes held my two ice axes out as wide as I could so I didn't hit the rope and climbed like I had never climbed before. All I could manage was 10 moves, 10 hits of each axe, then I was totally exhausted.

At one stage I wiped my goggles and through the smeared ice I could see the drop below me. It was almost 20 metres. I didn't look down again.

We finally made it over the top of the frozen waterfall. What elation I might have felt disappeared when I realised it was impossible to stand up or even crawl because of the wind. We had to slide on our bellies towards Gardiner Hut, which was about 30 metres away. The wind was probably over 100 knots. We all kept very low and used the rocks as wind breaks to give us some relief.

Finally we made the hut but the door was frozen solid. We had to spend 10 minutes cutting the ice free. Well, Paul and Milo did – I was frozen, a bit of a mess and not much use to anyone.

When they finally got the door open, we all piled into the hut. Ever practical, it took only minutes for Paul to have a brew on the go. He handed me some crackers and cheese. I just stood there shaking with a huge smile on my face.

In his own understated way Paul said, 'Well now, that's the worst weather I have ever climbed in with a client …'

Milo followed it up with, 'Oh my god! That is the worst weather I've ever been in in my entire life!'

I still couldn't speak and was focused on trying to prise my frozen goggles off my face.

Once I finally managed to get all my gear off, including the goggles, I climbed into my sleeping bag to thaw out. To help me warm up, Paul brought me over a hot drink and dinner. I was still grinning. What a day!

The weather didn't let up that night, and for the next two

days we were trapped in this tiny little hut. It's supposed to sleep eight people but I'm very glad there were only three of us there. The time passed quickly, as we played cards and Milo and Paul entertained me with climbing stories.

On the third day, the weather had finally settled and we decided to carry on up the mountain. Our goal for the day was to make the three- to four-hour climb up to the Empress Hut. We climbed via the lower Empress Shelf. Even though it wasn't a long day's climbing, Paul had us nearly running some of the way as he was concerned about possible avalanches after the recent bad weather. On the way up, the cloud rolled in down the valley below us and I could hear the roar of avalanches lower down the mountain. Paul's fears suddenly became a whole lot more real to me.

Empress Hut was a lot bigger than Gardiner Hut and I was pleased to see that it was perched on a rocky outcrop safe from avalanches. The hut was reasonably new, having been built in 1994, but it looked a bit battered. I asked Paul about it and he said that he had been standing outside the hut a few years back when a huge chunk of ice broke off Mt Hicks. The ensuing avalanche blast knocked him off his feet and peppered the hut with fist size ice rocks.

We spent the next day cutting steps into the ice over a pass called Earl's Gap. This pass led to the Hooker Face of Mt Cook, a huge ice face that seemed to touch the sky. I looked at it in awe, wondering how good you would have to be to climb that face. I was also wondering where we were going to climb.

Almost as if he was reading my mind, Paul looked at me and said, 'Mike, you seem very fit, so we are going to climb

the Hooker Face. I've always wanted to do it with a client.'
I didn't know what to say, but I felt very nervous.

Every hut has a hut book, where climbers write their
intended routes and notes on their climbs. That night, back
in the hut, I read the sad story of a climber whose climbing
partner had fallen while climbing down Porters Col a couple
of weeks before. They had been getting ready to abseil when
the rock they were anchored to gave away, one of the pair
fell all the way down the col and then into a crevasse. The
mountain rescue team hours later managed to get him out
alive but he died. It was spine-chilling reading.

We all went to bed around 8pm, as we were going to get
up at 2am to start climbing. I couldn't stop thinking about
the story in the hut book so sleep didn't come easily to me.

It wasn't long before I woke to the sound of Paul and Milo
bustling around the hut. I like being really organised when
I go climbing so I slept in my climbing clothes. I got out of
bed, put on my harness and was practically ready to go.

It was such a clear night, very cold. As we roped together,
I was very excited but I had no idea what the next 48 hours
had in store for us. What I did know was that what we were
about to attempt was very dangerous.

We walked and climbed up the steps we'd cut in the previous
day and finally arrived at the bottom of the Hooker Face at
6am. To reach the face itself we had to scale a very scary looking
vertical section of ice that appeared to be over 30 metres high.
It was different from the one we had climbed a few days before.
I looked at it and I could feel knots in my stomach twisting
around. 'There is no way I can climb that, Paul.'

'Yes you can, Mike, I know you can. I'll go up now and you watch.'

Paul left me with Milo, who had a real insight into how I was feeling. He started talking to me as we watched Paul climb. The more Milo talked the more I could feel my confidence building up. I can do this. Well, maybe.

Paul made it up the icefall and then disappeared over the top. Two tugs on the rope signalled that he had set up the anchor and it was my turn to climb.

My focus was intense. I didn't look down. I concentrated only on things within a one-metre radius of me. Milo was shouting encouragement as I dug both my axes in hard, each move, each stroke, rock solid. I made the final move over the lip where I could see Paul, who had a huge smile on his face. As I looked back down at what I had just climbed, I was beaming as well.

Once Milo arrived, we all started climbing the actual Hooker Face, which seemed like it was thousands of feet high. Paul and Milo took it in turns leading; each time they would put an anchor in, sometimes ice screws, sometimes a v-thread, where a short section of cord is threaded through two holes above an ice screw forming an anchor.

Each time I would climb up to the new anchor, clip in and make myself safe, then Paul or Milo would head off again. This process gave me enough time to rest, eat some food and apply sunscreen.

This went on all day. We had arrived at the bottom of the face at 6am and some 13 hours later we topped out on the summit ridge. It was summer and, at that height, the sun didn't set until about 10pm.

I looked over at the true summit of Mt Cook and it was still a fair distance away. I asked Paul how long it would take to get up there and he reckoned it would take about an hour and a half to get there and back. Thinking it would be dark soon, I told Paul I had no intention of carrying on.

But he wasn't having any of it. 'Mike, we are going to the true summit. No one climbs to the true summit anymore since the big landslide. Let's go.' And with that Paul led off.

In 1991, a massive landslide of snow and rock roared down the east face of the mountain into the Tasman Glacier. This saw the height of the mountain shrink by about 10 metres.

Paul was moving fast and just before the summit, he had used a cornice (an overhanging piece of ice) as 'natural' protection. He looped the rope over the ice so if I fell it would act as an anchor saving me from falling. It was a really good idea until I came along and couldn't flick the rope back over the ice cornice. I looked at Paul, who was about 10 metres away.

He shouted, 'Lie on your belly, slide up and flick it off.'

I lay down, making sure my crampons were digging into the ice, and slowly shimmied up. I reached up and grabbed the lip of the ice and pulled myself up and peered over the side. I almost had a heart attack. I looked straight down probably 2000 metres but, worse than that, I looked back towards my feet. I was lying on a tiny piece of overhanging ice cornice that was going to break at any second.

Petrified, I edged my way back inch by inch, very gently. I could hear Paul shouting, 'Get the rope, get the rope …'

'Get stuffed! It's a huge cornice. I'm not getting the rope, it will collapse.'

Paul waved me up and I moved up to him where I clipped into his main anchor and we pulled the line up. Milo wasn't keen to retrieve the rope either. There we all were – standing very carefully on the summit of Mt Cook. I had done it. I had climbed the highest mountain in New Zealand.

Even though we'd summited the mountain, we were only halfway through the climb. It was getting dark, it was almost 9pm and we had been climbing for 19 hours. I was worried but had no choice but to put my total trust in Paul and Milo.

Their plan was to simul climb along the summit ridge to Middle Peak, where we would stay for the night. Simul climbing is where one person leads out putting protection in along the way, with the rest of us moving behind them at the same time. This is very fast compared to stopping and belaying each person. The down side is that you are not as safe, and if you fall you can plummet a long way before the protection catches you.

Paul's instructions to me were very simple. 'We are going to simul climb. Don't fall.'

We climbed along the ridge, watching the spectacular sunset over the Tasman Sea to the west. At about 11pm with the last of the light fading, we finally arrived at Middle Peak Hotel. Far from being a hotel, it was just a crevasse in which climbers can shelter overnight. Middle Peak Hotel was made famous by Mark Inglis and Phil Doole, who spent 13 nights trapped there in 1982. Both Mark and Phil lost the lower parts of their legs during the time they spent trapped by the weather. The country was on tenterhooks, not knowing if the pair was alive or dead. Theirs was a true display of human courage, spirit and strength to survive.

Mike Allsop

Even in pretty much perfect conditions, Middle Peak Hotel proved to be a reasonably challenging place to stay for one night. Paul had brought food, coffee, Milo and a stove. We all huddled around the tiny stove and lay on our improvised mattresses made up of our packs and coiled-up ropes. It was freezing, probably –25°C, and we didn't have down jackets with us. We had tried to keep our packs as light as possible for the climb so left things like down jackets and sleeping bags behind.

I lay back and gazed at the stars as Paul cooked dinner … well, while he opened the tins of sardines. I asked Paul where the term 'bivi' came from.

'Bivi is short for bivouac and, bivouac is French for MISTAKE!' (it's not really)

We all laughed, laid back and snacked on our partially frozen sardines and lukewarm coffee … and froze our nuts off.

After an hour, none of us could get any warmth or sleep so we packed up, ready to get moving. As Paul was sorting out his gear he absent-mindedly put a karabiner in his mouth. It instantly froze to his tongue. He started pulling on it but it was locked on. He pulled and pulled, while Milo and I tried not to laugh. Finally it came off and when he shone his light on it, there were furry bits of his tongue left on the karabiner. It must have hurt.

We traversed along to Porters Col, where we stumbled across two axes and a few other bits of climbing gear. It was the site of the incident I'd read about in the hut book the previous night. It was a long way down.

152

We abseiled down the col and then, roped together, started making our way across the plateau. Halfway across Milo needed a pee. We all stopped while he did his business and the next thing I remember was him standing right next to me. I was so exhausted I had fallen asleep standing upright.

A few more hours' descent and we arrived back at the Empress Hut some 30 hours after we had left it. The bunks looked mighty welcoming but I had a big problem.

I had promised Wendy I would be out of the mountains when she arrived on Thursday morning. It was now Thursday morning and I was two days' walk away from civilisation.

I told Paul my problem. He said, 'No problem. Let's eat, sleep and then get going.' And we did just that. Unbelievable!

After about five hours, we made it down to Gardiner Hut, where a fellow climber took one look at us and told us to sit down while he made us dinner. We ate with her and then carried on down onto the glacier and navigated our way around the labyrinth of crevasses. We eventually made it onto the glacier moraine and then finally found a tiny patch of grass. There we unrolled our sleeping bags and seconds later, we were all fast asleep.

I managed to get a message to Wendy via various radios and people that I would now arrive in Wanaka before midday on Friday.

I was so exhausted that that night out in the open went quickly. When I woke up, I was still in the same position as I had been in when I went to sleep. I opened one eye slowly and there, just centimetres away, was another eye looking at me. I sat up in fright. It was a beautiful mountain parrot, a kea. It hopped back and let out an almighty squawk. I thought it was a pretty cool alarm clock.

But then I looked down at my sleeping bag. The little bugger had torn my bag to shreds. There were down and feathers everywhere.

Paul woke and shouted, 'Quick, chuck a rock at it. If he calls his mates, they will pester us all the way out.'

We didn't throw any rocks but waved our arms around and the kea took off, letting out cries as he went, telling his mates where we were.

We had finally run out of food so there was no breakfast. We packed up quick smart and got going. A few hours later we arrived back at Mt Cook Village. Once there we went into the Department of Conservation office to sign ourselves off the mountain and let them know we were ok. The department manages the mountain closely and is often the first to raise the alarm if climbers are late to return or don't check in at huts when they are expected.

It was at the office that I noticed people looking at us funny. Paul pulled me aside and told me that the DOC staff had a nickname for climbers – smellies.

Paul, Milo and I all went back to the mountain club hut and cleaned up, before hopping in the car and driving to Wanaka.

We pulled up and I saw Wendy standing in the Aspiring Guides office. She ran over and gave me a huge hug. Wendy pulled away just a little and I stared into her eyes, expecting her to say something romantic. But no. The next words out of her mouth were, 'Poo, you stink!'

We drove to our hotel via the supermarket where Wendy bought some industrial soap and a wire scrubbing brush. Back at the hotel, she ran the bath and insisted I sat in it and scrubbed myself until the smell had gone.

It was only when I was clean that I looked closely at my legs and feet. On one heel there was a chunk of flesh missing where a blister had simply worn though. One of my shins had a 10-centimetre long purple bruise on it where my boot had been rubbing.

I sat back on the sun lounger at the hotel while Wendy got me a beer and put dressings on my wounds.

Then she said, 'Close your eyes. I have something to show you …'

My heart stopped. 'You're not pregnant are you?'

'Just close your eyes, ok?'

With that I felt her drop a wad of paper into my lap. When I opened my eyes I saw it was a property contract. Wendy had bloody bought a house!

I quickly thumbed through the contract and it looked rock solid. She had used the power of attorney that I signed over before I went into the mountains. I couldn't believe it.

'Holy smoke! You bought a house. This is fully legal, we can't get out of it!'

She just smiled and let the news sink in.

We had put in a tender for this house a few months earlier but had been unsuccessful. We decided that it wasn't meant to be, and I had completely forgotten about it. But obviously, Wendy hadn't.

I was stunned for a little while, then really happy. Wendy had done really well buying it and it was a much better family home. The plan was to move out of the one we were renovating and keep it as a rental property.

That evening, I went to the Aspiring Guides office and gave Paul and Milo a bottle of wine as a thank you. We sat out on the veranda overlooking the lake and talked and laughed about the climb. Sadly, this was to be the last time I would see Paul Scaife.

UP ALPAMAYO

Having climbed Mt Cook, my dream to summit Everest was stronger than ever. I knew that if I was going to even attempt the world's highest mountain I needed to get some more altitude experience. The idea for my next adventure came from David Hiddleston, who I had met on Mt Cook. David was a very experienced guide, and he knew Everest well. He was the perfect person to have help me achieve my dream of climbing Everest myself.

David suggested that I join an expedition he was guiding on Alpamayo, a 5947-metre peak in the Peruvian Andes. Following our climb there, David and I planned to climb another nearby mountain called Huascarán. Standing at 6768 metres, Huascarán would be my training for Everest.

The expedition was planned for June 2003. Ethan would be nine months old. It was going to be hard being away from the family and I decided that I would ask Wendy to marry me before I left for Peru.

On the night before my departure, Wendy and I went to her parents' house to drop Ethan off for the night. There I pulled Wendy's dad, Brian, aside and asked for his daughter's hand in marriage. Tears welled up in his eyes and he was a bit speechless but he agreed.

Having got Brian's ok, I then took Wendy to our favourite Japanese restaurant for dinner. While we were having dinner, our conversation somehow got on to marriage. Wendy said with a tear in her eye, 'You're never going to marry me …'

At that precise moment, the lights dimmed with just one spotlight left on over our table. Wendy looked a bit confused. Then a waiter brought out our dinner platter. Among the many beautiful dishes on it, sitting on top of a rose was a diamond ring. The spotlight caught it and it sparkled like a star … well, a small – no, make that tiny – star!

Wendy's eyes lit up and a huge smile crossed her face. She turned to me and I said, 'Babe, will you marry me?' She then burst into tears and gave me a hug.

'So is that yes?' I asked.

'Yes, yes, yes,' she said.

I turned around to see all the restaurant staff standing behind us. I gave them a thumbs-up and they applauded.

After dinner I had arranged a red carpet rolled out to a stretch limo for our departure. As we walked out, Wendy saw she was on a special red carpet and thought it was for some movie star so jumped off it. I laughed and told her it was for her.

We hopped in the limo and popped open a bottle of champagne. The limo driver asked where we wanted to go.

I had booked a luxury room at a hotel but before I got a chance to direct the driver there, Wendy shouted, 'Mum and Dad's house!' The hotel room would have to wait.

The next day, Wendy and Ethan waved me off at the airport. Wendy had the wedding to plan while I was away and I felt good. I knew I had made the right decision, and was happy that I hadn't rushed.

After flying to Los Angeles then down to Lima in Peru, I met up with David and our other expedition member, Lily. Lily was another client on the climb of Alpamayo but it would be only David and me on Huascarán We stayed the night in Lima and the next day boarded a local bus for the 12-hour ride to Huaraz, the gateway city to the Peruvian Andes.

The bus trip was not nearly as bad as I thought it was going to be. It was in a luxury coach, complete with a toilet. The driver warned us to lock the toilet door as on his last trip he had jammed on the brakes and the poor chap who was sitting on the toilet came flying out with his pants down and ended up halfway down the bus.

I had been having Spanish lessons for six months and had quite a good basic grasp of the language, so I happily took part in an on-board game of bingo in Spanish to kill time.

With a population of about 120,000, Huaraz was a nice little town abuzz with plenty of tourists there to either climb or mountain bike. It sits at an altitude of 3000 metres and we spent a few days there doing treks up to about 3600 metres to help us acclimatise.

One day I went for a walk and stumbled upon a huge protest. As part of a national day of action, the local teachers were on strike and they were fired up As I walked through the crowd, the front line between the protestors and the police had already been drawn. Among the people carrying placards were some, carrying big sticks, who looked like they were preparing for a fight.

I must have looked very lost, as the crowd parted and someone ushered me out past the demarcation line. Then a policeman in full riot gear waved me over and pointed for me to go up the street. As I made my way through the police, they were strapping on armour, loading their tear gas guns and putting on helmets. They looked a little confused when they saw me. All I could do was smile and say, 'Hola!'

I was only about 200 metres away when a teacher started chanting on a loudhailer. This served to fire the crowd up. In seconds, the police started firing tear gas straight into the crowd. Boom, boom, boom. The teachers scattered instantly. The riot lasted about 10 seconds – the time it took for only one good chant. Those Peruvian cops were tough and didn't stand for any shit.

Having experienced as much excitement as I could stand in Huaraz, I was happy to finally head for Alpamayo and start our big climb. We took a taxi to the trail head and then arranged for a donkey driver to carry all our gear up to base camp. It took us two days trekking to be reunited with it.

We arranged for our donkey driver to stay and look after our gear at base camp as there were a few dodgy looking characters lurking around and we needed to leave our base camp tent set up here.

While we were climbing, I talked to David about Everest a lot. He told me about his first attempt when he got to the south summit but had to turn around. He eventually summited the following year. Listening to him talk about what it was like to actually summit Everest helped to inspire me towards my own goal.

It also gave me a chance to quiz David on the best way for me to attempt the climb. I had read *The Kid who Climbed Everest* by Bear Grylls, and I wanted to climb Everest in a way similar to his. He had worked with a man called Henry Todd.

Todd was a very experienced mountaineer who would provide you with all the camps, food and oxygen, but no western guide. You had to be able to operate independently and safely. On summit day, Henry would match you with a suitable super strong Sherpa who would carry your spare oxygen. It turned out that David and Henry were good mates, and David heartily recommended my planned approach.

Having made our arrangements at base camp, the time came to move up to Camp 1 on Alpamayo. It was a few hours' climb but we had no porters and the donkeys couldn't cope with the steep terrain. This meant we had to carry all of our gear. I really struggled at this altitude with my pack weighing about 35 kilograms. But mine was nothing compared to David's. I reckon his would have been over 40 kilos – David was a machine at altitude.

The next day was an acclimatisation day. We hiked up over a glacier and manoeuvred around some very scary crevasses. When it comes to safety, I'm a perfectionist, so I like things to be textbook. I think this was a little hard for Lily to take and we ended up having a few words.

David let me lead through some of the icefall, with Lily in the middle and himself at the back. I was insistent that the rope be run in a textbook manner. I can see that for someone not used to rope work, I must have come across like a complete pain in the arse to Lily. But David just smiled and kept saying, 'I like your style, Mikey.'

Despite the tensions, we all needed to work together as the next day was time to climb up to Col Camp and then go for the summit. As we were climbing, two really friendly Japanese climbers passed us. David asked them lots of questions, and they insisted they were ok and continued on. David was worried that they had come up too fast but watching them climb, they seemed very experienced.

Coming into Col Camp, I was totally stuffed, with the altitude, my pack weight and plain hard work taking their toll on me. Once we reached the camp, Alpamayo opened up unrestricted views of her summit. It has to be one of the most picturesque mountains in the world, with huge snow and ice flutes that are unique to the Andes.

The two Japanese had set up their tent about three metres from us and disappeared into it.

I thought I might have trouble sleeping as I was so excited but the second I lay down I was out like a light. Next thing I remember David was shaking me awake. It was 2am – summit time.

We set off across the glacier and up to the bergschrund. This was the hardest part of the climb. My heart sank. I had never climbed overhanging ice before. There was a huge drop off but because it was night I couldn't see all the way down. But I knew the drop was there.

Just before David set off to lead the pitch he said to me, 'Watch me, Mikey,' which is mountaineers' code for, 'I'm a bit nervous, so please pay attention on the belay!' He then disappeared around the corner and over the lip. Five minutes later there were two tugs on the rope and I was on my way.

When I got near the top, I took a deep breath and centred myself before edging out onto this thin lip of ice, with a massive drop below me. The ice seemed to hang over my head like a roof. I dug in one crampon, reached up and swung my axe hard. It hit just before the lip. I then pushed and sort of jumped, swinging my other axe, and it landed further up with a solid 'thwack'. Then my foot popped off and I was swinging mid-air held by my axes. Strangely, I felt fine. I swung my leg sideways and hooked the heel point in over the lip. This gave me a chance to take the load off one axe and reposition it. And that was it, I had done it, I was over the edge. Stoked.

I climbed up to David and heard him quietly say, 'Well done, Mikey.'

Dawn was just starting to break in the distance, and then over the lip came an ice axe, then a foot and then another axe – Lily had made it. David looked at me and said, 'Wow, she climbed that well.'

Now it was a long slog up the near vertical mountain. The flute narrowed at the top, and at the end of the flute was this huge cornice (overhanging ice) that looked to be about the size of a small house. I looked up wondering how we were going to make it around this monstrosity. We got all the way to the top of the flute to a dead end. On the left was a tunnel through the wall of the flute. We were all clipped into the anchor and David again said, 'Watch me this time, Mikey.' Then he disappeared.

A few minutes later came the familiar tug on the rope and I began climbing through this little tunnel of deep blue ice about five metres long. It opened out onto the flute system alongside. This was very steep and the vertical drop would have been 500 metres straight down. The ice was dark blue and almost bulletproof. I swung my axe and it just bounced off. I swung it again and it bounced off again. I looked for David but I couldn't see him, just the rope snaking up for 15 metres then disappearing.

I could feel the doubt starting to swell up inside me. It is a very strange sensation when you can actually feel the fear starting to take its grip on you. But I didn't have much choice but to harden up and sort it out myself. I told myself to relax, slow down and think. My feet had good holds in the ice and one axe was in solid. I looked up just above my head and then swung my axe again. It just bounced off. Unbelievable. How can an ice axe bounce off? Was it blunt?

I looked around and found one of the holes that David had made on his way through and I placed my axe in this tiny hole in the ice. I cautiously weighted it, expecting it to blow out at any stage. It held. I used this hold to get some balance, lifted my other axe and swung it high expecting it to bounce off. But it dug in with a nice thwack. Finally, I felt confident this would take all my weight.

That 15 metres or so of climbing was spectacular. I reached the top ledge and had to crawl on my hands and knees under the cornice to a small opening. I poked my head up and there was David – and the summit of Alpamayo.

It was awesome, the Peruvian Andes just opened up all

around, baked in glorious sunshine. The sense of achievement I felt was indescribable.

Lily soon turned up. She was a better climber than me and had no trouble getting up the vertical ice but she was very cold. I gave her my down jacket as I didn't need it. We stayed at the summit for a few minutes and then prepared to abseil down.

There was just one snow stake hammered into the ice on the summit ridge and everyone was abseiling off this one anchor. I asked David if this was ok with no back-up. He looked at it very carefully and after a few minutes decided it was fine.

We clipped in and kicked off down the parallel flute. We went past the little tunnel we'd climbed through and then there were these huge hollow ice caves. They looked like they were suspended in mid-air. They looked so dangerous, as if they were about to collapse at any time, and if they did collapse it would trigger a massive unsurvivable avalanche.

David was about 10 metres below me with Lily. I caught his eye and gestured towards the ice caves. We didn't need to speak. He nodded. It was simple. We needed to get the hell out of there as soon as possible.

We got down onto the glacier and then raced across the ice out of the way of any potential avalanche. We staggered back into camp at around 2pm – the climb had been 12 hours of hard work.

I tried to speak to David but I was so exhausted that I was slurring my words really badly. David told me to sit down and went and made some soup. He was knackered as well but didn't show it.

I looked around for the two Japanese climbers but they were nowhere to be seen.

The next morning was spectacular with beautiful weather and stunning views. We packed up the camp and set off back down to base camp. We climbed down the steep part of the glacier and worked our way through the crevasses, trying hard not to fall in. Once we could safely take off the ropes, David and Lily went ahead. I trailed behind as I was extremely tired.

Hours upon hours seemed to go by. I could see base camp but I had almost ground to a halt. About 500 metres out from base camp all I could manage was 10 steps, then I'd stop and rest, then 10 steps then stop and rest. It took me ages but I made it to base camp in the end.

Our loyal donkey driver was there waiting for us and our camp was intact. David had prepared a great meal and had made some new friends in the tent next door. They were two Israeli climbers who had been planning to climb that day but the woman had come down sick and her guide had stayed with her until she was healthy enough to climb in a few days.

The next morning I woke up to a bit of ruckus. There were a lot of people standing around talking. David went over to see what was going on. It turned out the two Japanese climbers had not gone climbing the previous day. They had stayed in their tent. One had had very bad altitude sickness and died. There had been a doctor up at the Col camp at the time and when he returned to base camp, David and I went over and spoke to him.

He said that by the time he knew there was a problem it was too late. Sometime during the previous day, one of the Japanese climbers came over and asked for help as his friend was having trouble breathing. They pulled him out of the tent and gave him dexamethasone shots but he stopped breathing shortly afterwards. The doctor performed CPR but it was no good.

David and I walked back to our camp. I could tell he was mad about it as he had known that they were going up too fast and wished he had tried harder to make them turn around. Even if he hadn't managed to talk them out of it, maybe we could have lowered him down the glacier somehow if we'd known he was sick. I'm not sure how we would have done it but the one thing I did know was that David could have made it happen.

That afternoon, the now solo Japanese climber walked into base camp, very distraught. There were a few Peruvians trying to talk to him. I looked at this poor man who had just lost his friend and I had no idea what to do.

David jumped up straight away, went over and simply put his hand on his shoulder and said, 'I'm so sorry …' The Japanese climber didn't speak any English or Spanish so communication was difficult, but he knew exactly what David said and bowed to him in thanks.

David then organised a horse to get the climber out quickly and somehow borrowed a satellite phone to speak to the Japanese embassy in Lima. I watched how caring David was to this man as he hugged him goodbye.

When David walked back over, I said to him, 'The poor guy must be devastated. How did you know what to say to him?'

'I didn't. I just spoke to him and showed him some compassion.'

The mood at camp that night was very sombre. We spent our evening talking to the two Israelis and a group of climbers from Argentina. There was a real sense of camaraderie on the mountain that night as we had all been reminded just how dangerous climbing could be.

The next morning we started early and headed back down the valley, enjoying the walk out. We all felt very strong coming down from altitude and were motoring along the track. After about 10 hours we arrived at the end of the track or the beginning of the road, whichever way you want to look at it. Eventually, a taxi arrived and David, Lily and I all piled in. We squeezed a German climber in as well. She didn't say much despite David's attempts to speak to her in German. I got the impression she was tired as she had just walked down from base camp as well.

The taxi was a Toyota Caldina. In fact, pretty much every taxi in this part of Peru was a Toyota Caldina. This particular one was very rundown, with a noisy exhaust, rust everywhere, and canvas showing on the tyres. Oh well, I thought, I'd survived the mountains, now I just had to survive the taxi ride.

After an hour's driving, we had all fallen asleep, with David, Lily and me in the back seat and the German in the front. All of a sudden, we were woken by a very loud bang. The front outside tyre had blown out. The German climber was screaming at the top of her lungs as the taxi swerved all over the place, finally coming to a stop on the other side of the road. We were so lucky there was no traffic coming the other way.

We arrived back in Huaraz tired and sore but our little family hotel felt just like home. After a bit of a rest, it was time to go out and celebrate. Lily went home after dinner and David and I went out in search of a South American dance bar where we could practise our moves on the dance floor with the locals. We found a cool bar with loud Latin dance music playing but when we saw all the Latin men dressed immaculately and dancing like flamenco dancers, well, we didn't want to embarrass ourselves and headed for the bar and had a few beers.

The next day, after saying goodbye to Lily, David and I prepared for Huascarán, the highest mountain in Peru at 6786 metres. I was excited to be climbing one on one with David.

After a few days' rest, we headed further north to start our climb. It was a few hours in a taxi to the start of the track where we would begin our trek to base camp. I had been coughing a little and not feeling 100 per cent, but I hoped I would shake it off. Unfortunately, after a few hours I started feeling much worse.

David was a long way ahead with the donkey and driver, who were carrying our base camp gear. I just seemed to be getting slower and slower. After six hours all I could manage were a few steps at a time then rest.

Eventually, I collapsed into base camp coughing and wheezing, unable to even speak. I lay on the ground and fell asleep for a few hours. David brought me some hot drinks and food but I was too weak to eat. That night was very rough, and I was feeling really sick. The next morning I told

David that I thought the wisest thing would be to descend. I was feeling a little better but didn't want to back myself into a corner at high altitude. If the weather changed while we were at a higher camp and I got any sicker, I could very easily die.

We relaxed for the morning at base camp before taking the long walk out. While we were there a team of Spanish doctors came down from the mountain. They asked what we were doing and I told them how I was feeling. One of them offered to listen to my chest with his stethoscope. 'Ah,' he said. 'Very wise decision not to climb higher, you have a very bad chest infection, my friend. Well done, now go down.'

David and I took all day to get back to the little village at the end of the road. There was a tiny cafe – well, actually a few tables and chairs in the front room of a house, with chickens running around outside. David went in and asked if we could get lunch – there was only roast chicken on the menu! I was still feeling sick and didn't feel like eating anything. David went in and ordered.

Next thing there was a horrendous noise and the distinct whack of an axe made it clear that lunch was going to be very fresh. David and I looked at each other and a few minutes later David said, 'It looks like you're getting chicken for lunch. There were six running around and now there are only four. Sorry. I must have said two in Spanish by mistake.'

Forty-five minutes later, two beautifully roasted chickens arrived at our table. Just the smell made me feel better and once I had eaten I felt like a new man.

David and I went back to Huaraz and spent a few days

relaxing. We had extra time as we had come off the mountain early and we couldn't change our flights.

One night we went to the pub and as we came home dared each other to eat guinea pig being barbecued by a street vendor. It tastes like chicken right up to the point where I thought of a cute little furry pet I used to have as a kid.

While we were waiting in Huaraz, we heard there had been a big accident on Alpamayo. The huge cornice had collapsed off the summit and gone flying down the route we had just climbed, killing everyone in its path – eight people in total. Then we heard their nationalities: Israeli, Argentinian and Peruvian. Without a doubt they were the climbers we had camped next to and spent time with at base camp on Alpamayo.

It didn't really sink in. The closest I can get to describing it is, it was like hearing someone you had met had been killed in a car crash. You feel very sorry for them and think of how sad it must be for their family, friends and loved ones. But it seemed somehow removed. Sure, I had been climbing the exact same route and mountain nine days ago but I didn't really think about getting killed myself. To tell the truth, I was worried about how my family would take the news in relation to my mountain climbing. I knew how dangerous it was but this would be a bit close for them.

I called Wendy straight away. She seemed ok, a little worried. I guess she simply put it out of her mind and accepted mountaineering and adventure was part of the man she was going to marry.

David and I eventually made it back to Lima for one night before the flight home. We wanted to go out, smoke a big cigar, have a drink then go to a Latin American dance club and have a dance with the locals. David had been in Peru the year before and told me about a place he had been to that was a full-on serious dance club. The only issue was that neither of us could Latin dance.

I paid $50 for two Cuban cigars, we toasted our success and also acknowledged my failure on Huascarán. To tell the truth, I'm not a smoker and although the cigar smelt and tasted nice, afterwards I felt like a squirrel had slept in my mouth.

After a few beers we plucked up our courage and went to find the dance club. When we got to the place David thought it was we found it had been shut down. A man dressed in a suit came up to us and asked if we were looking for the dance club. He told us it had closed down but he had a limo that could take us to a new, better and bigger dance club. He seemed very well dressed and very formal, so we agreed and hopped into the limo and off we went.

He had promised that the club was only five minutes away, so after about 10 minutes driving we both started to get nervous. David asked the driver to let us out. He was told not to worry, we were nearly there. His reassurance was enough to stop us worrying.

We looked up and this huge, three-car wide garage door was slowly opening revealing two men in suits standing there with Uzi sub-machine guns. I looked at David and said, 'Oh shit. I think this is a high class brothel! How much money do you have on you?' He said he only had about $100.

'Right, well, we are in the shit. We can't get out of this

easily. Let's go in and have a drink then try to get out safely. I have US$500 on me. Just follow my lead.'

We got out of the car with a false air of confidence and walked over to the reception desk. We each paid the US$50 entrance fee and went into the bar. It was the most luxurious bar I had ever seen, with mirrors and glass, leather booths and an amazingly stocked bar. There were beautiful women dressed in long backless ball gowns everywhere.

We sat down and some of the women walked over to us and we started chatting. As luck would have it, the lady that started talking to me asked in English, 'What are you two guys doing in here?' I was happy to think we didn't look like the place's usual punters. I explained what had happened and that I thought the best thing would be to come in, have a few drinks and then try to leave.

She said, 'You're lucky because if you had tried to leave, the guys with the Uzis would have robbed you of all your money and probably beaten you up as well. They did it to two guys just like you last night.'

I explained that all we wanted to do was try Latin American dancing and have some fun – but not *that* kind of fun. She laughed and assured us that if we gave her and her friend a good tip then they would look after us, dance with us and make sure we got out of the place ok. It was a little surreal as we actually shook hands on the deal.

David and I spent the next few hours dancing with our new friends. There was no pressure as the deal had been done. I think the girls were relieved as they knew they would get a good tip for a few hours' dancing. But they did have to work for their money as David and I both had two left feet.

Pretty soon we had run out of money and the two ladies walked us out of the club. The bouncers wished us a very polite goodnight, still with their Uzis slung around their necks. Once around the corner we thanked our hosts and paid the agreed fee, happy to escape without getting robbed or beaten up. And as a bonus we had a really fun night!

BEGINNINGS AND ENDINGS

Over the next few months Wendy was busy planning our wedding. I was just happy to be getting married so I just generally nodded my head in agreement. For me it wasn't so much about the actual ceremony.

Of course, before the actual wedding day I had to survive my stag do. I went with some good friends to Rotorua, about three hours' drive from Auckland, where there are amazing geothermal mud pools, mountain biking tracks and lots more.

The guys and I headed straight for an attraction called the luge. It's a bit like an engineless go-kart you drive downhill on a very fast concrete track. Just before the place closed, my friends were waiting for me at the top and said they had arranged with the management for one last ride for us all. They all took off on their luges ahead of me and as I rounded a corner they had blocked the track. As I climbed off my luge I was jumped on by six of my closest friends. Nice!

Within seconds, they had stripped me of my clothes leaving me completely naked in the middle of the track. I had no choice but to climb back on my luge and carry on to the bottom of the track.

As I raced down the track, my so-called friends were waiting for me at various stages and would give me a big slap on my naked body, leaving large hand prints. By the time I got to the bottom of the track, they were all gone, so I had to catch the gondola back up on my own – stark naked.

I got to the top and I could see my clothes all laid out waiting for me. I thought at least they were being a little nice to me. But no sooner had I thought that than the gondola stopped right in front of the hilltop restaurant full of people pointing and laughing. There wasn't much I could do but smile and wave.

Having survived my stag weekend, Wendy and I flew to Wanaka to meet up with David Hiddleston and his partner Anna for dinner. Wendy and David got on instantly and chatted away. Before long the conversation turned to Everest. Wendy asked David about a climber called Rob Hall.

Rob was an expedition leader during the 1996 disaster on Everest when nine people were killed on the mountain on 10–11 May, including Rob himself. Rob had tried to help a sick client down during a storm and had become trapped at the south summit of Everest. His client, Doug Hansen, died and while Hall managed to stay alive for a few nights, no one could help him. While he was stuck there, he managed to radio through to base camp and was patched through to his wife back in New Zealand. During that radio call they named their unborn child. Most of base camp was listening to the heart-breaking conversation. Rob died a short time later.

Rob Hall was awarded a medal for his bravery and he was one of the mountaineers I held in the highest regard. He was a friend of Paul Scaife's and Paul had told me many stories about him. David also knew Rob very well and spoke highly of him.

Wendy didn't hold back when she was talking to David. She was very straight up about what she thought of Everest and risking your life on the mountain, especially when young children were involved. I sat back and stayed out of the conversation as it was Wendy's time to talk to someone who had actually been on Everest and lost friends there. It was very hard to listen to her fears and worries, but at the same time I could see her understanding more about what drives someone to want to summit Everest. After dinner we said goodbye to David and Anna. David wanted to meet Ethan so we met up the next morning for coffee. That was to be the last time I would see my friend, he held my son's hand and played with him a little before giving me a big hug goodbye.

Before I knew it, it was our wedding day. I stood next to my best man Mat, my buddy Brendon (aka Pinky) and my brother Bob. We were surrounded by 70 of our closest friends and family. The orchestra started playing Pachelbel's Canon and Wendy's bridesmaids slowly walked in. They all looked so beautiful.

Then Wendy appeared. My heart almost stopped. She looked so stunning, all dressed in white with her beautiful dark hair flowing down her back. Tears welled up in my eyes, and I started to feel a little dizzy. Wendy walked down with her father Brian and stood with me in front of our celebrant, my best friend's father, Mike Blamires. Mike had been my senior school master and one day had actually kicked me out of his class for talking too much. We now laugh about it, but when I was 14 years old it wasn't funny.

Wendy and I stared into each other's eyes and exchanged our vows. I remember thinking about the life we would have together. It had sure been lots of fun so far. We had a great reception and danced the night away. My best man Mat, who was a world class photographer, set up a huge old antique golden (empty) photo frame with a remotely activated camera. Guests would stand inside the frame and activate the camera themselves. The photos got better and better as people drank more and more.

The next afternoon Wendy and I departed for Rarotonga on our honeymoon, leaving Ethan with Wendy's mum. We had a fantastic time and talked a lot about our plans for the future. I really wanted another baby, but Wendy wanted to wait a little bit. I got my way in the end as it was on our honeymoon that our little girl Maya was conceived. It was quite a turnaround that I was the one who really wanted to have a baby and not Wendy.

A few weeks later Wendy realised she was pregnant again; this time I knew what to expect. By now it was getting close to the end of 2003 and I had some leave owing. Wendy's family have a large beach house right on the water's edge in Tairua in the Coromandel, so we would spend every moment possible at the beach.

On New Year's Eve, we heard there had been a bad accident on Mt Tasman in the South Island's Southern Alps. Six people had been hit by an avalanche and four of them had been killed. I heard it on the radio news at midday then went off for a trek up a nearby mountain and sat on the summit thinking about the avalanche and hoping it was no one I knew that had been killed.

When I got home I sat down to watch the television news at 6pm. It was the lead story – six climbers had been caught in the avalanche. The news presenter then said the words I had been dreading. 'The names of some of the dead men have just been released. They are David Hiddleston and Paul Scaife. The names of the two other climbers are yet to be released.'

My heart sank. Wendy screamed out, 'Nooooo!'

I just couldn't comprehend the information. It didn't make sense. The news story finished. I got up and walked down to the beach. Pretty soon I started to cry. I couldn't believe it. How did two of the world's best climbers get caught in an avalanche? Wendy came down to the beach and we cried together.

The next day I rang Aspiring Guides and was given the details for Paul and David's funerals. Then I rang Air New Zealand and spoke to the pilots' duty manager, John Mathewson. I explained what had happened and told him I wasn't in a fit state to be flying. John was so nice and spoke about the loss of some of his friends, then said there were tickets for Wendy and me on his desk for us to fly down to Queenstown for the funerals. I quite often think about that conversation with John; the way he spoke and the compassion he showed meant a lot to me.

A few days later Wendy and I flew to Queenstown for the funerals. We drove over to Wanaka and I went straight to the Aspiring Guides office. Jean, who ran the office, jumped out of her chair as soon as she saw me and gave me a huge hug. We both cried. She told me that David's body was at his home and I should go and see him. I didn't want to as I knew it would be so upsetting but I also knew I would regret it if I didn't. I asked Wendy to come but she said it would be too upsetting for her. I understood that.

Jean sat me down and told me everything she knew about the accident. According to her, there were three guides and three clients all climbing together as a team on Mt Tasman's north shoulder. They had just set up an anchor system and the three guides were above the clients ready to belay them up. One of the clients had just set off when the avalanche triggered. The slope was very steep, almost 60 degrees, so in theory it should not have avalanched. Another experienced climber was on a ridge overlooking the avalanche site. There was a bit of cloud around so he didn't see the actual accident. There was speculation that Paul and David's view of the route they were going to climb on the north shoulder was obscured by cloud so they couldn't clearly see it. Perhaps if they could have seen it they may have taken a different route or climbed it two at a time. The speculation didn't change the facts … my friends were no longer here.

I drove out to David's house at Lake Hawea. I sat outside in my car for a little while trying to gain some composure. I hadn't done this sort of thing before. I wasn't sure it was appropriate and I didn't know if I would be too upset.

I walked into David's house and saw a friend of his and asked if it was appropriate for me to see David. He put his hand on my shoulder and said, 'Absolutely, my friend, this is why we brought him home. He is out the back in the sleep-out.'

I walked out the back and there were two of David's friends already in with him. I sat in the garden trying not to intrude on their grief but I could hear how upset they were. I had tears streaming down my face and was trying to hold myself together. They came out comforting each other and it was my turn to see David.

I took a deep breath and walked into the sleep-out. His coffin was in the middle of the small room and as I walked, I tripped on a step I didn't see. I landed right on David's coffin almost knocking it over. I held on to it tightly and steadied myself. My heart was pounding, imagining knocking him out of his coffin. I then thought how David would have found it funny, and a smile came across my face.

I sat next to David's coffin on my own for a little while and paid my respects privately. For the relatively short time I knew him, he had a big influence on my life and I was very grateful for that. I said my goodbye and then left.

The next day was the day of both funerals. First was Paul's in the morning. It was held in a park and everyone sat around his casket for the service. Most of Wanaka and the climbing community were there. Everyone just looked shocked. Paul was so well known, such an amazing climber and such a great person. I sat with Wendy and held back my tears as best I could. I did well until the speaker invited Paul's friends to place a rose on his coffin and say their goodbyes. I couldn't hold my tears back any longer and cried and cried.

That afternoon was David's funeral. It was held in the local community hall and it was packed to capacity. His father spoke of losing a son, his brother spoke about losing his brother and his partner Anna spoke of losing her love. Some of the old climbers spoke as well. They told some really funny stories about David. I found myself smiling and laughing at the stories and then it was time for the final goodbye. The Neil Diamond song 'Holly Holy' played really loud and David's loved ones carried out his coffin. I didn't stay for the wake. I just wanted to be with Wendy.

After Paul and David's deaths I couldn't face going into the mountains and put everything on hold. I took time to clear my head. Did I really want to keep climbing? Was it worth the risk? If two of the world's elite climbers can get killed what chance do I have with my experience? These were all very hard questions to answer.

After a few months I contacted David's father. I had lots of photos of David from our Peru expedition. I flew to Wellington on a duty as I had changed aircraft fleets with Air New Zealand and was now a domestic jet B737 pilot.

I met David's father in the hotel where we stayed and we went to the bar and had a drink. I was a bit nervous about giving him an album full of photos of his son. David's dad was a retired banker and we chatted about David. When I eventually handed him the album I had made, he slowly turned the pages. I could see the emotion on his face. He turned to me and said, 'You know, this is the nicest thing anyone has done for me in a while. I don't have any photos of David in the mountains. They are all his photos of other people. Not of him. Thank you so very much, Mike.'

The next morning I had arranged to meet one of the climbers who had survived the avalanche. I had arranged it through Jean from Aspiring Guides as I didn't want to intrude on their grief and their recovery, but he was happy to talk to me about what had really happened.

We met and had a coffee and he went through the whole event. It was spine-chilling to hear first-hand how my friends had died, their final moments. I tried not to ask too many questions and let him speak; some things were just too hard for him to speak about and I left them alone. Looking back this all helped me come to terms with losing my friends and mountaineering mentors.

A short while later I called Aspiring Guides and went ice climbing for a weekend with a guide called Murray Ball.

Murray was a Kiwi but spent most of his time in Chamonix in France. He liked hard climbing and didn't like baby sitting clients. Climb hard or go home, I'm not here to baby sit you, seemed to be his attitude. At first he was a bit harsh but then I really warmed to him and liked the way he climbed. He was very thoughtful, as safe as possible, but hard. After the ice climbing weekend, I booked a summit week with Murray around the Mt Tasman area but not until the next climbing season.

At this stage, Wendy was about ready to pop with our second child. This time we had both found out the baby's sex at the scan stage and had already named her Maya. This pregnancy had been a little more difficult than the first one and Maya ended up being overdue.

Wendy and I had been trying all the natural methods to encourage Maya to come along but to no avail. On Friday, the doctor said that if she hadn't arrived by Monday, she'd have to be induced. That night we got an extra hot curry from the local Indian restaurant hoping that a spicy meal might move things along.

Wendy woke at 4am with a really sore tummy.

'You're in labour,' I said. Wendy reckoned she wasn't as the feelings were completely different to the last time.

I phoned Wendy's sister Penny, who was going to be our support person. The initial plan was for Wendy to be in labour at home for a few hours then go to hospital. We didn't want to spend 8–10 hours in hospital waiting. But we weren't planning a home birth.

Wendy was a bit angry as she was still convinced she wasn't in labour, but after a few minutes it was very obvious she was having contractions. Huge random contractions. They were four minutes apart, then 30 seconds, then three minutes.

Penny arrived and I was in the lounge rubbing Wendy's back. She took over but according to Wendy she couldn't rub it the same way I had so I had no choice but to stay there in my undies, rubbing Wendy's back with one hand and talking to the midwife on the phone with the other.

I told the midwife what was happening and she told me to get Wendy in the car and drive to hospital right away. Wendy reckoned she still wanted to stay at home for a little bit. I couldn't believe it.

I wasn't risking it. 'NO! Get your shoes on. We are going to the hospital NOW.'

I was surprised that Wendy just waddled off down the hall to get her shoes. No sooner had I put the phone down from speaking to the midwife than there was a horrendous scream from the bedroom.

'THE BABY'S COOOOOMING!'

I ran down the hallway and into the bedroom to find Wendy bent over the bed in total agony. I pulled down her pyjama pants and she instantly swung around and slapped me across the chest, shouting, 'Don't pull my pants down!'

Holy shit, I thought. How was she going to have a baby with her pants on?

Wendy soon forgot about her pants when her waters broke and she started another contraction. Maya was now in a hurry to arrive.

I shouted to Penny, 'Quick! Get some boiling water and towels.' I don't know why that would have been even remotely useful but I had clearly been watching too much TV. Unfazed, Penny ran off to do what I'd asked.

I dialled 111 and just as the operator answered, Wendy let out a bloodcurdling scream. I could hear the operator shouting, 'What's going on?'

I looked down and what I saw made me drop the phone. Maya was face up, eyes closed, with the umbilical cord wrapped around her neck. Her face was completely blue. Out of nothing but instinct I grabbed the cord and pulled it clear of her neck. There was no genteelness now. She had to come out right now.

'Ok, Wendy, the head is out. Big push, big push on the next contraction.' The contraction started in a few seconds and I just pulled Maya out. Wendy slumped forward and passed out semi-conscious on the bed.

I now had the most precious little baby in my hands; she wasn't breathing and she was blue. This horrible feeling came over me. It was the identical feeling I'd had just before the Twin Otter crash. The only way to describe it is like it's the true moment of life and death and it could go either way.

I gently shook Maya with one hand and hoped she would start crying; with the other hand I picked up the phone and shouted at the operator, 'My wife has just had a baby, it's not breathing, you've got to tell me what to do ...'

'Sir, I need you to take a deep breath,' was the initial response. Not what I needed to hear. I threw the phone across the room.

I then flipped Maya over onto her tummy and gently shook her again, but she was still not breathing. I gently put my little finger into her mouth to see it there was any gunk in there stopping her breathing. I was worried about potentially pushing something further down her throat. I briefly thought of gently sucking out anything in her mouth but by this stage a few minutes had gone by and it was now time to start mouth to mouth resuscitation. I couldn't wait any longer. I rolled her back over in my hands and gently wiped down each side of her nose and cheek. It was covered in afterbirth and I wanted to make a good seal over her tiny little nose and mouth. Just as I leant forward to begin mouth to mouth she let out this huge cry. My heart filled with total joy.

I was still in my undies and T-shirt so I lifted up my shirt and put Maya against my chest and I could feel her trying to suckle. Wendy was still lying face down semi concious, With one hand, I flipped her over onto her back as I knew she needed to get the placenta out within the next few contractions or there could be major complications. The next contraction started and I gently pulled on the umbilical cord, exactly as the midwife had done last time. Wendy didn't like it at all and sat up really quickly, shouting for me to stop.

At that very moment, the midwife turned up and went straight to Wendy. She could hear Maya crying under my shirt and knew she was alive. The midwife took over looking after Wendy while I went to give Ethan – now 22 months old – a bottle. When I came back into our room, there was Wendy breastfeeding Maya, holding her with one hand and cutting her own umbilical cord with the other ... I couldn't believe it.

Wendy looked at me and said, 'Well, that was easy; I'll have another baby no problem ...'

I thought, 'I'm never having sex again let alone another baby.' To say I was a little traumatised was a massive understatement.

Wendy's oldest sister Melody came over a few hours later. I asked if she was hungry. When she said yes I told her there was some breakfast for her on the stove. She opened the lid and almost threw up on the spot. In the pot was Wendy's placenta!

From the first sign of a contraction to Maya actually arriving was only about one hour, really amazing when you think about it. After a few days of being looked after at Birthcare, we brought our very precious cargo home. Wendy was a fantastic mum and life was a whole lot busier with two kids. We were all now living in the house Wendy had bought while I was climbing Mt Cook.

Climbing took a back seat for a while and it was actually Wendy who encouraged me to go climbing again. I think she knew what made me happy and didn't want a grumpy husband moping around.

It was now time for me to head back down to Wanaka for my week's climbing with Murray Ball. Murray and I drove over to Franz Josef town ready to fly into the mountains by helicopter. When we arrived in Franz Josef village, we pulled off the main road and headed to the alpine club's hut just behind the village.

Out of the blue a pukeko, a large blue bird, ran out in front of the car. At the last second, it tried to fly away and hit the front grille, flying over the bonnet, feathers everywhere. We stopped and it was a mess with a leg missing and a wing torn almost completely off. The most humane thing to do was to put it out of its misery and quickly.

Murray ran to the back of the car and grabbed my climbing axe. He was so intent on what he had to do that he didn't notice a carload of little old ladies that had pulled up to see what all the fuss was about. He hit the pukeko so hard, its head came off instantly. There was a scream of horror from the watching car. Murray looked up and saw the elderly ladies. 'Sorry, ladies. I didn't realise you were watching. But it was the best for the poor bird.' They didn't look impressed. And neither was I. My axe was covered with bits of bird. I asked Murray why he used my axe when it was right next to his. He just looked at me and said, 'Because I'm not silly!'

The next day we flew by helicopter up over the Franz Josef glacier to the Centennial Hut, which is situated on a rocky outcrop high on the glacier neve, where the snow turns to ice. The view was just out of this world – huge crevasses, towering chunks of ice the size of buildings all flowing downwards.

We landed at the hut, had a quick cup of tea and we were off. We took our rock climbing shoes to use if we had to, but at −2°C it was a bit cold. Murray looked around and pointed to this huge buttress tower a few hundred feet high and said, 'That's us!' Simple as that.

'Has it been climbed before?' I asked. 'Who cares?' replied Murray.

We crossed the bergschrund and got onto the rock. The first pitch – a pitch is a rope-length normally about 50 metres or 150 feet – was fine. It was vertical but had good handholds. We climbed this pitch in our plastic climbing boots but at the anchor, we changed over into our rock climbing shoes for the next pitches.

The climbing just got better and better, pitch after pitch. I really got into the flow, the movement, the concentration, the challenge. My mind was focused on what we were doing. I looked around and the mountains were so beautiful. There was no one else around. It was such a beautiful yet hostile environment. The final pitch was a crack system where you had to jam your hands in and lay back with straight arms.

I came up to the anchor and Murray was sitting there belaying me up. He had a huge smile on his face and said, 'It's not true what they say about you – you can actually climb rock really well!'

'What do you mean?' I asked.

'Just saying. Rumour had it that you were average on rock. But it's not true. You can climb really well.'

While some people might have been a bit offended, I was chuffed. It was a great compliment from a hard-core climber.

I looked at my hands and my knuckles were all busted up and bleeding but I couldn't even feel them as I was so focused on the climb. I couldn't feel my toes for that matter as they were very cold in my rock climbing shoes. Murray looked at my hand and said, 'A little bit of claret never hurt anyone.'

We abseiled back down the buttress and as we walked back to the hut, Murray said, 'I think that is a first ascent. No one has climbed that before so we should name it. How about Busted Knuckle Buttress?' I was stoked to be part of a first ascent, even a relatively small one.

After a few little climbs, we decided to climb a 3070-metre peak called Haidinger. The weather forecast was perfect for the next day, so we got all our gear ready.

I woke at 3am to Murray brewing a coffee in the hut. Pretty soon, we were all roped up and moving across the glacier to the start of the climb. There was a very steep ridge or arette covered in snow and ice, which led to a beautiful long ridge. It was very thin and precarious in some places, but once we'd traversed it there were only about four pitches of steep climbing to the summit. But the biggest difficulty was getting over the bergschrund.

Murray led. Lying on his stomach, he gently edged himself across the thin ice layer that looked like it could collapse at any second. I belayed him off a very solid anchor we had built. Next it was my turn. I was probably 10–15 kilos heavier than Murray and I was convinced that the ice layer wouldn't hold me. As I edged across Murray shouted words of encouragement and it held … just.

We then started moving up the steep ridge. All the way along Murray was talking to me. Do this, do that, try moving your feet this way. He was constantly giving me tips and advice. I just lapped it up.

We got to the ridge and the real climbing began. Murray wanted us to move fast. 'Come on, no rest, hurry up, this is how real mountaineers move, I'm not here to baby sit you, move faster …' It went from positive encouragement to directly telling me to move it. I loved it and went as fast as I could over the terrain. There was another team of two climbers on the ridge and we left them for dust.

The final part of the ridge before the summit pyramid was so thin that we had to put one leg on either side of it and shuffle along. The exposure or drop on each side was just outrageous, thousands of feet straight down.

We made it to the summit pyramid and started climbing with our two axes up the steep slope. Whack. One axe in. Whack. The other goes in. Then a good swing of the boot and you feel the crampon biting into the ice, then the other … I found my flow and was enjoying myself until a helicopter flew past and circled back around and hovered about 30 metres from us. I was a bit mad but I could see the passengers clearly. They were Japanese and they were waving furiously at us. I waved back a little reluctantly. They were guests in our great country, after all.

Next thing the pilot stopped waving and broke away quickly. I looked up and Murray wasn't having any of it. He was giving them the finger and gesticulating wildly. We were back in beautiful silence.

A few minutes later I reached the summit to a warm smile and a handshake from Murray. The Southern Alps were spectacular, beautiful peaks everywhere, and the Tasman Sea looked like it was at our feet. Mt Cook was very clear. It looked huge and very difficult. I had climbed it from the other side. My eye then caught Mt Tasman. My heart sank as I could see the very slope that had avalanched and killed David and Paul. I thought about the guys and sat on that summit feeling completely at peace.

I looked over to the south face of Mt Douglas, a very technical climb that I had been aiming towards. I asked Murray what he thought about me climbing it. Without hesitation, he said, 'You will need a few more bullets in your six-shooter before you try that.'

I had thought I had done very well climbing fast and hard but strangely I wasn't disappointed by his comment. I really appreciated his honesty. It was what I needed – someone to mentor me and give me honest feedback on my ability.

We climbed back along the ridge and simul climbed down

to the glacier. We sat on the glacier, opened our lunch and ate it, looking at the mountains towering around us.

Murray said, 'Mike, get your camera ready. There is going to be a big avalanche soon, right there …'

Yeah right, I thought, but got my camera ready to be polite. A few minutes later there was a crack in the distance and a huge avalanche streamed down a slope in the distance.

'Wow! How did you know that was going to happen?' I asked.

'The slope we came down was a bit unstable when we were climbing up, that's why I wanted to move fast. See how we are sitting here now and the sun hasn't hit the slope we just came down. It would be too dangerous to climb down it once the sun had heated it up. All the snow over there is also unstable. You watch as the sun hits that slope. There will be other avalanches soon.'

Sure enough there were a couple more avalanches triggered. Murray had experience and knowledge that you could only get from spending years in the mountains.

We returned to the hut and the next day flew out to Wanaka. I had a great time climbing that week with Murray but most importantly I had found my mojo again. I was ready for the Himalayas.

TO THE HIMALAYAS

When I had come back from climbing in Peru with David, I had contacted his old friend Henry Todd, who I was keen to have support my Everest climb. He had been very sad to hear of David's death as they had been great friends at Everest base camp a few years in a row.

While it had been Bear Grylls' book, *The Kid who Climbed Everest*, that had first given me the idea of contacting Henry Todd, David's enthusiasm for his style of climbing confirmed my thoughts. I wanted to climb Everest unguided.

Todd would provide me with all the logistics, camps, food and oxygen. The only assistance I would get would be one of his super strong Sherpas to carry spare oxygen for me on summit day. Basically, I had to know how to look after myself as there was no babying on his expeditions.

For me the real reason I wanted to climb on Todd's

team wasn't to do with Bear or even David. It was Henry's experience. He had been to Everest every single season since god knows when. In his decades of experience, he had seen life and death on Everest like no one else. You can't buy that sort of experience – well, you can actually, just climb on his team.

He was a bit fussy who he would take up Everest so I booked an expedition with him to climb Ama Dablam in October 2005. This expedition required some hard-out training and equally hard-out saving.

In the meantime life was going on. I had been promoted to first officer on a Boeing 767 and was now flying all over the Pacific Rim. This was great as it allowed me lots of time overseas to buy climbing gear.

Wendy was now a full-time mum and she would quite often come away with me on work trips, bringing one of the kids at a time. Wendy and I talked a lot about a third child and decided the time was right to try.

One morning Wendy walked into the kitchen and said, 'I have a surprise for you,' and handed me a pregnancy test pen. It had two lines on it and I knew full well what it meant. But it didn't compute. There was less than a week to go before I left for Nepal to climb Ama Dablam, which at 6849 metres was the hardest mountain for me yet.

I must have looked a bit stunned and spluttered out, 'Does this mean I can still go the Nepal?' Wendy gave me a look that didn't even need to be backed up with any words.

'You mean that's wonderful news. And, yes, you can still go to the Himalayas.'

'Oops, sorry … aaahhh … I mean, that's fantastic. Sorry, babe!'

The night before I was to depart, I had a very bad moment. For some reason I was really scared. I wasn't sure that I should be going climbing in the Himalayas with a young family at home. I tossed and turned all night and couldn't sleep.

The next morning, I talked to Wendy about how I was feeling. She simply said, 'You have to go. If you don't, you'll regret it for the rest of your life. We'll be fine here, Mike. This is something you know you have to do.'

Wendy dropped me out at the airport and I said goodbye to her, Ethan and Maya with a tear in my eye. This was my biggest adventure yet but I was going to miss them terribly.

After a night in Bangkok, I arrived in Kathmandu, Nepal. What a place! The drive from the airport to the hotel was just amazing. I was in sensory overload. There were hundreds of people going about their day's business, sacred cows wandering along in the middle of traffic, dogs, goats and lots of monkeys everywhere, and tons of motorbikes zipping in and out of traffic.

I had arranged the whole climbing trip through Henry Todd and I was to meet him at Ama Dablam base camp. He told me that if I wanted to trek in with someone, I should contact Victor Saunders, who had a team of clients climbing Ama Dablam out of Henry's base camp.

That night I caught up with Victor for dinner and we got on like a house on fire. He had a team of three Brazilian climbers and four English guys all heading up to Ama Dablam. The next morning we headed to the domestic airport, which was fantastic. It looked like total chaos, yet when you stopped and actually watched, everyone had their own task and beavered away at it.

Before we knew what was happening, we were bundled up by a little Nepalese person who, with the greatest of urgency but total politeness, ushered us onto a bus and out to a waiting plane. It was a 19-seater Dornier 228 STOL (short field take-off and landing) aircraft. Within a few minutes, we were airborne and as we climbed out over Kathmandu, the city looked huge. In the distance I could see the Himalayas getting closer and closer, the roof of the world. The excitement was growing inside me like a little kid going to Disneyland. I was going to be climbing in the Himalayas right next to Everest. I could barely believe it.

The pilot climbed to about 16,000 feet and there was no oxygen. In New Zealand, you have to have supplemental oxygen or be in a pressurised aircraft above 10,000 feet. We skimmed across the tops of a few ridges by a few hundred feet, which got my heart pounding. Then we spiralled down through a hole in the clouds to begin our approach into Lukla. The airport at Lukla is known as the most dangerous airport in the world. The biggest issue is there is no overshoot as there is a huge wall at the end of the runway and a massive mountain behind that. The airport has a 16-degree uphill slope for landing and, to top it off, it has a short runway.

We landed on the tarmac with a thump and the pilots had to put the power on to get up the slope of the airstrip. One engine was shut down, the other one left running to save cycles on the engine and we were herded off the plane quickly. The pilots who fly the route into Lukla are truly brave souls and do such a fantastic job. I would love to get a job flying out of Kathmandu … perhaps in another life.

Once off the plane, a Nepalese policeman blew his whistle and pointed to the arrivals area. We identified our bags and then walked up over the end of the airfield to a small teahouse called Paradise Lodge. Here we sat down and had a cup of milky sweet tea – a drink I would come to love in the coming weeks.

The first night we spent in a tiny village called Monjo, and then next day we tackled our first challenge – the Namchee Hill. Here we went from 2500 metres (8000 feet) to over 3440 metres (11,280 feet) with most of the altitude gain in going straight up on a very windy track.

Once you arrive in Namchee, it's a whole different world, something very special. It is a very large village of about 800 permanent residents, situated in a steep horseshoe valley. All the buildings are made out of perfectly crafted hand-carved granite. The streets are tiny and heaps of yak trains wander through them giving it the feel of a place that has been lost in time.

We spent a couple of nights in Namchee before heading off on the 13-hour trek to Pangboche, which would become my favourite village in the Himalayas. It is the last village that is inhabited all year round on the way to Everest. Most of the Sherpas on Everest come from Pangboche and, sadly, when you start talking to the local people you realise the toll that Everest and altitude have had on this tiny community. Everyone has either lost a close family member to Everest, Ama Dablam or altitude sickness as Pangboche is about 4000 metres (13,074 feet) high.

Overlooking Pangboche is Ama Dablam. It seems to tower over the village with its arms wide open. The name means 'mother's charm box, where the mountain welcomes you into her heart'. It is a very sacred and special mountain.

We arrived in Pangboche and then had to walk another 20 minutes up the hill to Upper Pangboche where we would be staying with the local lama. His name was Lama Geshe and he was the head teaching lama for the entire area. He had escaped Tibet during the Chinese invasion in the 1950s along with the Dalai Lama. It was such a privilege to be staying in his home.

The next morning I woke early and went down to the tea room and sat down. Lama Geshe came in and gestured what I thought was 'good morning'. He only spoke Tibetan and Sherpa (a very similar language). Next thing, his son came into the room and said to me, 'Sir, you are sitting in the Lama's chair.'

I was horrified. I jumped up and moved away apologetically but Lama Geshe wanted me to sit next to him. We ate breakfast together and even though neither of us could understand a thing the other was saying, we had a very interesting conversation.

As Pangboche is so high it was the ideal place to acclimatise to the altitude. That day was a rest day and we spent it milling around the village drinking tea and looking up at Ama Dablam, the mountain Sir Edmund Hillary had once famously described as unclimbable.

That night, Lama Geshe noticed a book I was reading called *My Quest for the Yeti* by Reinhold Messner. The first man to climb Everest without oxygen, Messner was also the

Mike Allsop

first person to climb all 14 peaks above 8000 metres – all without oxygen. But this book wasn't about his climbing. While in the Himalayas, Messner said he'd had an encounter with an animal that stood up on its back legs right in front of him, and then circled around behind him. He also says the creature then chased him for miles. These sightings sparked Messner's 20-year hunt to find out what the animal was – an undiscovered bear or the missing link?

Lama Geshe pointed to my book and through his son, I asked if he had ever seen a Yeti around Pangboche. Next thing, Lama Geshe and his wife got into a heated discussion. Well, actually she got heated, Lama Geshe just laughed.

Their son relayed the discussion to me. 'Dad is saying the Yeti attacked Mum's friend at the back door five years ago and Mum is saying, "NO! It was nine years ago!"'

While the Yeti is a creature out of folklore in the West, it seemed to be a very real threat to the people of Pangboche. One thing was for sure, I wasn't going walking out at night on my own around this village now.

Later that evening, Victor told me about the famous Pangboche Yeti hand and skull that had been stolen from the monastery in the 1990s. The person who stole it not only took a precious artefact from the village but also robbed the monastery of its small income from people who would pay a few dollars to look at the Yeti remains.

The next morning our little unofficial team sat down and were given a formal blessing from Lama Geshe. He chanted mantras and told us we were now blessed and would have a safe journey – but I noticed he didn't say it would be successful.

After our blessing we departed for Henry Todd's camp, which was situated on private land over the hill from the somewhat crowded Ama Dablam base camp. As I came into base camp I could see Henry. After everything I'd read and heard about him I was a little nervous to finally meet him.

He walked over to me larger than life and I put out my still gloved hand. He grabbed my hand and tore off my glove saying, 'I don't shake good people's hands with a glove on!' He had a huge smile on his face.

The base camp was set up in a large meadow where the landowners would keep their yaks in spring and autumn. There were a few yaks walking around but they didn't seem to be bothered by us. We each had our own tent, and each had a very thick foam mattress. Compared to other camps I'd stayed at this one was quite luxurious. I felt right at home.

The plan was after a day's rest to go up to Camp 1 and spend a night, then descend back to base camp. A few days later go back up to Camp 1 and the next day climb up and touch Camp 2 then return to Camp 1 for the night before descending back to base camp the next day. After reaching Camp 2, even though we didn't stay at Camp 2 we would be fully acclimatised and ready to go for the summit.

That evening, while there was still some light, Henry asked me to go for a walk with him. We walked together and chatted about life and death in the mountains. Henry had lost many friends to the mountains. I spoke about David and Paul. It was really good to talk to someone who had such an understanding of the mountains and their risks, and why people continue to climb knowing those dangers.

I told Henry about my desire to climb Mt Everest. Normally people would climb Ama Dablam then an 8000-metre (26,000 feet) peak called Cho Oyu to get some experience at that extreme altitude. The media call above 8000 metres 'the death zone' but climbers don't – they simply talk about being above 8000 metres.

Henry said he'd see how I performed on Ama Dablam before he could say whether he thought I needed to climb Cho Oyu before Everest. I explained that cost and time were both issues for me. He said he'd only had one client go straight from Ama Dablam to Everest and that was Bear Grylls. Gee, no pressure there then ...

After a rest day spent practising our rope skills, I planned to head for Camp 1 – a 12–14-hour climb with an elevation gain of about 1000 metres (3200 feet). I would be carrying most of my gear with the Sherpas carrying only my sleeping bag for me so that they would have Camp set-up by the time I got there.

Victor was staying in base camp for a few more days with his team in order to acclimatise a little more. There was one other independent climber called Tom. He was moving a lot faster than me so he went ahead with the idea of helping complete the Camp 1 set-up. Henry planned to come up and meet us at the camp later in the evening.

I naively planned to carry only one litre of water for the day and before leaving base camp one of the Sherpas had given me some boiling water to which I added an electrolyte drink sachet. After an hour of trekking on my own I opened my water bottle for a drink. To my horror it had congealed into a goo-like liquid that smelt really bad. I guess the electrolyte mixture was not designed to be added to boiling water but it was too far to go back for water so I told myself I had to drink it. Each time I drank it I almost vomited, but there was no option so I persevered.

After a few hours, I looked up at the climb to Camp 1 and I realised I didn't have a climbing harness. Henry had said not to worry about bringing one. The climb looked a bit intimidating and there was no way I wanted to attempt it without protection. I had a karabiner and some thin rope in my pack so I made myself a harness and used the karabiner to clip into the fixed lines. With my improvised harness, I climbed really carefully all the way to the camp.

When I got there I said to Henry, 'Bloody hell! You told me not to bring a harness.'

He laughed and said, 'By tomorrow, you'll be running around up here like a mountain goat.'

I looked at the steep drop-off and thought no bloody way.

That night was pretty rough for me. I woke up with a massive headache and feeling really ill. Henry wanted me to stay at the camp for two nights but I just wasn't up to it. I told Henry I was going to head back down to base camp.

I asked him for some water for the six-hour trek back to base camp. He poured half a litre into my water bottle.

'That's not a lot of water, Henry.'

'We didn't carry fuel all the way up here to boil water so you can use it to descend. You'll be ok.'

I was a little shocked. 'What about some food?' I asked.

He leaned forward and poked me in the stomach and said, 'I think you'll live!'

I was a bit scared but I didn't have any choice so off I went to walk six hours on half a litre of water and no food. Henry was right. I turned up at base camp just fine. At base camp my headache went away and I felt a lot better.

I spent the next few days at base camp then climbed back up to Camp 1 for a night. The next day I went up and touched Camp 2 and then descended all the way back to base camp. The plan was to rest up and wait for a good weather window.

About a week later one came along, so I was off up to Camp 1 for one night. We would miss out Camp 2 as it was too cramped to stay there, being perched on a tiny little tower with massive drop off either side. Henry arrived in Camp 1. 'Be ready at 7am,' Henry told me the night before I was due to climb. I had read lots of Everest books and the biggest lesson I'd learned was that successful climbers were always on time and organised. So I was ready at 6.30.

When Henry arrived to see me off, I was standing there with my pack on, harness on and itching to get going. There were a couple of other climbers around and they were still packing their gear. I could see Henry was not impressed with them.

He walked over to me, put his hand on my shoulder and said, 'You're fired up, aren't you? Ok, off you go on your own but be careful. The Sherpas will catch you up.'

It was all the encouragement I needed and I was off climbing the fixed lines on my own. I had developed good rock climbing skills and I knew the most important skill was moving quickly and safely while using minimal energy.

The route up to Camp 2 was mostly rock; above Camp 2 is where the ice started.

As I climbed along the rock, I looked down and the exposure was just amazing. It was straight down for hundreds of metres. Having realised that, I simply concentrated on the rock in front of me. After a few hours of climbing and still no sign of the Sherpas I reached the first tower – an overhanging piece of rock over 30 metres high.

There was a single strand of rope hanging down and climbing with it was the only way up. I thought about it for a minute. Was it safe? Who put the rope in? What was the condition like further up the rope? How long had it been there? Was it going to snap when I put my weight on it?

But there was only one way to find out the answer to any of these questions – clip into the rope and start climbing. I clipped my jumars into the rope and started climbing. Jumars are a device used to climb up ropes; they will slide up one way but clamp the rope the other way so you don't slip down.

I gently eased my weight onto the rope and then swung out hanging under the rock wall. I briefly looked down and the view was spine-chilling. If the rope snapped I was dead, no ifs, no buts. My pack with all my gear for the summit climb weighed heavily on my back and threatened to topple me backwards; I engaged my core hard to stop it. I took a few deep breaths and started climbing up the rope, pushing the top jumar up and holding on then bending my knee and sliding the bottom jumar up. Pretty soon I got into a rhythm and hauled myself over the lip at the top of the tower. I rolled over onto my back and just grinned to myself. I'd done it.

Camp 2 was right at the top of the tower and it was tiny, with space for only two or three tents. Thankfully, I wasn't planning to stay here. There was nowhere to go to the toilet and turds littered all the rocks around the place. I was heading straight up to Camp 3.

After Camp 2 the snow and ice began so I put my crampons on, making sure they were perfectly attached to my boots. If I lost a crampon up here it could cost me my life.

There was a narrow ridge that led to the bottom of a bigger tower, known as the yellow tower. This was almost 100 metres high, and was a mixture of rock, snow and ice. I eased out onto a lip that was only big enough to fit my feet and inched along. I looked up and as there were a few climbers coming down I had to wait. I knew that climbers had been killed right here by rocks dislodged by the climbers above. No sooner had that thought crossed my mind than a rock flew past my head at lightning speed, hitting the rock below me with a familiar zing. It was only about the size of a golf ball but at the speed it was travelling it would have killed me instantly had it hit me.

There was a French climber next to me who spoke no English but we both looked at each other and didn't have to speak. We just pushed our heads into the ice to avoid the flying rocks, we were protected by a small outcrop of rock and ice. As the climbers descended, more and more rocks flew by mere inches above our heads.

Finally, the climbers were beside us and we were all trying to pass each other on this tiny ledge. They looked absolutely exhausted. They had blisters on their faces and sunken eyes. It took some time before I recognised them as Victor and his Brazilian clients who I had shared base camp with. I asked how they were going. 'Terrible. We are terrible.'

The answer to my next question seemed obvious already. 'Did you make it?'

'No. None of us made it.' I said, 'I'm sorry to hear that, are you ok?'

'Yes yes we are fine, it was a beautiful climb my friend, good luck to you.'

Another climber came down shortly after them and I quizzed him as well.

'I made it but only just. It is so much harder than Everest.' I must have looked shocked as he quickly added, 'Oh, but you'll be fine.'

For a split second I was really worried but quickly snapped out of it as it didn't make any difference. I was still going up.

Soon came my turn to climb the tower. It was easy climbing with nice big handholds. The only issue was that I was climbing with my crampons on. They scraped and graunched against the rocky parts of the climb. As there was rock and I had to wear my crampons, it's called mixed climbing.

After a few minutes I came to this huge chunk of rock the size of a motorbike. It was secured to the main rock face with some ropes. Some previous climbers had obviously tied it up but it was only a matter of time before it fell on whoever was below. I thought about cutting it away with my knife but when I looked down there was a queue of people waiting to climb behind me so I left it where it was and hoped that the ropes would hold.

The next part of the climb was a technical climber's dream. There was mixed ice, snow and rock climbing, followed by a super exposed long ridge of ice to traverse, then a 70-degree slope of ice to climb up leading to a mushroomed ridge – all with the most extreme exposure beneath your feet.

I could barely believe it. Here I was climbing one of the world's great mountains all on my own, actually doing it and doing it safely and well. I had the biggest smile on my face.

Climbing along the ridge was, shall we say, interesting. On one side it was freezing cold, probably –20°C with a very strong wind of about 20 knots, so the wind-chill just zapped me to the bone. Once I crossed over to the other side out of the wind and into the direct sun I felt like I was roasting. I wasn't sure of the temperature but the contrast was massive.

The key to moving quickly and safely was to never stop for long. On the cold side of the ridge, I would pull my Buff Headwear up over my face and ears and zip up my jacket hood. As soon as I crossed over to the sunny side, I would unzip my jacket and pull my hood off and pull my Buff down. I never stopped moving while I did this and motored along the thin ridge.

Just before I got to Camp 3, there was an overhanging ice mushroom and a queue to climb it. At this point, Victor caught me up after dropping his clients off at Camp 2. It was here that Henry's Sherpas, who were going to summit with me, finally met up with me. They seemed shocked that I had managed to get so far ahead of them.

It was soon my turn to climb the ice mushroom. The climber before me had clipped into the safety line and used two ice axes to climb over the overhanging obstacle. He was a very good climber and made it look easy. I thought, that's how I'm going to climb it too. So I clipped into the line and started climbing with my ice axes. After a few moves and hanging backwards off my axes I was exhausted and had to use the rope and my jumars. I had forgotten that I was climbing at 6300 metres where every move is exhausting. I made it over the lip and walked up to Camp 3.

A few minutes later the Sherpas turned up and set up camp. I remember looking up at this huge hanging serac, or column of ice, above the camp. It didn't seem like a great place to have a camp, but there was really no other place to stay the night. We simply had to hope not even the tiniest piece of the serac came off during our stay.

It was getting dark and I could hear the Sherpas talking to Henry. My ears pricked up when I heard my name mentioned. One of the Sherpas who I didn't know was telling Henry that I was very fast and very strong. I felt chuffed that a super tough Sherpa thought I was fast and strong.

That night, I shared a tent with Tindu Sherpa. He had climbed Everest twice, and was a super strong climber. I got into my sleeping bag, freezing and shivering quite badly. Ama Dablam is a very cold mountain and I didn't have a down suit like climbers on Everest wear. Tindu handed me a bottle of hot water and said, 'Put it on your nuts.'

What? I must have looked a bit confused.

'Put it on your nuts,' he said again and then got his own bottle and put it between his legs, then pushed it up, well, there's no other way to say it, on his nuts. If it was good enough for him … So I did what he said and within seconds I was toasty warm. Amazing! The Sherpas really know how to stay warm. Afterwards I found out that the bottle was heating the femoral artery that runs up both legs and into the core, instantly warming you up.

I asked Tindu Sherpa what it was like at the top camp on Everest. 'Same, same,' he said with a smile. I rolled over on my side and he hopped into his sleeping bag and pushed his back up against mine. This is another way the Sherpas keep warm.

The next day was summit day. But instead of starting out before the sun was up, I didn't set off until 9am. The early starts are so that the bulk of the climbing is done while the snow and ice is firm, giving you the maximum amount of time to reach the top. But Ama Dablam isn't like other mountains. There it is so cold that you have to wait until the sun comes up before you can attempt the summit.

There was a small team of us ready to go for the summit – Victor and his two clients as well as Tindu and me. Straight out of Camp 3 is a very steep ridge and we started climbing up. Almost instantly I began overheating so I took off my down jacket. While the rest of the team carried on, I couldn't seem to get into a rhythm and was playing catch-up with the other guys.

As I got to the top of the ridge, there was a very large bergschrund where all the other guys were waiting. I was exhausted and sat down. Within seconds, I could hear terrified screaming.

Victor spotted where the screams were coming from – about 300 metres below us on the ridge we'd just climbed. About halfway along was a woman dangling off the side of the ridge on one of the fixed lines. There was nothing below her feet except thousands of metres of air.

I was horrified. Victor was really calm though, saying, 'Don't worry, I know the guide. He's onto it. He'll save her if she stops thrashing around. Let's watch how he does it.'

So we all watched the unfolding drama. It was gut-wrenching, but the guide calmly and methodically set up a new anchor and abseiled down to the climber, clipped her into the new safety anchor and they both climbed back up onto the ridge. I was amazed at how quickly the guide acted to save his climber's life. It just goes to show how valuable a fully qualified mountain guide is.

Once we knew the climber was ok, we turned and started crossing the huge bergschrund and then on to the final climb. The final slope wasn't too steep but it was long. I was at the back, but was still getting slower and slower. Victor asked me if I was ok and then put me up the front so I wouldn't fall behind. We climbed straight up for what seemed like hours and hours. At one point Henry, who was watching with a telescope, radioed Victor to ask if everything was ok. The rest of the team were encouraging me over and over. One step up, a few breaths, one step up, a few breaths … on and on and on.

Finally we made the crest of the summit. I'd made it but my next goal was even clearer to me from that high point – in the distance I could see Everest. It looked so close, towering above us by 2000 metres. I just stared at her for a while wondering what it would be like to be on that mighty mountain.

We were all overjoyed to have made it to the top of Ama Dablam but we didn't spend long on the summit. Our descent was pretty straightforward and everyone made it back to Camp 3 just fine. I regained my strength and felt ok on the way down.

We stayed that night at Camp 3 and planned to head down to Camp 1. But then I found out that the Sherpas usually go straight from Camp 3 to base camp in one day. It's a huge day, but I was determined to do it too. I wanted to prove to Henry that I was strong enough to climb Everest and to make up for my less than top performance on summit day.

After descending to Camp 1 with Victor's crew, I was on my own from there down to base camp. I really enjoyed being alone in the mountains. It gave me a huge sense of achievement and this additional confidence gave me a real spring in my step even though I was exhausted.

But my happy place didn't last all the way down to base camp. Clouds rolled in and it began to snow, dropping the visibility to only a few metres. The track was not well formed as it crossed private land over the last 10 kilometres. As I walked along, the visibility fluctuated badly. I was so worried about getting lost that whenever I saw a part of the path I recognised I would focus hard on it and move forward until the clouds and snow made it disappear and then I would stop and wait until I could see it again.

This worked well for about an hour but soon night began to fall and the visibility was still very poor. I started thinking about plan B – the dreaded bivouac. I had a sleeping bag and an emergency blanket so it wouldn't be a big deal but I really would have preferred to be snuggled up at base camp!

I kept descending along the path as much as I could, checking my altimeter watch constantly to make sure I hadn't descended past the base camp by mistake.

Just as the bivouac seemed inevitable, out of the mist popped a figure and I heard a soft voice say, 'Hi, Mikey.' It was Tindu Sherpa. Boy, was I glad to see him.

'Can I take your pack?' he asked.

'No thank you, buddy. I'll carry it. I want to finish what I started, but it is so good to see you!'

Within 15 minutes, I could hear shouting and clanging. The mist and snow showers parted and all the cooks and Sherpas were banging pots outside base camp to help me find my way in the murky conditions. They were very happy to see me. Another 20 minutes and I would have been staying out in the hills for the night. Before long I was sitting around an open fire with the Sherpas, listening quietly to their stories. It was a beautiful way to finish the climb.

The next morning I got up early and left for Namchee. Passing through Pangboche I decided to go and see Lama Geshe, and thank him for keeping me and my friend safe on our climb. I knew he didn't really see people he didn't know but I thought I would try anyway.

I knocked gently on his door and his daughter Tashi answered. She went and asked if he would see me and he agreed. I entered his tea room and bowed down low before him. He welcomed me with a huge smile. It's hard to describe but I felt this sense of calm or relief on seeing him. We spoke for a little bit, with Tashi translating. I told him that Wendy was expecting our third child. There was a bit of discussion and Tashi said, 'My father would like to name your unborn child.'

I must have looked a bit shocked as the next thing Tashi said was, 'Father says you don't have to if you don't want to.'

'No, no! I am honoured but my wife doesn't know you.'

'Father says, "Go home and tell your wife I have named your unborn child, but do not tell her the name. Once the child is born the first question she will ask is, "What's his name?" and she will agree to the name."'

Lama Geshe started chanting a mantra then he stopped and spoke to Tashi. 'His name will be Dalha. His name means like you, one who is better than the rest and God which protects against enemy.' I was so honoured.

I stayed for a cup of tea and then wished Lama Geshe goodbye. I felt so at peace after seeing him and walking down the valley on my own, I was happy. I looked up at Ama Dablam towering high above me and I felt proud. There was no one else around but I didn't need recognition from anyone else, I was happy within myself.

I arrived in Namchee and met Tom, the other independent climber, in the local pub. He'd summited as well so we toasted our success. That night, I met a guy called Rob Casserley. Dr Rob Casserley to be exact. We hit it off instantly – it was like we had been mates forever. Dr Rob had already summited Everest twice and he was on his way up the valley to climb Ama Dablam.

As we talked about climbing, he told me that the previous year he had been high up on Everest when the friend he was climbing with died of a massive heart attack. He tried to help him but a storm came in. Rob faced the dreadful reality of leaving his friend where he fell, knowing that the storm could kill him too. As hard as this story was to listen to, the lure of Everest was so strong, all I could think was that I wished Rob would be on Everest the same time as me.

Rob left the pub early as he was trekking up to Ama Dablam base camp the next day, but Tom and I stayed on and had a few more beers. There was a large group of trekkers that had just come in from Everest base camp and we sat around sharing our climbing stories from Everest and Ama Dablam.

After plenty of beers and stories, Tom and I headed back to the separate teahouses where we were staying. I was feeling a bit smug when I said goodbye to Tom because his teahouse was miles away and mine was just around the corner.

When I got there, though, the doors were locked. I knocked and knocked but no one would open up! I had no idea what to do so I decided to go back to the bar where I bashed on the door really hard. Eventually the bar owner grudgingly opened the door and I explained my problem. He took me back to the bar and gave me a thin blanket and pointed at one of the couches. It was in no way comfortable but I was so stuffed, I just lay down and fell asleep instantly.

The next morning when I woke up, there was a bucket beside me (unused) and a nice bottle of fresh water. Talk about service! I gulped the water down but the smell of smoke and alcohol was so overpowering I had to get out.

I staggered out of the dark bar and into the strong sunlight. It was quite a shock to the senses so I put my hand up to block the sun. Namchee's a pretty small place and I heard someone talking about me.

'Holy smoke! That's that climber guy, Mike.'

I squinted up and saw the trekkers I'd been in the pub with the night before.

'Have you been in the pub all night, Mike?'

I didn't want to spoil the illusion they had of me being some super tough climber. I croaked in a husky voice, 'Yep, see you in Lukla.' I then walked off back to my lodge for a shower.

After freshening up, I set off for Lukla, some 30 kilometres and eight hours' walk down the valley. It was a lovely trek and I felt great. Truth be told, I hadn't drunk that much beer the night before. I was so exhausted from the climb that the few beers I'd had felt like ten. I just let the trekkers think what they liked.

I arrived in Lukla and met up with Tom for dinner. We'd heard about a teahouse that had a pizza oven so decided to head over there for dinner. On the way there, we noticed huge numbers of Nepalese soldiers all busily digging fox holes and putting up razor wire around machine gun posts.

When we arrived at the pizza place, we asked what was going on. I didn't expect the response I got.

'War!'

'What?!'

'War ... tonight. This is the front line now. Maoist rebels are in the hills all around us and they could attack tonight.' I had heard that the Communist Maoist forces had been trying to take over the country by force but this brought the unrest very close to home.

When we went to leave after dinner, a soldier stopped us

and pushed us back inside. 'No. You cannot go outside. You stay here now.'

'We can't. We have no blankets. Please can we walk back down to our teahouse?'

After asking very politely a few times an officer turned up and said, 'I'll take you but you stay right next to me, ok?' We agreed.

Out on the street there were concealed machine gun nests everywhere. The officer would call out quietly to each position and the guns would swing around and point directly at us. Everyone was on edge. I was so scared.

We zigzagged along the street, through the razor wire. We didn't speak at all as we stopped and waited for the officer to call out to the next position. I was so relieved when we finally arrived back at our lodge. If I'd had any idea of how dangerous the walk back was going to be, I would never have asked. An army officer risked taking us through his front lines just so we could sleep in our own beds – the Nepalese are so amazing and helpful. It was quite a surreal experience to end my first trip to the Himalayas on. But it didn't put me off. Nothing could have.

MAKING PLANS

Wendy, Ethan and Maya picked me up from the airport. It was so good to see them. Ethan was now three and a half and Maya was 15 months old. They had all grown in the month I had been away. Wendy just looked beautiful. She had this glow about her and a tiny little bump showing.

After I had arrived home and unpacked my bags with the help of two little toddlers climbing through my climbing gear looking for their presents, it was time to tell Wendy about the name Lama Geshe had given our unborn child. I explained the story and that I had a name but I couldn't tell her what it was until the baby was born. She didn't look that impressed but at least she didn't say no.

Over the next few months, life returned to normal. I was still flying the Boeing 767 around the Pacific Rim and my longest trip away was only a week. This was a lot better for my family than when I was flying long haul. Even so it wasn't easy leaving my family for that length of time on a regular basis. But it was the price I willingly paid to be doing a job that I loved.

With Wendy's due date nearing we went to see the midwife. There was a discussion about being at home for some of the labour, as the plan had been for Maya's birth.

I couldn't believe it. The trauma of Maya's birth was still vivid in my mind. I could see this tiny little baby, my daughter, lying limp in my hands not breathing. It was too much for me and I burst into tears. Both Wendy and the midwife got the shock of their lives as they were happily chatting away.

'I can't do it. I just can't! There is no way I can handle you being in labour at home. I'm sorry, I just can't risk going through that again. The first sign of labour I want us to go to hospital,' I gulped with tears streaming down my face. The plan was quickly changed to go straight to hospital with the first signs of labour.

Our son was born in hospital without incident after a very short labour. Thank bloody goodness. After his arrival, Wendy's first question to me was, 'Is he ok?' I told her he was fine.

As Lama Geshe predicted, Wendy's second question was, 'What is his name?'

'Dalha,' I replied.

And so it was that Dylan Michael Dalha Allsop came into the world on 8 June 2006.

Over the next few months we settled into the busy life of a family with three young kids, but my Everest trip was coming around fast. I had planned to make my attempt in

April 2007 but with Dylan's birth I had started to wonder whether it was a good idea.

Wendy and I sat down and talked about me climbing Everest. I told her I was happy to put it off for 10 years, that I didn't need to go now when the family was so young.

'No, I want you to go now when the kids are young. They will not remember you gone.'

I was shocked to get such a blunt response. 'You mean dead?' I asked, feeling a bit confused.

Wendy laughed. 'No! Gone for three months, silly. They're so young that they won't remember you being gone for three months. But when they're 12, 14 and 16 years old, their dad leaving the country for three months will be a huge deal. I want you to go now.' She never ceases to amaze me.

So it was on. In one year's time I would be climbing Everest … wow!

Since returning from Ama Dablam, I'd been in regular contact with Henry Todd. He told me that the Sherpas on Ama Dablam had been impressed with how fast I was on the day before summit day. Not wanting to hide anything from him, I told him about how rough I'd found the summit day.

I was mightily relieved when he said not to worry about the actual summit day. Then the news I'd really been waiting for came – he was happy for me to go on his Everest expedition in April 2007. I was stoked. Everything was falling into place.

Time flew by. I had a small diary and every day I made sure I did something that moved me closer to my goal of summiting Everest. No matter what it was, I noted it all down – training, buying gear, emailing other climbers for tips, keeping up with Everest news on the internet, buying climbing magazines.

Henry was insistent that to succeed I would need to have a deep core fitness that comes from constant activity. My physical training was intense in the months before I departed. I had two awesome trainers, a strength trainer and a cardio trainer. My strength coach Steve focused on explosive strength, bench pressing, doing squats and core strengthening. To measure my fitness, Basel my cardio coach put me on a cross trainer and would take my heart rate up 10 beats every five minutes. After each 10 beat block, he would take a small blood sample from my thumb and test the lactic acid levels. Once we'd established my lactic acid threshold, I worked hard to increase it to allow me to push harder and climb harder.

I was so busy thinking about what I needed to do, I somehow didn't stop to think about the impact my climb was having on the people around me. That was until my little brother Bobby came to see me one day. The minute I opened the door I could tell something was wrong. Tears welled up in his eyes and he looked straight at me and said, 'You can't climb Everest. I don't want you to do it. Please don't do it, I don't want you to die.'

We spoke for a bit and I tried to explain how I was mitigating the risks and doing things as correctly as I could, but I guess it doesn't make sense to anyone that doesn't climb. Eventually, we hugged and I fought back tears. Bobby was a pilot with Air New Zealand also and flew Boeing 737s. It was very hard for him to understand why I wanted to climb Everest so badly, I did my best to explain.

Being away from my family for three months was one thing, but being away from work for three months was quite another. The last link in the chain was getting permission from Air New Zealand to take leave in advance as I couldn't afford to take leave without pay. I wrote to my boss and explained that I had been accepted on an expedition, and that I had all the finance and experience I needed – now I just needed the time off.

They were amazing. I got a letter back fully supporting me, saying I could take all the leave I needed and would simply pay it back over the coming years. I felt so lucky to be working for such a great company.

I then asked the company's public relations department for permission to wear the company's logo, a stylised koru or fern frond, on my climbing suit. I felt that it would represent all my friends and colleagues from Air New Zealand who had supported and encouraged me over the years.

When it arrived, it was a perfect sized five-centimetre square koru. I held it in my hand with a real sense of pride – I would be taking this to the summit of the world soon.

Then I was given another package. This one contained a huge Air New Zealand flag. I wasn't sure what to do with it as I couldn't imagine standing on the summit of Everest waving a flag. It just wasn't my style. This climb was deeply personal. It was my journey. I felt so humbled to be actually attempting Everest. There would be no bravado, no media, no Facebook, no blog, no one following me except a few friends and family. When I mentioned the flag to my brother he told me to chuck it in my bag and forget about it. For once, I took his advice.

The night before I departed I wrote a letter to my best mate Mat. It contained very clear instructions about what I wanted done in the event of my death. If I died high up on Everest I didn't want anyone risking their life trying to bring my body down. I simply wanted to be left on the side of the mountain and let the mountain take me. I also wrote down my wishes for my funeral or remembrance service. It was one of the hardest things I've ever had to do. Even harder was handing it to Mat the next day. He knew what was likely to be in it, but I knew I could count on him to carry out my wishes – we'd been best friends since we were kids.

The day of departure came. To get to Nepal, I had to fly to Bangkok and then transfer to a flight to Kathmandu. Checking in 80 kilograms of luggage was never going to be straightforward. The staff looked shocked until I explained what I was doing. I'd budgeted that the extra luggage was going to cost me about $2500, which I was happy to pay to make sure that I had everything I needed for Everest with me. But the woman on check-in went away and spoke to her supervisor and they kept looking back at me. It's always a bit strange being the passenger and not the pilot.

Finally, the woman came back and told me that if I hadn't been wearing jeans she would have upgraded me but as it was they agreed to take all of my gear for no extra charge. She had a little smile when she said, 'You're a pilot, you should know better about the jeans!' I wasn't at all worried about not being upgraded, I was just blown away by Thai Airways' generosity.

As the time came for me to clear Customs and head for my flight, I hugged everyone goodbye, then kissed my three beautiful children and kissed Wendy. She held me tight, tears welling up in her eyes. We said goodbye and I turned and walked off. I got only a few feet and turned around and hugged her again, tears falling down both of our faces. I put both my hands on her face and whispered, 'Don't worry, I'll be fine.' Then I turned and left.

After security, there is a public viewing platform above the concourse. I looked up and there were Wendy and the kids waving goodbye. It was so hard to walk away from them but this was such a monumental moment of my life. I took a few deep breaths and waved then walked to the departure gate. While I was sitting waiting to board the flight, something then clicked in my head. It was time to focus on Everest. I had to stop thinking about anything else. I spent the next two flights focused on two things – the summit and coming home alive.

When I finally arrived in Kathmandu, I felt strangely at home. Despite all the hustle and bustle, a peace descended around me. The Nepalese people are so warm, friendly, open and honest. I've travelled all over the world and this is definitely the place where I feel the most welcome.

After checking in to the hotel, I called Henry. We arranged to meet for dinner that night with 'a bunch of Kiwis' at a bar called The Red Onion. The bunch of Kiwis Henry had been talking about weren't just any old Kiwis. They were Everest legends, Russell Brice, Mark Whetu and Mark Inglis. Russell and another climber, Harry Taylor, were the first to climb the Pinnacles on the north-east ridge of Everest. This was one of the last great unclimbed routes on Everest. As for Mark Whetu, every aspiring Everest climber has heard of him.

He's not only a great Everest guide but probably the best high altitude cameraman on the planet. Mark Inglis' story was one I was only too familiar with – he and Phil Doole were the two climbers who had been trapped at Middle Peak Hotel on Mt Cook all those years ago. As a result of that experience, Mark had had both his legs amputated below the knee. But that didn't stop him climbing – in 2006, he became the first double amputee to summit Everest.

It was a great group of people to have dinner with and I gathered lots of bits of advice without actually directly addressing climbing Everest. Russell had guided and managed hundreds of climbers to the summit of Everest. As we walked along the streets of Kathmandu, he said, 'You look nice and fit, Mike. Good luck with the climb. Henry will look after you.'

I spent a couple of days organising the last of my gear in Kathmandu before meeting up with the two guys I'd be sharing the same base camp with, Ward and Pat.

Ward Supplee was a very tall, strong, silent type of guy from near San Francisco. He kept to himself and when I asked what he did for a living, he said he was a carpenter. I suspected that he must have had a pretty successful career building or renovating houses rather than being a chippy. I hoped he would open up a bit more during the coming six to eight weeks we'd be climbing together.

Pat Hickey was from the other end of Carolina and was a completely different character. He was a professor of nursing at a university and loved to have a chat. He was extremely friendly and always seemed to have a story.

Together, we flew to Lukla. Thankfully, this time I knew what to expect and we landed without a hitch. As we walked over to the small terminal, I saw my two huge gear bags come off the plane and be grabbed by a Sherpa. With typical efficiency, they were heaved onto the back of a yak and I wouldn't see them again until I reached base camp in two weeks' time.

We met up with Henry and after a brief stop at Paradise Lodge for sweet, milky tea with the owner Dawa, we were off. The adventure had begun for real. After a couple of days' walking – including the dreaded Namchee Hill, where the track winds steeply up and you finally pass the 10,000-foot mark – we finally made it to Pangboche.

We were staying in a lodge called Sonam Lodge, owned by Nima Lamu and her husband, Gyurme. In November 2006, a massive serac collapsed on Ama Dablam resulting in an avalanche that took out all of Camp 3, the same place I had stayed during my climb in 2005. Six people were killed. Among them was Gyurme's brother. This was the final straw for his family. They no longer wanted family members to climb in the mountains so their only income would now be from running their lodge. Practically every family in Pangboche, and probably most villages in the Kumbu, have lost someone to the mountains. As more people want to climb in the Himalayas, more Sherpas are employed to help them and more lives are at risk.

We arranged to visit Lama Geshe the following day. I was really looking forward to seeing him. I can't really explain why. I just felt a sense of peace when I thought of him. I guess deep down I was very scared about what lay ahead for me, the uncertainty over whether I would live or die, whether I would make the summit or not. The only thing that was certain was that the next few weeks would be the most defining of my life.

As I walked up to Lama Geshe's home, I could feel the emotion welling up inside me. Tears kept building up in my eyes. I would wipe them away when the other guys weren't looking. We walked into his home and there he was sitting at his table, a huge smile on his face. I walked over and bowed down and offered the lama my folded white khata – a silk scarf that is given as a mark of respect. He placed it around my neck, said a short prayer and touched his forehead to mine, then welcomed me to sit down next to him. He then gave each of the others a similar blessing.

His daughter Tashi translated as I told Lama Geshe that my son now had the name Dalha. He smiled and laughed as Tashi spoke to him in Tibetan. He then started a mantra for our safety on the mountain.

Hearing the deep tone of Lama Geshe's chant was one of the most moving experiences in my life. Tears streamed down my face, I couldn't stop them. His prayer lasted five minutes and when it finished I wiped my eyes and a sense of relief came over me. I was now safe, blessed, I felt that I could now do what I had come to do. As I walked down the hill back to Lower Pangboche I felt like a weight had been lifted off my back. There was no more emotion, just excitement.

Henry didn't want us at base camp until he had everything set up so we had a few days to kill. Pat, Ward and I left Pangboche and headed up the valley and did some trekking and a bit of climbing. Returning to our tiny teahouse at the bottom of the mountain, I felt unwell. It was nothing major, I was just off my food and feeling a little lethargic. I spoke to Pat and Ward and they agreed I should descend to the next village down the valley so off I went on my own. I probably shouldn't have gone on my own given I was showing signs of altitude sickness but I made it down ok. The combination of being at a lower altitude, Panadol for the headache and Diamox for the altitude sickness had me fixed up in no time.

The next day I met up with Pat and Ward again and we made our way up the valley nice and slowly. There is a little teahouse at the bottom of Dugla Hill, run by a cool Sherpa called Mr T. Here we bumped into a well-known English climber called Kenton Cool – yep, that's his real name. I had read about Kenton in climbing magazines and Ward had been on an expedition with him before so we all sat down and had tea. He introduced us to his friend, the Swiss climber Ueli Steck. Kenton told us that Ueli had just climbed the North Face of the Eiger in 3 hours and 54 minutes – a record he has since broken. Unbelievable. It normally takes climbers a couple of days to do that climb and heaps of people have been killed just attempting it.

Someone pinch me – there I was sitting in a little teahouse in Nepal with two of the best climbers in the world. And both these guys were really open and friendly. We spent the next few days trekking up the valley with them. Ueli was accompanying Kenton to base camp to help him acclimatise for a major attempt on Annapurna, an 8091-metre (26,545 feet) peak in the west of Nepal. Meanwhile, Kenton had four clients on Everest and was using Henry's facilities at base camp and further up the mountain.

Kenton and Ueli headed up to base camp before us, but we were under Henry's orders not to arrive in base camp before 12 April, so we took it easy and stopped off and stayed at all the teahouses along the way.

EVEREST AT LAST

Leaving the last cluster of teahouses in a tiny village called Gorak Shep, I could see the massive Khumbu Icefall above base camp. The icefall is one of the most dangerous parts of the climb up the South Col route as the glacier that forms it moves so quickly – up to a metre a day – which means huge crevasses can open up with little warning. Crossing the icefall is so dangerous that it is the place on the south side of Everest where most deaths occur. It was also the main obstacle preventing climbers from summiting the mountain before Hillary's ascent in 1952.

As we got closer to the icefall, I knew that we couldn't be far from base camp. I was so excited to finally get there. Then suddenly, as we climbed over a moraine mound, there it was – a tent city that housed about 500 people on the side of the world's highest mountain. It was almost surreal.

When we finally reached the tent village, I asked a passing Sherpa where Henry's base camp was. Thankfully, all the Sherpas knew Henry and he pointed us in the right direction.

As I walked into camp – our home for the next six weeks – Henry came out of the cook's tent with a huge smile on his face. He walked over and shook my hand hard. He then put his arm around my shoulder, turned me around to face Everest and said in a thick Scottish accent, 'There's ya mountain, sonny. I'll give ya everything ya need to climb it but ya goonah have to climb it yourself.' These words I will remember forever. After years of dreaming, reading, research, training and climbing, I was finally at Everest.

At base camp, I met Mike Davey and Bo Parfet. Mike was a business consultant from south London. And Bo was an American guy, as he proudly stated, from 'the great state of Michigan'.

They had been on an unsuccessful attempt on Everest together with Kenton Cool in 2005 when one of their team mates, Rob Milne, had a heart attack high up on the mountain. When a storm came driving in, they had to leave their good friend where he fell. At altitudes above 8000 metres, it is almost impossible to move people who can't walk or have died. Despite having seen the devastation that Everest can bring, Bo and Mike were both determined to summit the mountain this time.

The first night I looked around the tent and listened to the laughter and camaraderie that was bursting out of the tent. Bo was very loud, very funny and loved telling stories. He had brought a massive barrel of food from home ... American food: his favourite mustards, cheeses, spreads and biscuits. He had factored in that it would be rude to sit eating all these treats on his own so he brought enough to share with everyone else. He even had this aerosol can of cheese – cheese in a can. Who knew?

To entertain ourselves in the evenings, we all sat around and played cards – a game that was sort of like 500 or euchre. It got so competitive that someone made a medal out of a Milo tin lid and this was the trophy for the evening's winners. I was totally useless at cards to the point that people would moan if they got paired up with me. It was like being picked last for a kids' sports team – 'Awww no, not him. Why do we have to have him?' It was all in good fun but I was determined to win the medal just once.

During our first few days at base camp, Henry took us into the lower parts of the Khumbu Icefall and taught us how to get across the ladders. The ladders were used to span the huge crevasses in the icefall and to climb the seracs. They were installed by a group of sherpas whose job it was to open the icefall and keep it open, they were called the 'icefall doctors'; a group of very brave sherpas as they had the most dangerous job probably in the entire world. I wasn't worried about the ladders at all as I knew I was a good climber and very co-ordinated. I thought to myself, this will be easy … a huge mistake.

The first time I went across a ladder that was traversing this huge crevasse, my legs shook badly – not because I was scared but because the ladder felt so unstable. I gingerly edged my way across and back a few times but I couldn't get comfortable doing these crossings. It didn't help that Pat and Ward just seemed to fly across. There were so many ladders in the icefall that all I could do was practise and hope I would get better quickly.

Before heading any further into the icefall, we were supposed to be given a blessing by a Buddhist Lama who comes to base camp every year. There is a very strong tradition on Everest that you shouldn't go onto the icefall – or indeed any further up the mountain – until you've received this blessing. But the Lama was busy with other teams and it would be a few days before he could see us, so we changed the rules a little … just a little. We changed it to not staying a night further up the mountain before having a blessing. This blessing was more of a team blessing where I felt like Lama Geshe had blessed me personally.

With that compromise decided upon, the next morning we all got up before dawn in order to go further into the icefall than we had before. Breakfast was cooked for us by the hard-working Sherpa cooks – porridge, eggs, fried Spam and plenty of other stuff to fuel us for the day ahead – and delivered to our mess tent. The food on Henry's expedition was outstanding as he knew the value of eating well and staying nourished.

Setting out up the icefall, we could see a tiny light ahead of us. Doctors way up the icefall working away. We walked for about an hour before coming to the first ladder.

All my practice didn't count for much. On my first crossing the ladder shook and rattled frighteningly. Bo and Kenton seemed to fly across it like they were walking along a chalk line on a concrete path. I kept telling myself not to worry, that

I'd get better. The further we went into the icefall the worse the conditions got. There were huge seracs hanging over us, and 'tiny' chunks of ice the size of a car. A lot of the icefall was very much a tumbling mess of slowly moving, creaking ice, if any bits broke free it wouldn't take much to get killed.

Eventually, I came to this place where there had been a massive implosion. It looked so unstable, with large boulders of ice everywhere and these deep holes that seemed to disappear into endless darkness. The Sherpas had strung prayer flags over this area to alert climbers to the danger. The flag colours represent the elements – blue for sky, white for air, red for fire, green for water and yellow for earth. On each flag, mantras or prayers are printed and when they flutter in the wind they release these prayers into the air.

I moved through this area, making sure to clip into all the safety lines, then up onto a flat area with deep crevasses running across it called the Football Field. From there, I carried on into the jumble of ice, seracs and crevasses. With every ladder I crossed, the scene seemed to get messier and more dangerous.

Another climber came past and we started chatting. He was a Kiwi by the name of Guy Cotter and he was guide for a team. He was a really experienced mountaineer and I'd been reading about his exploits for years. I told him that we were only coming into the icefall to get some experience but that I didn't like the look of the conditions and I was seriously considering turning around. It seemed too crazy to be taking these risks when I didn't have to be doing this as I wasn't going on up to Camp 1.

Guy looked at me and said, 'Why would you come all the way up here just to get some experience and height? Yeah, I agree, go down, buddy.' When someone with as much experience as Guy Cotter tells me to head back down, I wasn't going to hang around second guessing him. I managed to convince Pat to turn around as well and we headed off. The others were ahead somewhere.

I'd made it down to the Football Field again and started walking across it when I heard a sound so spine-chilling it's hard to describe. I turned and looked in the direction the noise had come from. A huge serac had broken free from the western shoulder of Everest. I was stunned. When it hit the bottom of the slope, the ground beneath my feet started to shake and this roar started. I looked to see a ginormous avalanche coming straight at me. I had two choices – stand still and take my fate, or fight by unclipping from the safety lines and running and jumping across some of the crevasses.

I chose to fight. I unclipped my karabiner and started running. I felt pretty clumsy as I had my climbing pack on full of gear but I sprinted like my life depended on it because, well, it did.

I raced across the ladder over the first crevasse, then jumped across the next two, which had no ladders just safety lines. I looked behind me and to my horror this huge avalanche was moving so fast up and over the ice seracs of the icefall that it sounded like 1000 freight trains.

On the far side of the Football Field was a large group of climbers who had been sitting, quietly having their lunch. As I ran past them, I heard their American guide screaming,

'BRACE YOURSELVES! THIS IS IT!' Amid the screaming that ensued, I heard another shout of, 'GOD HELP US!'

The dread of imminent death came over me. It was the same feeling I had had just before the Twin Otter crashed and again after Maya was born and was not breathing. At the end of the Football Field, there was a large, deep crevasse with two or three ladders spanning it leading down to a small ice landing then another two ladders to clear the crevasse. I thought about jumping down into the deep black crevasse and then looked back up at the avalanche.

Everything seemed to be happening in slow motion. Back on the Football Field, people were bracing themselves, some were yelling, some were running, some had started to run then turned back. Behind me was utter chaos. And in front of me was the crevasse. Would I survive the jump? Would I survive if I didn't jump?

Boom ... the ground shook. I looked back to see the avalanche hit the final ridge before the Football Field then dissipate into fine snow and ice, which seemed to rise up and hang in the air. With my heart still pounding out of my chest, I grabbed my camera and with trembling hands I took a photo. I'm not sure exactly why the first thing I did was to take a photo.

I paused for a second and then Pat walked up next to me. Until that point, I hadn't known where he was throughout the entire event. With no way out but down, we both started moving down back through the unstable area that was strung with prayer flags. I wondered how the avalanche had affected its stability. I nervously climbed down across the ladders again. Pat wanted to stop and take photos as we went. But I just wanted to get off the icefall as quickly as possible.

After another hour or so, Pat asked me to wait while he went back across one of the ladders so I could take a photo of him crossing it. My nerves were shot and the last thing I wanted to do was stuff around taking photos in the icefall, especially after our close call with that avalanche. I handed Pat's camera to another climber and took off on my own.

I got back to base camp on my own and a few other climbers who had seen the avalanche from the camp checked in to see if I was ok. Henry seemed pretty nonchalant about it, simply saying, 'Things happen in the icefall, man. Are you ok?'

Pat turned up a little while later. He wasn't too happy with me. 'Hey, thanks for leaving me in the icefall on my own!'

'Well, if you want to stuff around taking photos in such a dangerous place, you're on your own!' The truth was I felt a bit stink about leaving him on his own but I just wanted to get out of there.

Now there was *no way* I was going back into that icefall without a blessing from the Lama. I didn't care if it took a week.

Thankfully, we didn't need to wait that long. The very next day, the Lama came and performed the puja ceremony to bless our expedition. We all put our ice axes around a flagpole that held up the strings of prayer flags which spanned out over our base camp. The Lama chanted his mantra and blessed us all in order of seniority as befitted such a serious affair. The Lama chanted mantras and then threw rice into the air as an offering to the gods, then we all threw flour up in the air

237

as well, it was supposed to be out of respect to the gods but turned into a small flour fight. Everyone got covered in flour. Now we were blessed, I felt much safer!

The next few days were rest days for me and a few others but Kenton and his team of four went up to Camp 2 to acclimatise. Those of us still at base camp spent time playing cards, reading, walking near base camp and making the most of the fantastic base camp bakery. Yep, a bakery at base camp. A Sherpa called Dawa had brought up a baker's oven and was making the most amazing bread, apple turn overs and donuts.

Very soon, it was our turn to go on an acclimatisation climb up to Camp 2 with one night at Camp 1 on the way up. Usually, climbers would only go as far as Camp 1 then return to base camp to rest and then go back up to Camp 2. But the icefall was so dangerous this year that Henry felt it wise to minimise the time we spent going through it. It was a great idea, but it did mean less time to acclimatise.

Off we went, Bo, Mike Davey, Ward and Pat through the icefall again, rolling the dice with our lives. Dr Rob was with us, along with his girlfriend, Anna Shekhdar. She was a doctor as well. What she lacked in climbing experience, she made up for in sheer guts and determination.

Anna was ahead of me and started climbing up over the ice really quickly. I called out to her to slow down a bit. We climbed together for a couple of hours, before I headed off on my own, leaving Anna with some other climbers.

After negotiating the huge hanging seracs of Darwin's Corner – named after the English naturalist who came up with the theory of evolution, presumably because if you were dumb enough to dawdle in this area you'd get yourself killed, thereby improving the intelligence of the world's gene pool – I reached the top of the icefall. There the Western Cwm, or the Valley of Silence, opened up. The cwm is a glacial valley that runs from the foot of the Lhotse Face. It was absolutely incredible.

It wasn't long after reaching the cwm that I walked into the lines of tents that made up Camp 1. Ward, Bo and Pat were already there. It turned out that Pat was very fast moving through the icefall … when he wasn't taking photos!

I'd been in camp for about an hour when I spotted Dr Rob further down the valley carrying three packs. Something was really wrong. He obviously needed help so I got my harness on, grabbed some food and water and shot off back down to meet him.

When I got to Dr Rob, he asked if I could go down and help Anna and Mike, who were both really struggling. When I got to them, they looked absolutely stuffed. Anna sat down and I handed her some water. She said she didn't feel like drinking it. I knew she was dehydrated and it was vital that she got some liquids into her.

'I'll pour it in your mouth and spit it out if you don't think you can swallow it, ok?'

Anna nodded and tilted her head back and I poured a little water into her mouth.

'Ok, now I need you to eat these raisins. They'll give you some energy.' Again she said she didn't feel like it.

'Just put them in your mouth and spit them out if you want to. Please trust me, you will feel better.' Anna put the raisins in her mouth and managed to swallow them.

I tried the same tactic with Mikey. He refused to take any water or raisins no matter what I said. Mikey was a very experienced mountaineer and had been on Everest two years before so I couldn't understand why he was so affected by the altitude. But altitude sickness doesn't care how experienced you are, it can hit you at any time.

While I was trying to convince Mikey to drink, Anna recovered enough to start walking towards Camp 1. Seeing Anna go seemed to give Mikey a second wind. He got up and slowly started walking. When we got to the next steep climb, I put my hand on his lower back and helped him up by pushing him. As we got to the top I knew he would want to walk into camp without me pushing him. I asked him if he wanted me to keep pushing. Mike looked at me and slurred, 'I don't care.' I kept pushing.

When we got up to Camp 1, Mikey was settled into a tent with Dr Rob and Bo looking after him. Dr Rob gave him medication to fight the altitude sickness, while Bo made sure he had enough to drink so he could rehydrate. Even with the best of care, Mikey didn't recover as quickly as we had all hoped. Anna, on the other hand, was absolutely fine.

As the sun started setting, it became clear that Mikey needed oxygen – and we didn't have bottles with us. We called Henry and he despatched a Sherpa with some oxygen from Camp 2, which was about four hours up the Western Cwm. Dr Rob and I geared up with harnesses and head torches before heading off to meet the Sherpa halfway.

Walking in the moonlight up the Western Cwm in the middle of the night was so cool. There was a crisp crunch as our crampons touched the frozen snow. The cwm was lit by the full moon. On one side was the 7860-metre Nuptse and on the other side was Everest. I felt so humble to be walking in the footsteps of some of the greatest climbers in history.

After about an hour we could see this small light in the distance. It was the Sherpa with the oxygen. He had come three-quarters of the way down in the time it had taken Dr Rob and me to make it a quarter of the way up. We greeted each other warmly then the three of us returned to Camp 1.

When we got back to camp, Dr Rob administered the oxygen to Mikey. He improved instantly and was soon fast asleep. Dr Rob slept in the tent with him. Bo was supposed to share their tent but Mikey had puked on his sleeping bag so he joined me, Anna and the Sherpa from Camp 2 in our tent. It was a little cramped but it had been a long day and sleep came easily.

The next thing I knew Bo was shaking me. For a start I thought I was dreaming so I ignored him. He shook me again, harder this time. Grudgingly, I opened my eyes. 'Wha ... what?'

'What's the time?' Bo asked.

Surely he hadn't just woken me to ask me the time. Didn't the guy have a watch? 'It's 6am. Did you just wake me up to ask me the time?' I grizzled.

Bo looked at me and with a big grin said, 'Yeah.'

I muttered profanities under my breath, rolled over and tried to get back to sleep as Bo crashed around the tent before disappearing out the door. He was off to Camp 2 on his own, no mucking around.

It was another hour before the rest of us were up. I was relieved to find Mikey feeling much better. But he couldn't risk staying at altitude so he headed back down to base camp to get checked over by the Himalayan rescue doctors.

Setting off from Camp 2, it soon became apparent why Bo left so early. As the day wore on the heat in the cwm started building. Even though the air temperature was freezing the heat that reflected off the walls of the valley was building. I've heard a story of a climber getting his tongue and the inside of his mouth burnt by the reflective heat in the cwm, which made it even more difficult for him to breathe. That combination of heat and cold was really weird.

After an hour, our team had spread out with each climber travelling at their own natural pace. Looking up the valley a little, I could see a group of people bringing something down. As they got closer I could see they were carrying a body.

It was a group of Sherpas bringing one of their own down the mountain. I stood aside to let them pass, tears welling up in my eyes. The Sherpas called me and waved me past them. I couldn't look as I walked past.

A few metres further on there was a dip into the start of the crevasse. I couldn't go on. I sat in the snow and cried and cried. Three more Sherpas came past and each one of them rubbed the back of my head. The first two did it in silence then the last one said, 'It's ok. This happens sometimes, it's ok.'

I appreciated their support but, well, it wasn't ok. This poor Sherpa was dead, his wife and family destitute, all because westerners wanted to climb Everest. I felt incredibly guilty.

I knew I had to keep going so eventually I stood up and started walking to Camp 2, on the eastern side of the cwm. It was another few hours before I arrived at camp. Dr Rob and Kenton were there already. The Sherpa had been killed by a rock fall and it was Kenton who found his body hanging from his ropes. They could see I was upset so I spoke to both of them about how I was feeling. Their support made me feel better, sad but better.

At Camp 2, I was sharing a tent with Kenton. Despite it being so cold my breath crystallised on my sleeping bag, I slept well that night, which at that altitude of almost 6300 metres is not easy.

The next morning, Kenton headed back down the mountain base camp as he had already stayed two nights at Camp 2 and the rest of us got into a discussion about doing an hour-long acclimatisation walk up to touch the Lhotse Face. Lhotse is the fourth highest mountain in the world and is very close to Everest. The Lhotse Face is an 1125-metre wall of glacial ice on the western side of the mountain. The face has to be climbed to reach the South Col of Everest.

I knew the route had not been opened up yet, so there were no ropes set up and none of the crevasses had been marked, it was still early in the climbing season. I questioned the safety of heading up there before the route had been marked properly. The rest of the team seemed quite happy to take the risk. I knew we didn't have any rope we could use for glacier travel, where three people rope together with about 8–10 metres between them. Being roped together is much safer because if someone falls into a crevasse, the rope cuts into the side of the crevasse and the climbers above can halt the fall.

For a split second I agreed to join the expedition up to the face but then I heard someone talking about climbing some way up the face. Alarm bells started to ring loud for me. I told the others that I wouldn't join them. It seemed like too much of a risk to take when the route would be opened up in a day or so. Once I'd made my decision, I went back to my tent.

Dr Rob came over to see if I was ok, then another guy came over and asked if he could borrow my axe.

'Where's yours?' I asked.

'Back at base camp,' came the answer. I couldn't believe it.

'What are you planning to do if someone falls in a crevasse? With no axe you are useless, and that someone could be me.'

My logic didn't seem to have any impact. 'You're very right, Mike. I see your point, now can I have your axe?' I gave him my axe and off he went. At least I tried.

I watched them all depart Camp 2 and I wondered if I was just being a big softy or if I had real cause for concern. After all, quite a few of these guys had been on Everest before and this was my first time. But then I looked up and my question was answered. A group of British Special Forces guys, who we'd met at base camp, were traversing the glacier all roped together perfectly, exactly the way Paul and the other Aspiring Guides had taught me.

I was surprised to see the army guys coming back to camp about 45 minutes later. One of their team had fallen into a crevasse but he'd survived because they'd all been roped together. It made me worry even more about the rest of our team. Thankfully, my worry lifted when they all came back 10 minutes later. They'd decided it was too dangerous to continue up the glacier without ropes.

That afternoon I watched the Sherpas at work. They were sorting out loads of gear that had been brought up from base camp, getting them ready to go up to Camp 4. The Sherpas were incredibly strong. They could bring a load of around 40 kilograms up from base camp to Camp 2 and then return to base camp in a single day. I would love some TV channel to make a reality show where tough guys were given a job as a Sherpa on Everest for a season but I'm pretty sure it would have a 100 per cent fail rate.

The next day we headed back down to base camp for a three-day rest. Climbing back down the icefall, I felt better and my confidence was higher now I knew what the climb up to Camp 2 held in store. No sooner had I thought that than I came across a huge recent ice collapse. There were massive blocks of ice everywhere, tumbled and jumbled all over the place. The icefall doctors had already been there and rerouted all the safety lines, so it was safe for me to continue down.

The three days at base camp flew by, spent playing cards, fine tuning gear, drinking coffee and eating donuts at the bakery. Having fully rested – and still not won the Milo tin lid cards trophy – it was time to go up and spend a night at Camp 3 at an altitude of 7000 metres on the Lhotse Face.

One of the things I'd been refining during our acclimatisation was hydration. One of the Himalayan rescue doctors told me that I'd lose 200 ml of water per hour at 5000 metres just from breathing, even more when I'd be huffing and puffing while I was climbing. To counteract that, I made sure I drank a litre of water during the night and another litre in the morning before departing for Camp 3. I then carried two litres of water and drank a mouthful – about 150 ml – every 15 minutes. Then every 30 minutes I would eat half an energy bar. I got good at eating and drinking without stopping so I wasn't putting myself in additional danger especially in the icefall.

I was now pretty well acclimatised so there was no need for me to stay the night at Camp 1, so I headed straight through to Camp 2 in one hit. It took me about 12 hours and I was stuffed when I got there. I sat in the mess tent and Pasang Temba, the camp cook who happened to be deaf, brought me sweet tea and food. Temba's deafness meant he'd developed such an acute sense of people's reactions that he could tell if you didn't like his cooking. After that day's climb, I'd have eaten anything!

The plan was to rest here for two nights and then go up to Camp 3, where we would spend a night without oxygen as peak acclimatisation before heading back down to Camp 2 to wait for a summit window.

Henry was constantly watching the weather and I knew our plans could change at any stage. The thought of summiting Everest sometimes overwhelmed me. To beat my fear, I would focus on what needed to be done on each single day ahead of me. Henry had a good plan for us and I had full confidence in him.

The team had naturally split into two groups, Bo and Ward in one and Anna, Mikey, Pat and me in the other. Dr Rob was planning on being in both summit teams, summiting Everest twice in one season, a super human feat. Ward and Bo were much faster than the rest of us and I knew they'd get the first shot at reaching the summit. I really wanted to go with them as I knew that if we didn't make it I'd have a second chance at climbing with the rest of the team. All I could do was hope Henry had seen that I was a strong climber and that the only reason I didn't keep up with Bo and Ward was because I spent quite a bit of time helping the others.

Climbing the Lhotse Face up to Camp 3 was where the real mountaineering would begin. I walked to the start of the Lhotse Face and looked up. It was massive. At the bottom of the face, there was an area littered with rocks and someone pointed out the place where the Sherpa had been killed a few days earlier.

A few nights before a Korean team on the western shoulder of Everest had pushed on when their Sherpas had warned them not to. Two of their climbers were killed by falling rocks. Their bodies were clearly visible from where we were. It was a stark reminder of how fragile life was on the mountain.

Approaching the Lhoste Face there were about a dozen people waiting clear of the debris area at the bottom of the face. Other than me, there was only one other person wearing a helmet – an American guide. I went over and said hi. He smiled at me and touched his helmet, not saying a word. We were both thinking the same thing. Why wasn't anyone else wearing a helmet in such a dangerous part of the climb.

When it was my turn to start climbing, I went as fast as I could past the rock fall area and up onto the face. Then

I clipped in and started jugging (pulling myself) up the face using the rope. You are not really supposed to use the rope to pull yourself up but it's hard not to. I tried to use my legs to push myself up as much as possible.

In parts the face is very steep but there are huge foot holes where hundreds of other climbers and Sherpas had been so it was a bit like climbing a ladder – a very steep, difficult ladder.

It took hours and hours to get up the face but when I did the view was breathtaking. The Western Cwm opened up and I could see the summit of Nuptse and the western shoulder of Everest was in full view. But the best thing was that from here, Everest herself opened up and I could almost see the true summit. It just seemed to be there waiting for me.

When Camp 3 finally came into view, I strained my neck looking up at it. To get there, I was taking one step then resting, one step then resting and so on. Kenton was already at camp and greeted me heartily. It lifted my spirits to hear a real Everest legend say, 'Well done, buddy!'

My tent was almost on the edge of a crevasse. It looked like a really dangerous place to sleep but that was par for the course for Camp 3 and was as good as it got. I went into my tent and started melting snow straight away for drinking water.

After an hour or so I had recovered, having drunk a good amount of water and eaten some food. The meal was a boil in the bag meal, it actually tasted really good and I was surprised to have an appetite at this altitude. I decided to talk to Kenton over at his tent. The area between our tents was flat and looked ok. I took one step out of the tent and stood up. My feet went flying and I scrabbled to stand up for a few seconds before I finally landed on my knees. I was lucky not to have slid off down the face to my death. But I was embarrassed to have made a stupid mistake. I knew that a Taiwanese climber had been killed at Camp 3 during the 1996 Everest disaster because he was walking around in his boots without his crampons on and he slipped straight off the face. Apparently, quite a few people have been killed like this. It's the kind of place where you have to be conscious of every decision you make.

I crawled back into my tent and reappeared with crampons on my feet and sheepishly walked over to see Kenton. The pair of us chatted as Pat, Anna and Dr Rob arrived at camp. By this stage Bo and Ward had already been up to Camp 3 the night before and were slightly ahead of the rest of the team with their acclimatisation.

As night fell, it brought the most amazing sunset I have ever seen. As an airline pilot I have seen my fair share of sunsets at altitude but I'd never sat outside at 7000 metres (23,000 feet). The sun changed colours as it slipped below the horizon of mountains. I watched a shadow form lower down the valley, then rise up and go past where I was sitting. Instantly the sun left my face the temperature plummeted and I got cold … it was an amazing sight.

I shared a tent with Anna and Dr Rob. I couldn't have asked for better tent-mates – both doctors, one of them a two-time Everest summiteer. When we turned in for the night, Dr Rob and I played 'who's got the darkest pee game'. Because it was so cold, it was easier for us to pee in bottles than to go outside to go to the toilet. Poor Anna couldn't play and had to go outside to pee. While it was easy enough for us guys to pee in a bottle, the trick was in not spilling it.

Peeing was the least of my worries though. We were spending the night at altitude without extra oxygen. Well, there was bottled oxygen available but the plan was to use it only in an emergency.

I was just about to nod off when I looked over at Dr Rob. It looked like he wasn't breathing. I watched for a few seconds and sure enough he wasn't breathing. I quickly shook him and he woke up gasping, 'What are you doing?'

'You're not breathing,' I said.

'I must have been having a Cheyne-Stokes,' he replied.

Cheyne-Stokes breathing happens when the carbon dioxide in your blood gets out of whack. Because you are breathing so hard and fast at altitude the carbon dioxide level in your blood changes and lowers. The body's first trigger to breathe is because of a build up of carbon dioxide, but when this is not working the second trigger kicks in, lack of oxygen to the brain. This trigger is much later, so you stop breathing for a little bit and then wake up gasping for air. I'd experienced Cheyne-Stokes before at Alpamayo but on Everest I didn't seem to be getting it.

Dr Rob rolled over and went back to sleep. I tried to but it was too weird lying there waiting for my mate to stop breathing. The next time he stopped, I knew it was a Cheyne-Stokes so I waited and waited and waited but he didn't wake. It seemed ages so I shook him hard again. He gasped again and said, 'Bloody hell, mate, I'm fine, stop waking me up!'

I had to trust that he knew what he was talking about so

I rolled over so I couldn't see him, put some earplugs in and went to sleep.

When I woke, Dr Rob was already up making porridge and tea for Anna and me. He is a bit of a freak at altitude – there aren't many climbers in the world with his kind of strength and ability to think clearly at extreme altitudes. I could see why he had been called on in medical emergencies high in the mountains many times.

Once we'd had breakfast, it was time to make our way back down to Camp 2. I felt confident as I had good rope skills thanks to Paul Scaife and David Hiddleston. I descended most of the face with a karabiner clipped into the rope, which I then wrapped around my arm. Called arm-wrapping, this created friction and slowed my descent down to a safe speed. When it got too steep, I turned around and abseiled down backwards.

All was going well until I came over a small lip of ice that had been blocking my view of the lower slope. Once I got there I could see dozens and dozens of people coming up. I descended a little more and met an American guide. I pointed at the crowd coming up and he nodded with an expression that said everything.

I was shocked to see that all of those climbers were on one single piece of line. And I was attached also to the same rope. I counted and there were 50 people attached to it. The tension on that piece of climbing rope was huge. I then looked at the anchor and it seemed that all the force of those climbers was on one ice screw with a back-up snow stake. The snow stake was supposed to be sharing the load of the anchor equally, but it wasn't. I touched the stake and it came straight out of the ice in my hand.

I shouted to the American guide and he looked horrified. We both knew that if the anchor failed, both of us as well as the other 50 climbers would slide straight down the 60-degree slope for about 300 metres (1000 feet). It would be a totally unsurvivable fall that would have left the 1996 disaster in its dust.

There was a second piece of rope that trailed all the way down parallel to the other climbers so I quickly transferred my safety over to it. The American guide put another screw into the ice and tried to split the load between it and the other ice screw. His confidence can't have been great as he made sure he was free of the whole anchor system himself.

Just as I started off down the face, I could see a woman having trouble. The foot holds in the ice had run out and she had to dig her crampons into the ice to get traction. I watched in disbelief as she tried to slam the side of her crampon into the ice repeatedly. I swung over a little, said hello and grabbed her boot. I turned it 90 degrees so the front point was facing the ice, then I pulled her foot back and swung it into the ice so that it held. She smiled and said thanks then did the same with the other foot. It astounded me that someone could be so far up the Lhotse Face with such limited ice climbing skills. It really made me question the ethics of some of the guiding companies.

Once I was abseiling down the next piece of rope, I heard a commotion above me. I looked up to see a climber falling down the face. He was still attached to the rope but had lost control of his abseil. As he fell, he was knocking people off the other

252

rope, one after another leaving them dangling on their jumars. He ended up hanging upside down a couple of metres above me. I thought about going back up to help him but I could see other people helping him so I abseiled away as quickly as I could in case he fell and took me out. What a mess!

The next section was 10 metres (30 feet) straight down vertically. I abseiled down and as I was switching to another rope, a voice came from above me. 'Hey, do you think this is ok to arm-wrap?' I couldn't believe it. I couldn't believe people were up here with such bad rope skills. They were not only putting themselves at risk but they could easily kill other climbers.

I shouted back, 'Knock yourself out! Just wait until I'm out of the way so you don't kill us both.' I think he got the hint as he turned around and abseiled down safely.

When I got back to Camp 2, I told Kenton what I'd seen. He didn't seem surprised and just said, 'Welcome to Everest, my friend.'

The next day we all descended to base camp to await our summit window. Henry announced the teams via Dr Rob. I was in the second team and I was really pissed off about it. I didn't know how to approach Henry and instead of dealing with it straight away, I mulled it over for a day. When Henry came into our mess tent, I hit him up for a place in the first team. I didn't know that he was suffering from the flu but let's just say the conversation didn't go well. Henry shouted at me and stormed out. I then stormed back to my tent, feeling even more pissed off.

Poor old Dr Rob was left trying to be the peace maker. He came over to my tent and said, 'Mike, you have to go and talk to Henry.' I wasn't having a bar of it.

Bo then came over and said, 'Allsop, you having a few troubles, eh?'

'Yeah, I'm in the second team. I'm as strong as you guys – I should be with you.'

Bo was a bit younger than me but he was surprisingly worldly wise. His words to me were brutally honest but what I needed to hear.

'You were always going to be in the second team. Right from day one, you've been running around like a boy scout trying to help everyone. The truth is, none of us is here for anyone else but ourselves.'

Wow. In response, I asked a pretty full-on question. 'Well, now I wish I hadn't. I wish I'd just looked after myself like you did. If I'd fallen into a crevasse, would you have even stopped to help me?'

'Hell no. I wouldn't help you because I would have been two hours ahead of you. If I saw you fall in, of course I would help you. That's the point, Mike. Don't you get it?'

I realised he was right. I was here to climb Everest for myself, not to help anyone else do it. Now I had stuffed a possible second chance at reaching the summit so I had to hope I would get there on my first attempt.

My happy world seemed to be collapsing around me. I didn't want to be fighting with Henry. I liked the guy but he had really pissed me off. I felt like crap and I was desperate to talk to Wendy. Thankfully Mikey could see what was going on and he let me borrow his satellite phone to call home. As I stomped out of base camp, with tears welling up, Henry waved me over to his tent. I couldn't speak and I certainly didn't want him to see me so wound up. All I could manage was to put my hand up to him to indicate that I didn't want to speak. This just made everything a lot worse.

Once I got out of camp, I rang Wendy. It must have been hard for her to hear me so unhappy and so far away. There wasn't a lot she could say or do but I just needed someone to listen to me. Her words of advice were pretty simple. 'Just do what you think is right, Mike.' It was great to talk to her, I felt a little homesick but wouldn't allow myself to dwell on it.

Back in camp, Dr Rob came flying into my tent. 'Oh my god, you've done it now. Henry is furious with you. You have to go and apologise to him, Mike. You have to or he'll kick you out of camp.'

I walked into the kitchen tent to find Henry. He was having his dinner but when he saw me, he walked over to me. As I went to speak, he grabbed me and gave me a huge hug and said, 'Hey, man, I care about you. I want you in the second team for your own safety. Trust me, it's better this way. All of those guys in the first team have been up to about 8000 metres before but you haven't. It's safer for you to go second because the trail will be broken by then and there'll be more resources up there for you.'

He was right. I should have trusted him. I felt a little silly, I apologised to Henry and told him how much I enjoyed his company. We talked for a while and the air was cleared between us. I was happy again.

The first team – Bo, Ward, Dr Rob, Kenton and two of his team – would now stay at base camp while the rest of us – Pat, Mikey, Anna and I – descended to the villages lower down the mountain to rest and wait for a good weather window for our summit attempt.

There is only about a two-week window on Everest each May and an even shorter window in October when the jet stream winds move slightly north. In order to make the summit during these short stretches of good weather, you need to be high up the mountain waiting for this window to open. Predicting the weather forecast is critical and I'd learnt from 20 years of flying that when it comes to reading the weather, experience is the key. You can't buy it or get it from any university, you have to live it. And that is why I trusted Henry – he had been on and around Everest more than anyone in the world.

We said our goodbyes and wished the other guys luck. Dr Rob was planning to climb with both teams, and Kenton was going to do the same with his clients. There was only one western climber who had summited Everest twice in one season before and it had only been done a few times by Sherpas.

I'd read books that said you could feel the thick air as you descended lower down the mountain where there was more oxygen. I had thought it was rubbish until I got down towards the village of Pangboche. I took a deep breath and the air actually did feel thick. It was amazing but unfortunately at the same time my stomach started to rumble in a very bad way, I wasn't sure what was causing it.

On that particular stretch of track there is nowhere to go to the bathroom. There is a cliff on one side going straight down and one going straight up on the other side. I had no choice but to climb down the cliff, hang on to a tree and stick my butt out. Diarrhoea isn't pleasant at the best of times but if you're on a cliff hanging on to a tree, it's hideous. And worse was yet to come.

I was obsessed with making my pack as light as possible, to the point that I cut the head off my toothbrush and removed the unused buckles on my pack. Unfortunately, this obsession with lightness had extended to my toilet paper supplies. I only had three sheets ... eeek!

As soon as I'd used those three precious sheets I needed to go again, then again and again. When I was sure I'd finally finished, I realised I had absolutely no toilet paper. It was time to be a bit inventive. I racked my brains to work out what I could use when inspiration hit me. I might not have had toilet paper but I had my wallet with me. Out came a 10 rupee note, then 20 rupees then 50 rupees. I was just about to use a 100 rupee note when I realised it was cheaper to use a US$1 bill. Talk about spending a penny – I spent about NZ$4. I laughed to myself. The things you think about when you're hanging your arse off a cliff with a bad bout of diarrhoea.

I turned up at Sonam Lodge and there was Gyurme and his Sherpa friends. Nima, Gyurme's wife, had gone to the US for a holiday so he was in charge of the lodge. We ordered chicken, which was deep fried then roasted. There was no chance of getting sick from eating this chicken – it was well and truly cooked. After being on the mountain for so long, it was delicious.

The time spent in Pangboche was great. We ate, drank the odd beer and played a lot of cards. This time, the loser had to wear a pair of broken glasses with no lenses and thick black rims the whole of the next day. They were only allowed to take them off when someone else lost at cards. Naturally, I ended up wearing the glasses for a day, but the funniest thing was seeing Gyurme Sherpa wearing the glasses one day, and having to explain to other Sherpas what was going on.

We'd been in Pangboche a few days when a friend of Mikey's stopped in the village for lunch. Fi was working as a doctor on an expedition with the adventurer Bear Grylls. He was going to attempt to paraglide over Mt Everest – something that had never been done before. It was a weird coincidence because it was through reading Bear's book, *The Kid who Climbed Everest*, that I first heard of Henry.

Bear's team arrived first. Neil Laughton, who had climbed Everest with Bear in 1997, was the team's safety officer and Gilo Cardozo, a world champion paraglider pilot, was going to fly with Bear over Everest. Once Neil and Gilo found out I was a pilot, we got talking about flying. I had just started to tell them about my Twin Otter crash when Bear walked in.

He came over to the table where we were sitting and grabbed my water saying, 'Man, I'm thirsty. Whose water is this?' Then he helped himself before I could say anything. I just thought, 'Dude, I've seen you drinking the fluid out of elephant dung … you can have my water!'

Bear sat down and listened with the others as I told my story. Just as I was getting to the climax of the crash, someone farted. I looked at Neil and said, 'Did you just fart?'

He laughed and said, 'No, but I'm about to shit my pants! What happened?' Once the laughter subsided I finished telling my tale.

After Bear's team had left, Mikey gave me grief. 'So super star Bear Grylls turns up and you hold the floor with one of your flying stories. Bloody hell, Allsop!'

Every second night, we would call Henry and he would update us on the latest plan. It was looking like a short summit window so both teams would have to summit within a few days. Even so we had to wait in Pangboche until Henry gave us the word to come back up to base camp.

During that week I spent a lot of time at the monastery in Upper Pangboche. There I would just sit quietly in the corner of the courtyard with my eyes closed, imagining being on the summit, trying to conjure up the feeling of standing on the roof of the world. Then I would imagine myself back safely at base camp.

It was a technique that a friend at Air New Zealand had taught me. I would then picture the worst case scenarios, like an avalanche, seeing dead bodies or even getting injured myself. I would let myself picture this to the point where it felt almost real, to where tears would build up in my eyes. Once I got to that stage I would picture myself coping with everything that was thrown at me. It was a way of training my sub-conscious mind to believe that I could cope with anything that might happen to me.

I also worked on training myself to believe that I would go from Camp 4 to the summit, back to Camp 4 and then all the way down to Camp 2 in one go. There are only a few climbers in the world that could do this, including Dr Rob and Kenton. I knew I wasn't in their class, but the theory was that my sub-conscious mind didn't know this. Over and over again I would think – and sometimes even say aloud – 'Camp 4, summit, Camp 2 … Camp 4, summit, Camp 2.'

I had no intention of actually doing all of that in one go but by convincing myself that it was possible, when I did stop at Camp 4 after summiting, I would have more energy to look after myself and others if required.

Pat was starting to get a chest infection and as a health care professional he knew how important it was to get on top of it straight away. We knew Mikey's friend who was the doctor for the paragliding team would have antibiotics, so a couple of us trekked up to see them and ask if we could raid their drug kit.

When we got there, Bear was filming but he came over and chatted for a while, and told us to grab whatever medical supplies we needed. Bear had been on Everest with Henry almost 10 years ago to the day and he understood just what was in store for us.

The days passed and each morning I would go to the monastery and sit quietly. The caretaker would take me inside and put me in front of the huge gold Buddha as he thought I was praying. I smiled and let him think that.

After a very nice week of rest the call finally came. Henry wanted us all back at base camp. This was it. We were going for the summit.

THE SUMMIT

As we walked up the valley the next morning the usual silence was broken by the sound of engines. Bear and Gilo had taken off from their camp at Pheriche and were circling around in their powered paragliders. Pheriche was about two hours from Pangboche and we hurried along hoping to see their attempt to fly over Everest unfold.

In order to climb to altitude, Bear and Gilo had paramotors strapped to their backs. These looked like big windmills and were powered by single rotor, four stroke engines. No one had ever attempted anything like this on Everest before.

After about an hour, the noise of one of the engines changed and we could see a tiny canopy floating back down to earth. When we got to their base camp, one of the paragliders was on the ground but the other one was still going strong.

We found out from the ground team that both Gilo and Bear had made it up to about 8300 metres, where the temperature was about −60°C before Gilo's engine developed a fault just 300 metres below the summit. It was Bear who was still up there and the images being transmitted from his cameras back to camp were mind blowing. You could clearly see Everest, Lhotse and the rest of the Himalayas laid out before him. The vistas took in Nepal and Tibet. Incredible.

We watched him descend and land in the field below. He had broken the world record – an amazing achievement. By the time I got to the spot where Bear landed, he already had a bottle of champagne in hand. He shouted, 'Hey, Mike, I've seen the world from your office!' before giving me a big hug.

'Yeah, but you were sitting on the outside, you crazy bugger!' was my reply. I would have loved to have stayed and partied with Bear, Gilo and the team but I was on my own mission. Everest awaited.

At base camp, Henry greeted us all and gave us a briefing. Bo, Ward, Dr Rob and Kenton were all at Camp 4. They would leave for the summit at 9pm. That night, I nervously wondered what it must be like climbing through the night high on Everest as soon it would be my turn.

The next morning the weather was fantastic and everyone gathered in a tent and listened for the first sign of any progress. The radio crackled into life. 'Hey, Henry, it's Bo. I've run out of road.'

'Congrats, Bo. Now please don't stay too long.'

A muffled voice came over the radio, 'Ok, Henry, will do. Kenton is just behind me.'

Over the next few hours all our friends made the summit and all over base camp I could hear gongs or pots and pans being clanged together when each team heard one of their friends had made the summit. It was now a nervous wait for everyone to get back safe.

Sitting in the mess having breakfast, Kenton radioed in to say there was a Sherpa lying in the snow just below the south summit. Henry asked Kenton to see what he could do.

A few minutes later, Kenton reported back, 'He's one of ours. He's lying on his back with his mask off and his arms are flapping in the air.'

As a pilot I knew only too well what that meant. Part of my training involved spending time in an altitude simulator. The experience simulated the same height as Everest – 8848 metres (29,000 feet). Once we'd reached that height we took off our masks and extended our arms out in front of us. If our arms began to flap involuntarily, it was a sign that the body wasn't coping with the lack of oxygen in our systems. When this happens it's because the body is trying to protect the brain by diverting oxygen away from the limbs and into the brain. It is a very dangerous condition and it sounded like our Sherpa was showing signs of it.

Henry called Dr Rob who was on the summit and asked him to get down to the south summit as soon as possible. He didn't elaborate any further as the last thing Henry wanted was to spell everything out over the radio as there were many people listening and any news was disseminated over the internet almost instantly.

Sitting in our mess tent, it was hard to listen to the drama unfolding just below the summit. Kenton tried to give the

Sherpa some oral dex but it didn't help. When Dr Rob arrived, they radioed again to say that they'd administered injectable dex but it hadn't helped. The Sherpa was trying to take off his clothes.

When in the final stages of hypothermia, victims can feel like they are overheating. This was probably why the Sherpa was trying to get undressed. It was a really bad sign.

There was a long pause and then Henry calmly radioed back, 'You might have to start preparing to leave him, Kenton.'

There was silence on the radio and in our mess tent.

At that altitude, if you can't walk, you're dead. It's as simple as that. There's no way anyone else can come and rescue you – they'd die themselves if they tried to carry you back down. This is something people who haven't been to extreme altitude find hard to accept and I can understand why. I struggled with it myself and I was there.

I left the tent and went for a walk. It was just all too much. Henry knew that it would be extremely difficult for Kenton or Rob to leave anyone, let alone one of our Sherpas, on the mountain to die. I guess he just wanted them to start thinking about the possibility of having to do it.

When I got back to the tent, there was better news. The Sherpa had managed to walk a few feet. Kenton and Rob kept radioing in ever improving updates. A bit more than half an hour later, the Sherpa was walking well and trying to convince other climbers to let him carry their packs.

After a few days at base camp, we finally got news that a good weather window was coming. We were to head up to Camp 2 for a couple of days and wait our turn there.

Stopping at Camp 1 for a bit of a rest, I set about boiling some water for the four of us. After about half an hour, I'd managed to get about a litre melted when an American woman came into our tent asking for water. I thought she was in trouble so I gave her half of our water. She then asked for more, so I asked her if she was ok. Her reply shocked me.

'Yeah, I just want to get going up to Camp 2.' The bloody bitch! I wasn't having it.

'There's four of us keen to get to Camp 2 as well, so you're welcome to stay and use our spare stove to melt yourself some snow,' I said.

I thought she'd get the message, but apparently not. 'No thanks. Can I please just have your water? You can melt some more yourself.'

I told her I'd given her half our water already and that we would be drinking the rest whether she liked it or not. She clearly thought I was a bit rude, and then walked off muttering to herself, without a word of thanks. I couldn't believe her attitude.

A few hours along from Camp 1, Anna started throwing up and slowed right down. She looked terrible. We were only halfway along the Western Cwm and it was hot, so vomiting meant that Anna would be losing all her fluids.

Two of Kenton's clients, Tori and Ben, were climbing with us. Ben radioed Henry and he despatched a couple of Sherpas with hot tea to come and help us. Once they got there, we continued slowly to Camp 2. Anna was tough but it looked like she had a chest infection, which would probably end her expedition.

At Camp 2, one of the doctors with the British army checked Anna over. Her blood oxygen saturation was terrible so he put the oxygen on for the night and gave her a radio. I felt like I should have stayed with her but I was worried about catching whatever germs she had. It's one thing to have a chest infection at 6300 metres but getting one at 8000 metres in a few days' time could be life threatening.

The next morning Anna was a little bit better – at altitude you heal much more slowly if at all. She was taking antibiotics which seemed to help a little. Everyone seemed to be coughing and spluttering in the mess tent, so I would quietly get my food and sit outside, hoping not to catch anything.

During our rest day at Camp 2, Dr Rob and Kenton arrived. They had had only one night's rest at base camp and then had come back up for another summit push. Legends!

The weather forecast was looking good for a summit push in a few days but at the moment it was so windy that I could hear the jet stream screaming up high. It sounded like a train or a jet engine running. Despite the wind up high, we set out for Camp 3 the following morning.

I was on the way to the summit! Getting to Camp 3 was still hard but knowing what to expect along the way took some of my nerves away. When I arrived I brewed some tea then sat down and tinkered with my oxygen mask.

One thing I had learnt from reading every book about climbing Everest was to be prepared. Don't start late, get your gear ready and set out on time were consistent messages that had been drummed into me. So I watched the magnificent sunset over the Himalayas and went over all my gear again before settling in for the night. A guide had once told me that my summit bid would start from Camp 3 so I was determined to make it count.

The next morning I got my down suit and oxygen mask on and off I went. There wasn't much use in the whole team staying together as we would all be meeting that night at Camp 4 and the Sherpa teams coming up from Camp 2 would be passing us along the route.

I left Camp 3 and started up on the fixed line. The route is very steep up a 60 degree slope which is the Lhoste Face, it then crosses the yellow band then over to the Geneva spur. There was so much history with the route I couldn't wait.

It was the first time I'd climbed with the oxygen mask on and it took a bit of getting used to. I only took two steps and felt like I was suffocating so I grabbed the mask, pulled it off and took a huge gasp of air. I tried again and the same thing happened. I started to worry that there was something wrong with my kit but I checked everything and it was all going as it should have. I realised I'd been going too fast so I tried once more but moved more slowly. Before long I got the hang of it and got myself into a nice rhythm.

I started up the Lhotse Face and it was all going well. It was such a beautiful day. I soon hit the famous Yellow Band, a distinctive yellowy brown band of marble and sedimentary sandstone. Tiny fossils had been found in the rock that 140 million years before had been in the sea bed. When the tectonic plates that sit beneath India and China collided the seabed was driven up and up … and up to 7500 metres.

Once I'd crossed the Yellow Band, I stopped, had a drink and checked my oxygen bottle. I was shocked to find that I was running out of oxygen. I checked all over the bottle and regulator and could hear a faint hiss coming from the thread where the bottle connected to the regulator. I had to think as clearly as possible. I wasn't worried about dying or getting into real trouble, I was just worried about exhausting myself and not being in good shape for the summit push later on that night so I turned my oxygen flow rate down to half a litre per minute and started climbing again. The oxygen system we were using was state of the art so I had a lot of confidence in it. But at the end of the day you are relying on a metal thread on a regulator or a thread on a refilled bottle or a rubber hose. Things break and fail, I knew this very well from my years in aviation.

The Geneva Spur, a large rock buttress named by the Swiss team in the early 1950s, was just in front of me. Before attempting to climb the steep spur, I sat down and rechecked my oxygen – it was nearly out. I calculated I had about 30 minutes left, which should take me up the steep spur ahead before hitting slightly easier ground through to Camp 4.

I could see a large team coming down along the spur so I turned off my oxygen to save what little I had and waited for them to pass. I couldn't quite believe it. I was here on my own actually sitting on the Lhotse Face on my way to the summit of Everest.

My reverie was interrupted by a voice from above me. 'Bloody hell, Kiwi, what are you doing here on your own?'

It was one of the British army guys. I told him about my leaky oxygen bottle and without a second thought he took off his oxygen mask then his backpack and pulled out his oxygen bottle. He disconnected it and handed it to me. 'Here you go, buddy, turn it up to three litres per minute and enjoy yourself!'

'What are you going to use?' I asked, feeling slightly overwhelmed.

'Ah, don't worry, I'll use what's left of yours, mate.' I handed him my bottle and he rigged it up.

I knew those boys were tough, but this was extraordinary. They then wished me good luck and off I went up the Geneva Spur. My renewed oxygen source meant that I did enjoy myself the rest of the way up to the next camp.

Camp 4, or the South Col, is a desolate place in between Lhotse and Everest, where the wind funnels between the two mountains, blasting the camp. It is also right on 26,000 feet (7924 metres), which is the point where the oxygen in the atmosphere doesn't have enough pressure to push it into the capillaries in your lungs and oxygenate your blood. Even on 100 per cent oxygen, there still isn't enough pressure to get the oxygen into the blood. This lack of pressure in the air at this altitude is why as airline pilots we have the option of pressurised oxygen in the flight deck in our emergency masks in case the aircraft depressurises. These masks are pressurised and force the oxygen into your lungs and from there into your bloodstream. Unfortunately there isn't anything like that for climbers.

I had made good time between Camp 3 and Camp 4 so it was midday when I arrived. Outside our tent was a body wrapped up in a sleeping bag. I couldn't make sense of it. Who was it? Why did someone die? Was it Mikey? Mikey had come up the day before us to spend two nights at Camp 4 before attempting the summit. I was almost scared to call out, 'Mikey, are you here?'

As I unzipped the tent I heard his voice, 'Yeah, buddy, I'm here. Come in.' Boy, was I relieved.

'Who's that?' I asked, gesturing towards the body.

'It's a Sherpa woman who died the other night.'

I only thought about her for a split second, and then focused on what I needed to do. 'Oh, ok, is there any water?' It seems a rather cold reaction, looking back, but that's the reality of life this high on Everest.

'Here you go, buddy,' said Mikey, handing me a litre of freshly melted water. It must have taken him hours to melt it. It was quite a gift.

The South Col is littered with dead bodies. You have to look hard to find them but they are there. That very fact made me uncomfortable so I stayed in my tent for most of the day, checking and rechecking my gear.

Kenton was already in camp when I got there, then Dr Rob and Anna turned up. As the day wore on we all got more worried about Pat. Finally we heard him shouting, 'Henry's camp – hello!'

We unzipped the tent and called him over. He looked shocking. Mikey and I pulled him into our tent and lay him down. He had been out there all day and had run out of oxygen. Looking at him, I seriously wondered how in a few hours' time, at 9pm, he would be able to attempt the summit.

But Pat was tough and once he'd had a drink and some food, he perked up considerably and was preparing his gear for the summit.

I lay there thinking about the next few hours – these hours would be the most defining moments of my entire life. Would I make the summit? Would I get killed? Would I lose my fingers or toes and never hold a pilot's licence again? All these questions started closing in on me but I realised I couldn't afford to think like this. It served no purpose and wouldn't help me anyway. I put my earphones on and listened to some music while visualising myself standing on the summit, then heading back to Camp 4 before continuing on to Camp 2. My plan was still in place.

To be brutally honest, I was scared – really scared. I didn't know whether I would live or die but in some strange way, I didn't care. I was going to the summit and I would meet my fate whatever that might be.

My mother had written me a letter, not just any letter – a very emotional letter. I read it while I waited at base camp. She wrote about how I was destined to be on Everest and that I had to go forward and follow my destiny. In the letter she included my small cardboard birth tag that she had kept for 37 years and asked me to leave it at the summit of Everest. I also planned to release locks of hair from each of my three children, Wendy and me from the summit.

Soon it was 8pm – time to get ready. I slowly got into my down climbing suit. I was covered from head to toe in Icebreaker clothing, which is made from fine Merino wool. It's the perfect fabric for climbing as it's a natural fibre and it breathes against your body. It keeps you very warm in extreme cold. I looked like a walking Icebreaker ad – I was wearing their underpants, long johns, socks, first layer top, jumper, liner gloves and balaclava. Over all of this were my fleece jacket and then my down climbing suit. For some strange reason I had this confidence when I thought about my Icebreaker gear.

I also had these chemical heat pads that generated heat when exposed to oxygen. They could generate over 50°C heat but when it's −40°C that only warms you up to 10°C. It might not sound like much but it's better than nothing at altitude. I had these pads on my fingers, toes, shins, lower stomach, chest, and finally one on the outside of my underpants.

I pulled up my balaclava and then fitted my oxygen mask snugly to my face making sure it was tight. I put my lucky thick woollen hat that I wore on my first climb with Paul Scaife over the top. Then I put my goggles on my forehead and finally pulled my down suit hood over all of that.

I came out of the tent bang on time at 9pm and was met by a Sherpa. He told me his name was Lhakpa and he would be my Sherpa. I greeted him and the two of us headed off. He had a radio and four bottles of oxygen in his pack. His pack must have been incredibly heavy as each bottle weighed four kilograms. I had just the bottle I was using and some spare gloves and it felt like quite a lot.

The route to the summit goes over the Western Cwm for a few hundred metres before it gets steep – really steep. When I looked up all I could see was a line of lights from climbers' head torches going straight up. There were about 15 climbers and Sherpas ahead of me.

We had only been going for a few minutes on the flat part when I started to overheat. I had to take off all my gear to get my fleece jacket off. Then I had to put it all back on again. Better here on the flat than up the mountain, I guess.

From here on up, it was steep all the way and it was a hard slog all night. I climbed one step, took five breaths, then another step, another five breaths and so on. It was very hard but after a while I got into a steady rhythm and was making good progress. There were fixed lines all the way up anchored in every 50 metres or so.

I had stopped for a small rest on the the lower couloir (gully) when something caught my eye. Turning to my left, the light from my head lamp shone on something that didn't look right. It was a person on a rock, lying back slightly with their arms down by their sides and a backpack over their head and shoulders. The lower part of the body was covered in snow and ice. I looked again in disbelief. I wondered if my mind was playing tricks on me due to its slightly oxygen starved state. I turned my light away and took a deep breath.

From reading accounts of the 1996 disaster, I knew that Scott Fischer had been left in a similar position somewhere near here on the mountain. Fischer was a professional guide and climber who had been the first American to summit Lhotse. He had been caught in the same snowstorm that killed Rob Hall and seven other climbers on 10 May 1996. Fischer is thought to have died of extreme altitude sickness and his body was left where he died in accordance with the wishes of his family.

I looked down at my feet and slowly looked back again. Sure enough there was someone sitting right there frozen in time. I began to feel upset and scared. If it was Scott Fischer, he was an amazing climber and guide, yet here I was climbing past his dead body. It felt completely insane.

I knew I had to keep going but I'd lost my confidence. I took one step up and struggled, breathing hard – five, six, seven breaths then another step and even more breaths. I muttered to myself, 'Keep it together, keep it together, come on, come on.'

After a little while I found my rhythm again. I passed two climbers, one of whom pointed out another body. I didn't look, I just put my head down and kept climbing. I couldn't risk losing my stride again. I'd been climbing for about six hours but I couldn't tell how high up I was because it was so dark. I pulled out the water bottle that I was carrying on the inside of my down jacket. I was shocked to find it had frozen solid.

Next thing a huge gust of wind hit me. It was at least 70 knots and it almost knocked me off my feet. I leant forward into the face and dug my axe in. The gust passed then a few minutes later another one hit. When these gusts hit you, you couldn't move at all. I hoped this wasn't the jet stream coming south. A few years before the jet stream had shifted south back onto Everest, blasting the mountain and killing anyone that was left on it. Surely it can't be, I thought.

Then there was a flash of lightning from over my right shoulder, towards Tibet. The wind gusts became more frequent. Each time I would dig my axe in and hold on. A group of climbers ahead of me turned around and descended past me and then another two did the same. They were all turning back. I couldn't believe it.

I'd come so far and there was no way I was going to get turned around now. I focused on the next anchor and when I got there I stared at my toes. Can I feel them? Yep! I checked my fingers. Can I feel them? Yep. All was ok, so there was no reason to turn around. No sooner had I thought that than another gust hit me. I held on and headed up to the next anchor and reassessed things there. I decided that I would do this all the way to the summit if necessary. Thankfully, that was the last gust of wind. As quickly as the storm had come up, it disappeared.

An hour or so later I made it to The Balcony, a platform on the south-east ridge from which the snow ridge rises 300 metres to the South Summit. It was the perfect place for a bit of a rest and to meet up with the others. Dr Rob was there and said, 'Well done, everyone. This is a great time to be here.' We had made very good time.

Lhakpa left a full bottle of oxygen here for our descent and we carried on by torchlight. A few hours later, I heard Pat shouting my name. I ignored him. I was so tired that I didn't want to stop and start again. He shouted again. I finally stopped and turned around.

'Look! The dawn is breaking …' I looked to my left and the huge pyramid shadow of Everest was rising over the Himalayas. I struggled to get my camera out and snapped a photo, and then I put my head down and kept going.

At the top of The Balcony the climb gets steep again and there are two difficult rock bands to cross. As I climbed past them I thought, 'It's going to be difficult getting down these rock bands.'

Going up was easy but coming down would be difficult because you can't see your feet past your oxygen mask. I decided that I'd deal with that when I got to it.

I looked up and there was Dr Rob, filming with a TV camera the BBC had given him. Only Dr Rob had the capacity and strength to film, climb and guide people at the same time at that altitude. He is truly an amazing climber. I thought about speeding up so I could get him to film me so I would have some decent coverage of my climb but it was too hard and I continued at my own pace.

Soon I was traversing the ridge. It had huge drops on either side but thankfully the conditions were calm or it would have been even trickier. The climb along the ridge seemed to drag on but the excitement of being so high on Everest outweighed any negative thoughts about how hard it was.

I climbed up a little higher and there it was – the famous knife-edge ridge opened out before me. I was at the South Summit, a table-sized dome of snow. There was so much history along this tiny ridge. More than 40 people had simply vanished here and many dramas had been played out. It looked just like all the photos I had seen over the years. I couldn't believe I was here looking at it with my own eyes. From here, I could see the final obstacles ahead of me – the Cornice Traverse, the Hillary Step and the Summit.

I descended from the South Summit onto the start of the

knife-edge ridge. Lhakpa said he would meet me here. It was a good time to change the batteries in my camera. I had taped two AA size batteries directly onto the skin at the top of my leg near my groin to keep them warm. If I was going to make the summit, I wanted to have proof of it.

As I waited for Lhakpa I watched some climbers on the Hillary Step, the final obstacle and the hardest part of the entire expedition climb. I felt calm at the thought of climbing it. I knew I had the skills. But I also knew this was the place where Rob Hall had died in 1996. Rob received New Zealand's highest bravery medal for a civilian for trying to save his client.

Another Kiwi guide, Andy Harris, had also disappeared on this ridge that night. David Hiddleston had told me the story of how he and his friends back in New Zealand had waited for news on the night and the next day. When it came, it was the worst possible news. It was so sad.

Thankfully, I was distracted from the sadness when my radio crackled to life. It was Henry asking if anyone could see the Hillary Step as he had heard there was a bad traffic jam of climbers up there.

'Henry, it's Mike. I'm at the South Summit and I can see the Hillary Step. There are three climbers above it moving up, two are on it and another three have just descended. I'll be next, there is no issue. Over.'

'Thanks, Mike. You're doing really well, man. Keep it up, I'm so happy for you.' Henry sounded happy. This lifted my spirits even higher.

Soon after, Lhakpa turned up and off we went along the ridge. There was a bit of a track along it where other climbers had already walked – this was the safest place to be. At one point I poked my axe into the lip of the cornice and punctured it clean through to the other side – I could see all the way down into Tibet. Crikey.

Gradually, the Cornice Ridge got narrower and narrower, to the point where it was only a few centimetres thick. On one side to my right, 2000 metres straight down into Tibet, on my left 2500 metres down to the Western Cwm. Both views looked terrifying, but strangely didn't seem to bother me. I had a reasonable amount of climbing experience and seeing exposure like that is normal – still terrifying, but normal.

It seemed like only a few minutes later that I was at the foot of the Hillary Step – a 12-metre wall of rock, snow and ice that is the last obstacle before the summit. I gave Lhakpa my camera and asked him to take some photos of me climbing the step.

I strained my neck back and looked up the step. I could see rock on the left and snow and ice on the right. I clipped my jumar in and swung my axe high. It stuck well and there was a large foot hold from all the other climbers before me. I moved on to the step. I looked down between my legs and the view beneath me was just unbelievable – there was nothing but air beneath my feet. I kept climbing without looking down until I was at the top of the Hillary Step.

I climbed around a large rock at the top of the step and then up a very steep bit back onto the ridge. From here it is an easy walk to the summit. I was so close, I could feel the excitement building. I was going the make it.

I should have known better than to be so cocky. No sooner had I thought that than a strange feeling came over me, something didn't feel quite right. I started to feel disorientated and then I began staggering. I'd take one step then I would stagger again. My left leg collapsed, and then my right leg collapsed. I slumped into the snow, managing to turn around facing straight out towards Nepal; the Himalayas lay before me. I thought, 'This is what happens to people when they disappear. I'm going to disappear.'

Lhakpa knew exactly what had happened – I had run out of oxygen. He reached into my pack and changed my oxygen bottle for a new one. I took a deep breath and then I had instant clarity. I felt 100 per cent again. If it wasn't for Lhakpa, I would still be sitting there today – it's a great view, but …

I got up and walked around a big rock to find Dr Rob standing there with his mask pulled down, smiling at me. 'Mate, well done. You've done it!' He then reached into his pocket and handed me his sat phone. 'Here you go, buddy, call Wendy from the top.'

I still had a wee way to go so we said goodbye and I carried on up. Anna passed me as she was descending – she'd made it. Given how sick she'd been only a few days before, it was one hell of an achievement, but then she is one tough, determined person.

I started moving up slowly and there it was – the summit of Everest. I was a little shocked. A flood of emotion came over me, tears welled in my eyes, and a voice came into my head – it was me saying, 'You've worked so hard for this,

Mike. You deserve it!' A tear rolled down my cheek under my goggles.

Then it was like someone had flicked a switch. This was no place for emotion – it is too dangerous, I'm here to do my job. I turned to Lhakpa and shouted, 'Four photos and one phone call!'

He looked shocked but nodded and gave me the thumbs-up. There was no one else around, just Lhakpa and me. With the short summiting window, it's very unusual to have the summit to yourself.

I took the final few steps and stood on the roof of the world at 8.45am on 24 March 2007 – a day and a moment that changed my life forever.

THE DESCENT

Lhakpa had my camera out all ready to go. I put one foot up and turned towards him as he snapped the photo. I stood there for a minute and looked around. I looked at Makalu, the fifth highest mountain in the world, now far below me. Then I turned and looked into Tibet. The world seemed to go on forever. There were small clouds beneath me and it looked like the view out of the cockpit at work. I stood there for a little bit, mesmerised. The whole world lay at my feet.

I took off my pack and pulled out the large Air New Zealand flag. It had gone from the last thing I wanted to take to the summit to the main thing I wanted. This flag connected me not only to Air New Zealand but to all my friends and work colleagues, people who had supported and encouraged me so much. I held it up and Lhakpa snapped another photo. The wind started gusting a little and my down mitten flew away but thankfully I had it on a safety cord. I put the flag away and waved Lhakpa up to me so I could take a photo of us together. I put my arm around his shoulder and snapped a photo; he was cold as he had taken off his mask and gloves so he could take my photos.

The way I felt on the summit is hard to describe. More than anything, I felt humble to be standing there. I also felt a nervous knot in my stomach as I was way out of my comfort zone. There was still so much that could go wrong.

I wanted one more photo on the summit so I gave Lhakpa my camera and edged my way out along the narrow summit, then I slowly turned around and faced Lhakpa as he took a photo. This was a special picture because I was not standing there as a mountaineer conquering a mountain. Behind the mask and goggles, I was very scared and conscious of the fact I was only halfway. I edged my way back and there was one last thing I had to do – call Wendy.

Wendy was waiting for my call with lots of family and friends at our house in Auckland. Henry had been putting info on his website when he could so everyone knew when I was getting close to the summit.

Wendy had been waiting to hear from me all morning. It must have been terrible for her. She had gone to bed the night before knowing I was climbing high on Everest. I found out later that she managed to wait until midday before she poured herself a wine and sat for a while on her own.

I sat just below the summit, pulled out Dr Rob's sat phone and dialled my home number. I then realised I still had my hat, goggles and mask on. I put the phone down on my lap while I took off my hat, thinking, 'If I lose this hat, I'm going to lose my ears.' I tucked my hat carefully under my arm inside my jacket. Next I took off my goggles. Same thing, 'If I lose these, I'll be snow blind in a few minutes.' As I pulled my oxygen mask down, with the outside air at −55°C and a wind of 25 knots the condensation on my face instantly snap froze. It was excruciatingly painful. I clawed at the ice with my hands trying to wipe it away.

All this time, the phone line had been open and everyone at home was waiting with bated breath, listening to nothing but a huge, rushing wind noise. Finally organised, I picked up the phone and shouted, 'Wendy, can you hear me?'

Wendy shouted back, 'Yes! Yes! I can hear you, where are you?'

'I'm on the summit, it's really Wendy, windy.' I got my windys and Wendys mixed up.

Wendy said later I sounded really bad, slurring my words, with the wind roaring in the background – not the romantic vision she had of talking to someone on the summit of Everest.

I shouted, 'It's really windy – I've got to go …'

'Are you safe?' Wendy shouted back.

'Yes, yes, I'll call you from South Col. Bye, I love you.' I didn't wait for a response before ending the call. It was really difficult to speak in that temperature and wind.

Apparently, back in Auckland, my best friend Mat refused to celebrate until he knew I was down safe. Wendy's oldest sister Mel, who is always up for a celebration, wasn't having a bar of it and popped the champagne!

I put all my gear back on and sat on the summit again. There I pulled out the hair clippings from Wendy, Ethan, Maya and Dylan. I opened the small bag and released my beautiful family's hair from the roof of the world. I then took out the birth tag that Mum had sent me and tied it to a snow stake just below the summit. This was a special moment for me.

It was now time to head back down. As I moved off the summit I saw a large group coming up – my stay on top had been perfectly timed. As I got closer I saw Pat and Mikey on their way up. We shook hands as we passed.

Now I had the most dangerous part of the climb ahead of me – the descent. I knew that most of the accidents on Everest happened on the way down the mountain. I was feeling good and seemed to have plenty of energy left. The thing with the descent on Everest is you need to judge when you can arm-wrap and move down fast and when you must turn around and abseil down backwards.

I got to the top of the Hillary Step and clipped into one of the many ropes strung all over the place. The trick is choosing the newest rope. I turned around and leaned back, and then I turned and looked over my shoulder. The view took my breath away then it scared the wits out of me. I turned back and looked at my feet, which I couldn't see over my mask but I had a fair idea where I was putting them. I really didn't want to get tangled up in the ropes. This had happened to a few climbers before me and they had been flipped upside down. A few years before, the body of a climber that this had happened to was hanging upside down dead on the step.

I got to the bottom of the step, and then made it back along the Cornice Traverse and up the South Summit without once looking back. I had my head down and I was completely focused on what I was doing. I descended the Southeast Ridge and then it was time to get across the bands of rock of The Balcony.

Just as I started to descend, I saw a Sherpa in a yellow down suit disappearing climbing along The Balcony. Lhakpa had been in front of me and he had a yellow climbing suit. I got to the next anchor and by now it was getting very steep. I should have turned around backward and abseiled but I rushed and wrapped the rope around my arm and started off. I took about four steps down and hit the rocks. My feet flew out from under me and I fell, slipping down the rope. I strained hard and managed to hold on. I rolled over and clipped safely into the rope again. I just lay there, my heart pumping out of my chest. I was very close to getting the grand tour all the way into Tibet.

Another Sherpa abseiled past me and asked me if I was ok. I told him I was just a little shaken. He stayed with me while I fixed my abseil device to the rope.

The Sherpa in the yellow climbing suit was long gone. I couldn't believe it. Lhakpa had my spare bottle of oxygen and the thought of running out again really scared me. I descended a little and there was Lhakpa sitting there patiently waiting for me. I should have known he would never leave me. It was another climber in a yellow suit that I'd seen.

A little further on we came across two guys sitting in the snow, one with his oxygen mask pulled down looking half asleep. I casually said, 'Mate, it's not a good idea to be having a nap up here!'

He laughed a little and said they would be moving shortly, that they were just catching their breath. As Lhakpa and I moved off, I looked back a few times to make sure they were moving and not in trouble.

Lhakpa and I made it to the end of The Balcony and parted ways. He wanted to wait for his brother, who was descending at the same time. I decided I would be ok to descend the last few hours on my own. He helped me check my oxygen and I had a good amount left. Lhakpa kept a spare bottle in his pack in case anyone else needed it. He was a little worried about me continuing on my own, but I assured him I would be ok and I knew he would only be 30 minutes behind me.

I continued down and recognised the place where I had seen the body sitting on a rock. I looked around and saw nothing, no body, no backpack. I wondered if I had simply imagined it. With the lack of oxygen at this altitude, anything is possible. I'm still not convinced I really saw anything that night.

After a few more hours, I made it back to the South Col. Just as I was coming into camp a person ran up to me and gave me a big hug, shouting, 'Scott, you're alive, you're alive …'

'Mate, I'm not Scott, I'm Mike.'

'It's ok, Scott, you must be confused. We were so worried.' He was still hugging me and patting me on the back. I felt pretty stink as he was really convinced I was Scott.

'I'm not Scott, sorry, I'm Mike from New Zealand,' I said as I pulled my mask down.

He looked shocked. 'Oh no, you're not Scott. He had the same climbing suit as you, have you seen him?'

I told him I'd seen a guy in a similar suit sitting having a nap on The Balcony with another guy.

'Oh no! Did you try and help them?'

'Yeah, I told them it's not a good idea to sleep up there.'

'Is that all you did?' he asked, looking a bit shocked

'Yeah, they said they would move soon. I looked back at them a few times and they were moving ok. I'm sure they will be here soon.'

I might not have been Scott, but this complete stranger then walked me to my tent, unzipped it, helped me in and put my stove on and started melting snow for me. What a kind gesture.

I lay there for a few minutes before I called Wendy and told her I was down safe but the reality was I was nowhere near safe yet.

A short time later I was putting some more snow on the stove when I saw Lhakpa come into camp on his own. I put my boots on and hurried across to see if he was ok. He was lying spread-eagled on his back, not moving. When he saw me he got a shock and jumped up.

'You ok?' I asked

'No, no, I'm fine,' he assured me.

I think he thought no one was around so he could just relax for a second, then I came and spoiled it for him. He got into his tent and I went back to mine. It was now 1pm and I had been going since 6am the previous day – 31 hours climbing at this altitude without sleep. I closed my eyes and fell asleep easily. But I didn't get to sleep long before Pat turned up. He was in great spirits considering the state he had been in just before we'd set out the day before. He climbed into the tent and I gave him some water. He was grinning from ear to ear. He looked at me and just said, 'WOW!' That pretty much summed it up.

The wind was starting to blow and it was getting late in the afternoon and there was still no sign of Mikey. Despite being worried about him I was so tired I fell asleep. The next thing I knew a blast of wind hit me as my tent was unzipped. Then Mikey came flying in, his Sherpa almost chucking him inside. He collapsed on his sleeping bag and just lay there. 'You ok, Mikey?' Pat and I asked. He just moaned.

One thing about Mikey is that what he may lack in speed he makes up for in sheer guts and determination, but being out there for so long had taken its toll.

I let him sleep but after about half an hour he woke and asked me to take off his left boot. I sat up and started undoing his boot, pulling the outer shell off, then the inner boot, then peeling two layers of socks off. As I revealed his toes I thought I was seeing things with the torch light. His left big toe and the two toes next to it were a horrible dead grey colour.

I didn't know what to say but he could see in my face something was wrong.

'Ah, I think you might have a little frost nip, buddy,' I said, while actually thinking, 'Bloody hell, this is really serious.' I pulled his socks back on and gave him some water to drink. Mikey then asked me to go and get Dr Rob.

Even though Dr Rob's tent was only about five metres away, he wouldn't have heard me calling for him over the noise of the 40-knot wind so it took me about 20 minutes to get fully dressed, ready to venture out into the −40°C air.

Once I'd alerted Rob, it took him about 20 minutes to get himself organised to come over to our tent. His reaction to Mikey's feet was a little different to mine. 'Holy shit, Mikey. Look at your toes!'

Truth was, it was a serious injury and once his feet defrosted Mikey would be in serious pain. Dr Rob came up with a plan – Mikey would leave his toes frozen so he could get down the mountain and Dr Rob would assess them again down at Camp 2.

That night at Camp 4 was rough and to be honest scary. I woke a few times with the tent laying flat on my face. I then put all my gear on in case the tent ripped and blew away, it would be difficult to survive if that happened to you and you weren't prepared. I also had enough energy to boil water all night which helped the three of us in the tent. My plan of Camp 4 – summit – Camp 4 then Camp 2 worked. I was never ever going to continue down to Camp 2 in one go, I was always going to stop at Camp 4. But my sub-conscious mind didn't know this and I had heaps of energy.

After a rough night in the howling wind, I woke up feeling pretty good. I set off determined to make it all the way to base camp. Around midday I called Henry to ask him if I could continue down to base camp as I was feeling good. He said I had just missed the cut-off time and he would prefer it if I stayed the night at Camp 2. This time, I wasn't going to argue with him. At first I was disappointed but then everyone started rolling into camp.

That afternoon, everyone made it back to Camp 2 and we all sat around in the mess tent. By now, Mikey's toes had started to thaw and even though it must have been incredibly painful, he didn't complain. Quite by coincidence, a famous vascular surgeon Chris Imray was at Camp 2. He had plenty of experience of amputating climbers' digits and he was coming to have a look at Mikey's toes.

When Chris arrived, I recognised him as the guy who had thought I was Scott. 'Hi, I'm Mike from New Zealand, not Scott,' I said as I shook his hand. He laughed. Scott had turned up alive some time later the previous day.

He advised Mikey to get to base camp tomorrow and get an ultrasound there from the Himalayan rescue doctors to see how deep the damage was. If it was only on the surface, he would then have to get a helicopter from base camp straight down to Kathmandu as there could be a possibility of saving his toes. If it was really deep, then there was no chance of saving his toes and he could get a horse down from base camp.

The next morning I woke up to a beautiful day and managed to get going reasonably early. About an hour out of Camp 1, I heard the huge rumble of an avalanche and saw it tearing down off Nuptse on my left. It carved a path right across the whole Western Cwm, right across the track we were on. If I'd started out 30 minutes earlier, it could've taken me out – it wasn't worth thinking about.

We all regrouped at Camp 1, where good old Henry had left the camp in case of emergencies and so we could brew up. Then off we went, each at our own pace. Darwin's Corner came up quickly and I was so keen to get down, I ran past it. The rest of the Khumbu Icefall had changed so much I didn't recognise much of the route. The one thing that hadn't changed was that climbing down it still felt dangerous.

I walked the last part of the icefall with Dr Rob. Over the previous weeks, we had become good friends so it was a nice way to end the expedition. From the icefall Rob went to see his friends from another expedition and I walked back to base camp on my own.

The relief of being out of the icefall and knowing I had made it started to show. I began to stagger a little and bumped into a trekker who was visiting base camp. She looked horrified at the sight of me and asked sheepishly whether I'd come from the summit. I nodded. She asked if I needed help and offered to carry my bag. The concern on her face said it all. I told her I was fine and staggered off to our camp. I was at the end of my endurance but I had done it!

As I walked into camp Henry walked over and gave me a big bear hug. 'Well done, man, David would've been so proud of you.'

I finally lost it. I started crying great sobs and I just hugged Henry. He kept hugging me and saying 'Well done, man. Well done.' I just cried and cried. The relief, the emotion, missing my family and just making it all came crashing down. Not what you expect from a tough Everest summiteer.

Kenton came over, handed me a beer and gave me a big hug too. The beer was like giving a baby a pacifier – as soon as I started drinking it, I stopped crying.

Gradually the rest of the team rolled into camp. The news on Mikey's toes was bad – they were frozen deep. There was no point in getting a helicopter so a horse was booked for him to head down from the mountain the next morning.

I called Wendy from base camp. It was so good to hear her voice knowing that I was safe. Hearing her say, 'Mike, you are such a legend!' made me stop for a second and realise just how massive this achievement was. I'd never really thought about it that way. I couldn't wait to see her and I knew it wouldn't be long. She was leaving Auckland for Kathmandu that night to bring me home.

The next morning, I said my goodbyes to the Sherpas and took Lhakpa aside and gave him his well-earned tip. I said goodbye to Henry and set off to walk the 42 kilometres to Namchee. I walked most of the way on my own and as I rounded the corner just before Namchee I looked back at Everest. There was a plume of cloud coming off the summit showing the jet stream winds had moved back in rendering her unclimbable. How on earth did I climb that? It still hadn't sunk in.

After a night in Namchee, I walked to Lukla then flew to Kathmandu the following day. Wendy was due to arrive on the same day. I checked into our hotel and I realised my last two showers had been a while ago – one in April and one in May. Total. I was quite proud of that but I was pretty sure Wendy wouldn't be so thrilled.

I went and bought some soap, shampoo and shaving cream. Then it was back to the hotel for a good scrub and a long sit on a western style toilet before going out to the airport to meet Wendy.

The airport was the same as ever, hustle and bustle everywhere, it felt a little strange after being in the mountains for so long. I saw Wendy coming through Customs; she looked so beautiful. I hadn't seen her for two months. We kissed and hugged like there was no one else around, much to the amusement of the Nepalese.

We spent the next few days exploring Kathmandu before heading to Pokhara in western Nepal where we spent a night by the lake, watching water buffalo playing from over our candlelit dinner table. It was a world away from camping out on the slopes of Everest.

When we got back to Kathmandu, it was time to say goodbye to the rest of the team. Bo and Ward had already left, but we got to say goodbye to Kenton and Pat before they headed off. Mikey had managed to get his much needed medical attention in Kathmandu but there wasn't too much they could do. He needed surgery in England. Then it was time to say goodbye to Anna and Dr Rob. We had become such good mates, I knew I would see them both again.

Finally, it was time for Wendy and me to head home. As we took off I felt a little sad to be leaving Nepal, it is such a magical place. I wondered if I would ever be back.

RETURN TO EVEREST

Not long after I got home, Mum organised the most incredible surprise for me – a meeting with Sir Edmund Hillary. I couldn't believe it. I was going to meet the first man to ever summit Mt Everest and my hero.

Arriving at the Hillarys' house, I was very nervous. Lady June welcomed Wendy and me and shouted out to 'Ed'. Before I knew it I was standing there shaking Sir Ed's hand. I was surprised by just how tall he was. He looked a little frail and invited me to sit next to him by the fire. Wendy sat on another sofa and chatted to Lady June.

Sir Ed and I chatted away for a little bit about his recent visit to Nepal. Then Sir Ed asked if I'd just climbed Everest. I told him I had and showed him some of the photos I had had taken on the summit. He looked at the photos for a while and pointed out another mountain called Makalu that was in the background of my summit shots. Makalu is the fifth highest mountain in the world.

Sir Ed then spoke about his expedition in 1953. 'When I was on Everest, towards the end, there was no doubt that we were going to make the summit, so I turned my attention to Makalu and took lots of photos. That mountain was going to be our next expedition.' It was unclimbed at the time but was eventually first climbed by a French team in 1955.

I asked Sir Ed about the Hillary Step. He told me how he climbed up the crack of ice to the side of the rock on the step. That was exactly how I had climbed it 54 years later. Sir Ed seemed to like the fact that I had gone to Everest on my own and climbed with a Sherpa in a similar way he had on his summit day.

I politely asked if he could sign one of my photos and we both went into his kitchen where he signed my summit shot, then we had our photograph taken together. That single photograph means such a lot to me.

I could see that Lady June was about to prepare their dinner so we said our goodbyes and left. I just couldn't believe I had met Sir Ed and Lady June. I had asked Sir Ed questions he had been answering for 54 years and he had answered me as if I was the first person to ever ask him the question. From that moment I decided to do the same thing – if anyone asked me questions about Everest, I would answer them with the same respect and enthusiasm as Sir Ed had answered mine.

In the week before I went back to work, I had to have a medical to make sure I was ok to start flying again. My heart rate was very low due to all the extra red blood cells running through my veins and I had also lost 11 kilograms, most of which I'd dropped in the week when I summited.

That same week, I had a call from Air New Zealand to ask if I would like to come in and meet the company's chief executive, Rob Fyfe. I was chuffed to be invited to see him. I had never even been on the executive floor of Air New Zealand before, let alone met the big boss, so I had no idea what to expect. What I did know was that Rob had been a great CEO and had turned the company around in a very short time, making us all very proud to work there.

Apparently, one of Wendy's emails updating some of my friends on my progress towards the summit had been forwarded to Rob. He wanted to know how I came to be on Everest without anyone knowing. My fleet manager explained that was the way I wanted it.

Sitting in Rob's office, we chatted about Everest and the whole adventure. He said he couldn't believe that one of his guys climbed Everest without him knowing. He then asked me to talk to the management team. I thought he was talking about the top10 executives but then I realised he meant about 120 managers from all over the company. There was no way I was going to do it – I hated public speaking. But Rob wasn't having it: 'Come on, it will be a challenge!'

When I told him I'd prefer death over public speaking, Rob made me an offer I couldn't refuse. 'How about I give you a media coach? He'll teach you how to speak in public and then you could use that skill in the future.'

'Ummmm, unlimited lessons?' I asked sheepishly.

'Unlimited lessons,' he replied. I cautiously agreed and left Rob's office feeling both chuffed and scared about my upcoming speech.

That one meeting sent me off on a new direction in my life. I met up with Rob's coach, Kevin Simms, who turned out to be the country's leading professional development coach.

When the morning came for my speech, I was nervous yet confident. It was pretty humbling to stand in front of 120 executives from the company you work for all waiting to hear what you have to say. The speech went well and I got a standing ovation. I was then invited to speak to 350 people about my Everest climb at an Air New Zealand leadership conference in Queenstown and later to be the guest speaker at an aero medicine convention in Darwin, Australia.

This event was full of doctors, professors and even NASA's chief medical officer. Kevin Simms used to say that if you're not nervous you don't care. Well, I must have cared heaps because every time I had to speak in front of a crowd I was absolutely bricking it. After a while, I had so many invitations to speak that I had to learn to say no. It was quite hard for me but I had to find a balance between working, speaking and my home life.

After I got back it took a bit for me to adjust to life post-Everest. From climbing the world's highest mountain to going back to my day job and doing normal stuff like grocery shopping was quite a challenge. It took a bit of a toll on my relationship with Wendy. She'd had to hold things together while I was away and now I was back we had to return to so-called normal life. Thankfully, with a bit of hard work and time, we came out the other side stronger and more in love than ever before.

I'm brave enough to admit I learned a few cool things through the whole process. One was to stop focusing on what the other person was doing, and to start looking at what I was doing. I learned to forget about anything that Wendy was doing that bugged me and instead to address my own mistakes and issues.

The other cool thing I learned is called a 10:10. If you're having an argument with your partner then anyone can call a 10:10, then you both sit down and one person speaks uninterrupted and the other person has to listen. And you better listen good because at the end you have to reflect and repeat what they have said, with no judgment or opinions. If they say, 'The world is flat,' then you repeat it back – 'Ok, you said the world is flat.' No judgment, no opinions. I found this especially hard and had to bite my tongue many times. Then it's your turn to speak and be listened to uninterrupted. What tends to happen is whatever it is you were arguing about begins to seem really trivial when you hear yourself speaking about it out loud and uninterrupted!

In January 2008, I was in Fiji on a flying duty when Wendy called me with the sad news that Sir Edmund had passed away. It was a very sad day for New Zealand – a true legend had gone. I came home the next day and thought about how I could pay my respects to Sir Ed. At the time, 29 New Zealanders had summited Everest and only 25 of them were still alive. I liked the idea of the summiteers being involved in Sir Ed's state funeral in some way but I had no idea who to talk to about it. I decided to go straight to the top and I emailed the Prime Minister, Helen Clark. Within 30 minutes I got a reply from her private secretary.

'Dear Mr Allsop, The Prime Minister agrees with your idea of the living Everest summiteers being involved in the state funeral. Could you please provide us with the contact details of all of New Zealand's Everest summiteers.' I was stunned to get a response from the Prime Minister so quickly.

A few days later a formal invitation from the Prime Minister's office arrived. The day of the funeral came and Wendy and I headed to the cathedral and queued up with thousands of people. You had to have an invitation to get in. When I showed the security guard our invitation he said we were in the private chapel and pointed to a small church beside the cathedral.

Wendy and I walked over, and I saw Mark Inglis and said hello. Towards the back of the church there was a bench marked 'mountaineers'. I was proud to go and sit there. When I looked around there were so many dignitaries, world leaders and famous people. The service was a moving reflection of the great man's life. As I watched Sir Ed's coffin carried from the cathedral, I felt sad that a New Zealand legend had passed and I felt so privileged to have met him. There was a book of condolences for people at the service to write in. Humbled, I wrote, 'For I am a lucky man, I have stood on the summit of Everest and met Sir Edmund Hillary.'

*

Life quickly got back into its normal patterns. I loved my work, I loved being a dad and I loved spending time with Wendy, but thoughts of new adventures were never far away. One night when we were out for dinner, Wendy could tell that I had itchy feet. She told me that if I needed to climb Everest again, we'd find a way to do it.

I'm not sure if she really meant it but by saying I could go meant that she was giving me the space to work it out for myself. When it came down to it, I decided that my three beautiful kids needed their dad more than I needed to climb Everest again. Dads are so important and I should know because mine buggered off when I was 10 years old.

If I wasn't going to climb Everest again, I knew I needed to do something to refill the tank – maybe something that included the kids. I came up with the idea of taking each of my children to see Everest once they turned seven. Wendy thought it was a great idea – I would not only get to spend some magic time with Ethan but I'd also see my Sherpa friends again and spend time on Everest.

And so the planning began. Given I'd be exposing Ethan to altitude and to third world health issues, I went to see Dr Marc Shaw, who runs Worldwise, one of the world's best travel medicine clinics. He gave me some good advice, but it would mean about seven vaccinations for Ethan. He had the shots in two sessions and he was so brave and didn't cry.

There was getting all the gear and also a little training and before long it was time to go. So I bought Ethan some trekking gear, boots, poles and a sleeping bag. We would go training up and down Mt Eden, a small volcanic hill in our neighbourhood, also a bit of running and walking with a pack on. It had to be fun and cool, I was not going to be dragging a moaning child all the way to see Everest. But Ethan loved it and lapped it up.

Kids spell love – T.I.M.E.

On departure day, both Ethan and Maya had a Taekwondo grading before Ethan and I flew out to Hong Kong. I worked that morning and turned up just as the grading was finished. Ethan had been jumping up the gym steps and had missed one, smashing his face on the wooden step and knocking his two front teeth out. There was blood everywhere. After a quick clean-up, he surprised everyone by continuing his grading and gaining a 100 per cent pass. When I looked at Ethan's teeth and gums they were bad. His teeth had pushed up and punctured his cheeks and tongue. I took him to an emergency dentist who said that the teeth that had been knocked out were his baby teeth, so we would be fine to travel. What a relief!

After brief stopovers in Hong Kong and Delhi, we finally took off for Kathmandu. The flight was fine but looking out the window I could see thunderstorms building. Sure enough, Kathmandu airport was closed due to the storms. The captain informed us that we would divert to a small airport in northern India, refuel and return to Delhi. It wasn't the greatest start to Ethan's first visit to the Himalayas.

When we landed back in Delhi, there was total chaos with the airline struggling to arrange buses and hotel accommodation for us all. Ethan finally fell asleep on the bus to the hotel, where we were told we would be sharing rooms with at least two others. But I had a plan. Ethan woke up and I told him to pretend he was still asleep, which he gladly did. I then found the manager and politely asked for a room. He saw Ethan half asleep and assumed he was sick so instantly organised a room for us on our own.

The next day we checked out and headed back to the airport. This time there was a big problem. The army guards wouldn't let us into the terminal because our tickets had the wrong date on them. I explained that we had been diverted but it made no difference. We were told we'd have to go to the Jet Airways office and get a letter. The office was a four-hour return trip from the airport and we would miss our flight.

I made sure Ethan wasn't watching and I slipped the guard US$10. 'This way, sir, enjoy your flight ...' Problem solved.

This time our flight made it into Kathmandu. We collected our bags and were met by a rep from Himalayan Guides, the company who had helped me out with my Everest climb, who drove us into town. I sat and just watched Ethan taking in all the people and colour. After checking into my favourite Nepalese-run hotel, Hotel Manaslu, the pair of us headed off into town.

I'd explained the bartering process to Ethan and he was keen to try it. The first shop we went to, he was a bit shy but I insisted he went in on his own and I would wait outside. He did well and paid much less than the asking price for a small bag. The Nepalese just loved him and all the storekeepers kept saying he would bring them luck and would discount the price for him. By the end of the day Ethan had worked out he could get stuff really cheap. He'd taken to bartering so well that I had to have a chat with him about what's fair. I told him he wasn't allowed to go below half the asking price.

The next day Ethan and I went out to the local domestic airport. As we waited to board our flight, a man asked me how old my son was. I looked up to see Peter Hillary standing there.

'Wow! Hi, Peter, I'm Mike. This is Ethan. He's seven. I'm a big fan. You've done some amazing climbing.' It was pretty cool meeting him here given he'd first visited the country with his mountain-climber father, and here I was bringing my son to see the Himalayas for the first time.

Peter is an amazing climber and some of his expeditions have been among the boldest and hardest ever attempted. We chatted for a while. Ethan turned a bit shy and we said goodbye. As we got on the plane, Ethan said to me, 'I can't believe I met Peter Hillary.'

Even though I'd done this flight before, it was scarier because I had Ethan with me but again the local pilots did an outstanding job and we landed safely. We walked over to Paradise Lodge and met Dawa. She was thrilled to meet Ethan and she made a real fuss of him. And then Peter walked in – it turned out that Dawa was a good family friend of the Hillarys. We all sat down and had tea together. I knew Ethan would love a photo with Peter and he kindly got up and we took a couple of photos. Ethan was rapt.

After having a good catch-up with Dawa, Ethan and I were off trekking. We had a great day with many stops at teahouses along the way. It took me a while to work out that if Ethan went ahead and stopped when he wanted to we would cover much more ground. The key was keeping it fun. This was easy because there was always something different to look at – yak trains coming past, friendly locals who don't see many western kids, and, of course, the beautiful scenery … but no mountains yet.

We came across a small Sherpa boy herding a big yak. The yak was behaving badly and wouldn't do anything the boy wanted. Then, almost in slow motion, the boy raised a big stick. I thought, 'NO! Don't do it!' Then I watched the stick slowly fall and hit the yak really hard. At that point, everything sped up. The yak came running straight towards me and Ethan. We ran to the right, so did the yak. We darted left and the yak did the same. It was only metres away from us and moving fast. I grabbed Ethan by the scruff of his neck and threw him into a bush before jumping in after him. The yak thundered past. We were safe. We stood up, looked at each other and laughed nervously. 'Er, let's not tell Mum about that, eh, buddy?'

We paced it nice and slow, taking three days to get to Namchee. Dr Rob had recommended that we stay at a place called Namaste Lodge, owned by Palden Sherpa. It was absolutely fantastic with a real family atmosphere to it. Ethan and I rested there for a day and then walked over to the school in Khumjung. This was the first school that Sir Ed built. To get there was a hard walk up a very steep hill, which peaks at just over 4200 metres. Ethan did so well getting up there. As we came up to the top of the hill before the descent into the village of Khumjung, Mt Everest came into view. It was such a special thing to sit down on a rock and show my son Everest. He had so many questions. 'Wow, Dad, is that Everest?' 'How did you climb it?' 'How long did it take?'

After visiting the school at Khumjung, we went to the local monastery where they have a Yeti skull. Ethan was fascinated with the skull and this led to many days of questions about the Yeti. Then we stopped at the local bakery. Ethan had been having a few issues eating as he didn't like the local food much. He saw milkshakes on the menu and decided he wanted one. I asked the bakery staff about the milk powder and water they used and it all sounded ok so I ordered him one. He loved it.

When we got back to Khumjung Ethan had a good dinner of roasted chicken and went to bed early. It had been a long day for both of us. Later that night, he woke with a very sore tummy and really bad diarrhoea. I was really worried so I rang Dr Rob. He was climbing Everest for the sixth time and was due to come down from base camp for a rest so he agreed to come all the way to Namchee to see Ethan.

Since we'd met on Everest in 2007, Dr Rob had spent some time staying with us in Auckland. The kids absolutely loved him. He spent endless hours playing with them, wrestling or jumping on the trampoline. They weren't the only ones who took a shine to him. Wendy's girlfriends seemed to find a lot of excuses to come and visit while he was staying. I can't imagine what they saw in this handsome, charming British doctor …

The next day Dr Rob arrived in Namchee and Ethan was over the moon to see him. He treated Ethan with rehydration fluids only and spent the next few days hanging around with us.

It was then time to say goodbye. Ethan hugged Dr Rob and cried as we walked off down the valley. I tried to comfort him but he knew that Dr Rob was going back to climb Everest. And he knew that people got killed climbing. It was so hard for the young fella. It was also an eye opener for me – there was no way I would ever climb Everest again while my kids were still young.

The whole trip with Ethan was special. The reward for me was seeing the look on Ethan's face when he was telling the rest of the family the stories of what he had seen while we were away.

Kids absolutely love to have time spent with them. It doesn't have to be as massive as trekking to Everest – it can be anything at all as long as it's one on one.

To be honest, I think seven is a bit young to take a child on such a journey as it's a lot of work to keep them safe and healthy, but I've started something now and I will finish it by taking Maya and Dylan when they turn seven.

YETI

The trip with Ethan served another purpose. With plenty of help and advice from old Everest hands like Dr Rob, Henry and his wife Sue, I began planning a new business, a trekking business. My plan was to offer adventures to Everest base camp. I wanted to do things a little differently to most of the standard trek companies – all of our Sherpa guides would be Everest summiteers and we would stay only in small, family-run teahouses.

I opened the first trip up to Air New Zealand staff and within four days it had sold out. The team was made up of people from all over the company, including the CEO, Rob Fyfe.

One night, I gathered the team together so they could all meet and we could talk about what preparations needed to be done before we left for Nepal. With me that night I took a book that had a section about the Pangboche Yeti hand and skull. I began to tell the rest of the team about meeting Lama Geshe and about the impact that losing the artefacts had had on the village.

According to local lore, the hand and skull had been in the Pangboche monastery for many centuries. Visitors would pay the monks to allow them to see these rare pieces of the mythical beast.

In the 1950s Texan oil millionaire, Tom Slick, funded a large expedition to the area around Everest to look for the Yeti. He employed an experienced and well-known Yeti hunter, Peter Byrne, and it was Byrne who led the expedition to Pangboche. He dismissed the Pangboche skull as a fake but was more intrigued by the hand. In his opinion, it was neither human nor ape – it was, he believed, from an unknown species. The monks refused to allow the hand to be taken away for testing, saying that it was very precious and bad things would happen to the village if it was ever taken away.

Byrne returned to the village the following year and here's where the tale gets a little murky. According to some, he got the monks drunk and while they were sleeping he cut off the thumb and forefinger from the Yeti hand and replaced them with human bones. The monks were none the wiser.

Curious about this, I asked Mr Byrne, now in his 80s, and he said that he had negotiated with the monks and paid them a large sum of money to cut off two fingers and replace them. Whatever the truth, he ended up with two very rare specimens.

The bones were then taken to India and smuggled out of the country by the American actor Jimmy Stewart.

Apparently, banking on Customs officers not looking through a lady's underwear, Stewart's wife Gloria put the bones into a lingerie box and carried them in her luggage to London. When they arrived, their luggage was inspected by British Customs then forwarded to the couple's hotel. When she opened her suitcase, Gloria Stewart found everything had been searched apart from the lingerie box.

The bones were then examined by specialists at a university who pronounced them to have come from an undetermined species. The Yeti hunters were happy. The monastery was happy – they still had their hand and people would still visit them paying a small donation to see the artefacts. That was until the 1990s when an American TV network broadcast a story on the Yeti pieces and a short time later, the artefacts were stolen. The monks and the local villagers were devastated.

When I was telling the Everest crew the yarn of the Yeti hand, I mentioned that I'd thought about getting some replicas made that would encourage people to go up and visit the monastery. I'd never really done anything more than think about it but Rob Fyfe was determined that would change. He offered to introduce me to multiple Oscar winner Sir Richard Taylor at Weta Workshop, home of the special effects for *The Lord of the Rings* movies.

Rob emailed Sir Richard and he said he would love to help. I sent all of my photos of the hand down to the team at Weta Workshop and they got to work straight away. A week later, they called me to say that the replica hand and skull were both ready so I flew down to collect them. I was absolutely stunned at their appearance – they looked identical to the originals in the photographs. They really are miracle workers.

Through our website, www.returnthehand.com, I started a worldwide search for the original artefacts that had been stolen from the monastery. I started getting interest from all over the world, but most of it was from people who thought I was going off in search of the Yeti. That was the furthest thing from my mind – I just wanted to get the artefacts returned so my friends could get their income back. I also wanted to encourage visitors to go and see the monastery.

When the time came to take everyone on the adventure, I was a bit nervous as guiding people at high altitude can bring with it some unique challenges and risks. After two days in Kathmandu, we flew up to Lukla. As we approached to land, we seemed a little high on the approach. I looked out the window and we were crossing the end of the airstrip. Next I saw the touchdown makings float past. We hit hard, so hard that there were a few screams from the team, including myself – pretty funny since we were all airline employees! Once we'd taxied up to the gate area, the ground crew had trouble opening the door, possibly because it had twisted during the heavy landing. There was nothing else for it – the rear luggage hold was unloaded and we all piled out the tiny cargo hatch. If that wasn't weird enough, after we'd disembarked another 20 passengers squeezed through the hatch to board the plane.

Our head Sherpa guides, Ang Nuru and Nawang, were both Everest summiteers. Ang Nuru had summited twice – once without oxygen. He had also climbed Cho Oyu, the sixth highest mountain in the world, 13 times. Nawang had been on Everest in 1996 during the big disaster in May and had climbed up to Camp 4 to rescue several climbers. Ang Nuru and Nawang would be our guides for the two weeks.

Together we all trekked up to Monjo for the night. The next day we climbed the Namchee Hill and up to 3450 metres (11,319 feet). This is where we first started feeling the altitude. After two nights in Namchee, we headed up to Pangboche. It's the hardest day's trekking but this is where the Himalayas open up. From here, we could see Everest and Ama Dablam towering into the sky.

Of course I'd arranged for us to stay with my old friends Nima and Gyurme at Sonam Lodge. It was great to see them again. Once everyone was settled in, I asked Rob Fyfe to come with me to visit Lama Geshe. Even though he wasn't in charge of the monastery, I really wanted Lama Geshe to bless the replica Yeti artefacts.

When we arrived at his place, Lama Geshe didn't seem too impressed to have his evening interrupted by us. When we showed him the artefacts, he had many questions. I was glad Rob was with me as some of the questions were pretty full-on. I was shocked to hear Lama Geshe ask, 'Why do we need these things? Our village is peaceful and content. They might bring trouble to this village.'

I panicked that I might have misjudged everything and made a terrible mistake. Perhaps these people were not interested in money and the lost income from the replicas wasn't that important to them after all. Thankfully, Rob spoke to Lama Geshe at length and after a while he came around to the idea of restoring the artefacts to the monastery. Before we left I asked Lama Geshe to name my other two children, Ethan and Maya; he said he would consider the request.

The next day Lama Geshe agreed to formally bless the skull and hand before we took them down to present them to the monastery. The team gathered at the Lama's house and went inside for the blessing. As we entered his living room, we bowed our heads and each passed him a silk scarf with a small donation wrapped up in it. He then put the donation aside and placed the scarves around our necks. Each of us then touched heads with the Lama as he chanted a mantra. It was very special. Once we were all seated, Ang Nuru interpreted for Lama Geshe and he said he was very grateful for the replica artefacts. I was relieved when he thanked me, saying no one else had ever thought to do such a thing for Pangboche.

He then blessed us with the same mantra he had chanted when he blessed me on Everest four years earlier. I could feel the emotion inside me and a few tears started to flow. Lama Geshe then asked me to come forward and said he had named Ethan 'Tsering Dorjee', long life and strong like a diamond. He then said he had never named a girl ever but had decided to name my Maya, her name would be 'Namkha Dolma', blue sky green Tara, which means great goddess and enlightenment.

After receiving Lama Geshe's blessing, we all went down to the monastery to present the artefacts to the Lama there.

News about the replicas had spread and a small crowd of locals had gathered. The team met with the monastery council and the formal handover took place. I pulled out the skull and presented it to the head Lama of the monastery. He looked at it with great interest and then passed it down the line of council members. This was the real test as to how good the replicas were. The council members were astonished at the detail on the skull, pronouncing it to be just like the real one.

Then I brought out the replica Yeti hand, which was in a beautiful handmade Nepali wooden box, with the words 'From your New Zealand friends' carved on the base of it. I lifted the box and opened it to face the head Lama. His eyes opened wide and as he held the hand up in the air, there was a gasp from some of the local people. He said something in Sherpa and Ang Nuru turned to me, saying, 'He is telling everyone you have brought the real hand back.'

I was shocked, 'No, no!' I said. 'Zuma, zuma!', meaning 'Fake, fake!'

The Lama looked at me and I showed him that the hand was not made of real bone. He found it hard to believe as it was so much like his original artefact. I explained how I hoped that it might restore a small income to his monastery from people making donations to view the artefacts. The Lama thanked us all and we shared some tea.

As we departed, the head Lama shook my hand as Ang Nuru interpreted for us – 'He says you are very welcome to come back any time and view the artefacts – but bring a donation!'

I looked at the Lama and he laughed heartily. It was great to see that his joke had survived the Sherpa–English translation.

MAD, BAD AND DANGEROUS TO KNOW

About four years after I summited Everest, I started to get really itchy feet again. It was time for me to begin planning a huge new adventure, something that would scare me, something that seemed almost impossible. As usual, it was a book that provided my inspiration. I read *Mad, Bad and Dangerous to Know* by the explorer Sir Ranulph Fiennes. In it he describes his mission with Mike Stroud to run seven marathons on seven continents in seven days.

That was it! Running a marathon on a new continent each day for a week was made all the more impossible because I was a terrible runner. I mentioned my plan to Rob Fyfe and he offered me whatever help the airline could give me. That decided it for me – this was going to be my next big adventure.

But this time it had to be an adventure not only for me – I really wanted it to do some good for other people too. I was

314

thinking about possible charities to work with when Wendy suggested KidsCan. They provide thousands of New Zealand kids with breakfasts, lunches, shoes, raincoats … anything to give them a better start in life. It was the perfect fit for me and they really understood what I was hoping to do.

And so the 777 Project was born. I started planning furiously. If I was going to take on this crazy challenge, I was going to do my absolute best for myself and for the team at KidsCan. The more people I had onboard with me, the better it would be.

The logistics involved in getting me from one continent to another with enough time to run 42 kilometres on each one were a nightmare. Thankfully, my mate Torran Lepper at the Air New Zealand Holiday Shop in New Plymouth loves a challenge. He put in many hours' work to find flights that connected. Even as a pilot, I was pretty surprised to see how much flight timetables can change. The route Torran came up with in the end was to start the week in the Falkland Islands (Antarctica), then fly to Santiago in Chile (South America), on to Los Angeles (North America), then to London (Europe), then a hop across to Casablanca in Morocco (Africa), before heading to Hong Kong (Asia) and finally home to New Zealand (Australasia). Whew!

The question arose as to whether the Falklands were actually in Antarctica. My reply was to quote Sir Ranulph Fiennes, who said, 'The question has been asked whether the Falklands are genuinely part of the Antarctic continent or not. Well, they aren't part of South America and the Antarctic Dictionary assures me Antarctica comprises the continent and its surrounding seas and islands. Support came from quite another direction with the illustrious nineteenth-century botantist Sir Joseph Hooker writing about the Flora of the Falklands and South Shetlands in his *Flora Antarctica*. It was good enough for me.' And if it was good enough for Sir Ranulph Fiennes it was good enough for me too. It was all on in every aspect except one – training. Well, running, actually. The truth was that I'd never run a marathon before. Hell, I'd never even run a half marathon before. Talk about putting myself out there.

So what did I do? I read a few books on marathon training! Then I went on a five-kilometre run. I was fit. I went to a gym three times a week and I could trek to Everest base camp easily. How hard could running five kilometres be? Yeah, pretty hard. By the end of the run my legs hurt, my back hurt, everything hurt. I felt terrible. Seven marathons? The thought of just one scared me.

At my local gym there was a superstar trainer called David Bryson, who was the assistant conditioning coach for the New Zealand football team. He really knew his stuff and I started working with him. As well as getting some coaching I spent a lot of time working on correcting my running style, which helped a lot with the pain.

I slowly started to clock up the miles and before long I'd run my first half marathon distance. I felt ok while I was running it and I did manage to run the whole thing but at the finish I was completely exhausted and felt really sick. All I could do was keep running and stop worrying about doing seven marathons and just concentrate on doing one.

Interspersed with the training, I also tried to get some sponsors onboard to help support the project. Air New Zealand had pledged flights on the routes that we fly – in Business Premiere, which was a really great gesture. But this made up only three of the 11 sectors I was going to have to fly to cover all seven continents.

One of the first sponsors to come onboard with the project was Vodafone. I hoped they might support me with the cost of data and phone calls during the mission because it was vital that I be able to communicate while I was away so I could rally interest and donations for KidsCan. I was delighted to find that they were keen to support the project in any way they could and Vodafone joined Air New Zealand as my two key sponsors.

There was one company I tried hard to get onboard. It was a large vitamin company whose products I'd been taking for years, who I thought would be a perfect partner for the project. I couldn't get them to even acknowledge an email. I was pretty frustrated about it and I was talking to one of the other parents while we were watching Ethan play cricket one night.

I was a bit surprised when she said, 'We'll sponsor you, Mike.' I wondered if she really understood what she was promising me but then she explained she was partnered with an international company called USANA, who make health products to a pharmaceutical level.

Before long, a box of USANA products turned up and I started taking them. After a few weeks I honestly couldn't believe the results. I had more energy and didn't need a sleep in the afternoons after training, also I was recovering quicker. I knew this as I would take my resting heart rate each morning, I was recovering quicker back to normal. I called Paula and said, 'This has to be in my head,' to which she said 'No Mike, that's what supplements that are manufactured to pharmaceutical level are supposed to do.' USANA became a huge part of the 777 Project.

My training continued and I was now clocking up the miles and getting fitter and stronger.

A few months later I completed my first marathon distance in training. I was totally stuffed at the end. When I got home, I hopped into an ice bath, which helps with muscle recovery, and, boy, did I need it. Everything was shaking and I felt horrible. It was then I realised the enormity of the task I had set myself. It really scared me.

I kept running but once I had completed two marathons back to back, that was the peak of my long distance training. I didn't see much point in pushing my body any harder than that until I really had to.

The hardest thing for me wasn't finding or setting a huge goal – it was having the guts to tell people what I was planning to do. With climbing Everest, I didn't tell many people I was doing it so there wasn't much pressure on me. But the 777 Project was so public, I really felt the pressure on me mounting. So many people were relying on me – my sponsors, my charity, the media – and I was really feeling it.

And the 777 Project wasn't the only pressure I'd put on myself. I decided I needed to do something pretty extreme before I took on the project. I needed to find my inner strength, to push myself beyond my limits and to make sure I still had it in me. I wanted to get myself in a position where being strong was my only option. I was taking another team to Everest base camp so I decided to have a crack at breaking the world record for the highest marathon ever run.

I planned to start at 5639 metres (18,503 feet) then descend to 5030 metres (16,500 feet) before climbing back up to 5420 metres (17,782 feet) before finishing around 4500 metres (14,760). I had no idea if I could do it – I had never run at that altitude before.

Before we left for base camp, the Lama from the Pangboche monastery emailed me asking for some help. One of the stupas, or religious shrines, in the village had been destroyed by Tibetans who had come across the border looking for riches. They pulled the stupa apart looking for precious beads and gold that were rumoured to be inside. The Lama asked Nawang to email me and ask for my help. He said, 'The Lama says you are very kind to Buddhists. If you can help us you will have a good next life.'

With everything I had planned in this life, how could I say no to a good time in the next one? What they needed was 600 kilograms of cement to rebuild and repair the stupa. The only issue was that the nearest road was about 350 kilometres away. Airlifting it was the only answer but to get it carried from an airfield 40 kilometres away was going to cost $100 per bag of cement.

I emailed the first team I'd taken to Everest asking them if anyone wanted a good life. I sold 12 bags in about two hours, with each person putting their order in for what they would like to be in their next life, some of the requests were very funny. I sent the money over to Pangboche later that day, the only condition being that the next Air New Zealand base camp team be allowed to help paint the stupa once it was repaired.

With the stupa sorted, it was time to get back to thinking about running. I decided I needed to talk to someone who really knew what it was to push yourself to the limit. I got in touch with the ultramarathon runner Lisa Tamati. Lisa had done some amazingly tough races all over the world so I figured she was the perfect person to advise me on how to take on such a massive challenge.

I told her all my plans and asked her what she thought I should do. Her advice surprised me. 'Stop running marathons.' Eh? But I needed to train to do seven in a week so surely more was better? Then she explained that my body would take a month to recover from each one. I gulped. I'd done six in the previous month.

Lisa then asked how I was holding up. At that stage, everything was fine. I felt strong and fit and I had no injuries. I explained to her that I only had one more marathon to do before I had a scheduled six-week taper before taking off on the 777 Project. Then I rather gingerly mentioned that it was going to be the world's highest marathon. The great thing about ultramarathon runners is that not much surprises them. Lisa just urged me to be careful and suggested that I should turn up to the 777 start slightly overweight and slightly undertrained but, most importantly, uninjured.

With Lisa's advice in mind I departed for base camp with

another great team from Air New Zealand. On the day of my marathon, the plan was for the whole team to get up early and climb the trekking peak, Kalapatar. Once at 5639 metres, I would begin my record attempt. Of course, because I was running I decided to leave a couple of hours before the rest of them to make sure I was organised when the time came to start. There were four Sherpa guides and four porters looking after everyone so I was happy. A couple of the guys had decided not to climb so they headed down to Gorak Shep village where I'd see them a bit later on.

Ang Nuru was going to climb and run with me until we reached the high pass about halfway through the marathon. It was cold when we set off and the climb was steep and difficult. I asked Ang Nuru a few times if the team would be coming up this way. He assured me they weren't as it was too difficult for them. Eventually we reached the top of the peak, 5639 metres high, and I was exhausted – already! My heart was pounding, my legs felt heavy and it was difficult to take even a single step. The thought of starting a marathon seemed insane but I didn't allow myself to think about it. I just focused on the next thing I needed to do.

The sun was rising over Everest and it was pure magic. I put my headphones on and listened to some music to psych myself up. I was using two GPS devices to track my progress: a brand new Garmin watch that recorded data every second and was very accurate, and a Spot tracker which would ping a signal up to a satellite every seven minutes and would also update a map on my website so everyone back home could watch me live.

I pushed 'start' on my GPSs and Ang Nuru and I were off running downhill, trying not to stress my knees too much or fall over. We made it down to the frozen lake bed of Gorak Shep quite quickly. I kept running and Ang Nuru went in to see if the two team members who didn't want to climb up were ok. He caught me up shortly after and said they were fine.

I ran hard for the next hour and when I looked at my watch I found I'd only covered 5.5 kilometres but at least I was now at 5180 metres so I just kept going. I arrived in the village of Dzongla (4830 metres), had a quick cup of tea then started the climb up the Cho La Pass. Having just run a massive downhill, climbing up again was a killer.

There was a large avalanche just across the valley, which made both Ang Nuru's and my heart miss a beat. Crossing the Cho La Pass was very beautiful but incredibly cold. Unfortunately, the cold affected the battery on my Garmin GPS watch and it died around the 23-kilometre mark. I was gutted as I needed the GPS data to present to the Guinness world record people. I still had my Spot tracker going strong but the data from this wasn't accurate enough to provide the proof they needed.

Ang Nuru left me at the far end of the pass, pointing to a mark way in the far distance that I needed to head towards. The Cho La pass area is desolate, barren and very high. Ang Nuru said, 'Mikey, you must be careful. People disappear here, never to be seen again. Promise me you will be careful.' He looked very worried. I'd never seen him like that before.

For the next six hours, I didn't see another living person. It was difficult to run and give it my all when there was no fixed finish line. I went into survival mode and moved as fast as I could. After another three hours I found a little teahouse and the lady there asked if I was Mike. My friend Gyurme had been planning to meet me there but he had left 30 minutes before I got there, he thought I must have stayed in a teahouse somewhere as it was so much later. I figured I'd catch up with him in Phortse, the next village along the way, which I thought was about 10 minutes away. 'Oh no,' she said. 'It's at least two and a half hours away.' My heart sank. Since waking up at 3am I had been on the go for almost 15 hours giving it my all.

By 6pm I was still running. I still had food and water, and I was still able to keep warm, but when night fell I started to worry. Thick cloud rolled in and I could only see a few feet in front of me. It got dark very quickly. The night was so black that there was no difference between having my eyes closed tight or open wide. I had a head torch with me but because I'd started running in the dark that morning, the batteries had gone flat. Thankfully, I had a small emergency LED light but I knew the battery on it wouldn't last long. I'd been on the move for 15 hours and things were getting serious. I knew I was starting to stagger a bit so I could easily slip off the track and fall to my death. *I* didn't know where I was, but my Spot tracker was telling everyone at home exactly where I was. At least if I fell off the track they would find me – dead or alive … probably dead.

I marked the time whenever I passed an abandoned hut so I knew I could find shelter if I needed to. I set myself a time limit of 18 hours so I had until 10pm before I would seek shelter and hunker down for the night. In the meantime, I would keep going. I tried not to think about the Yeti. I'm not sure if I fully believe in the Yeti but it would be fair to say that there is something out in the Himalayas that makes a very strange noise, leaves large tracks and scares the crap out of the locals.

I came around a corner and almost bumped into a group of large thar, a type of Himalayan goat. I think one got more of a fright than I did and it took off crashing down a steep slope. I tried not to think about the Yeti or the Tibetan bears or the snow leopards … My mind was a bit of a shambles. I thought that I'd be fine if there were no rhododendrons around because legend has it that Yetis love rhododendrons. But then I shone my little torch up and I was smack in the middle of a large rhododendron forest. 'There's no such thing as Yetis, there's no such thing as Yetis …' and I took off.

It seemed like ages before the little lights of Phortse peeked through the clouds. I knocked on the door of a small house and asked for help. They took me to a little teahouse, where I told the owner I'd come from Kalapatar via the Cho La Pass. He said, 'Impossible. Not possible. I've never heard of anyone doing that and I've been here for 65 years.'

I didn't even know if I'd made the 42-kilometre distance but I was totally shagged! I tried to ring my Sherpa friends but the phone wouldn't work so I collapsed into bed with a thin blanket and I wrapped my Air New Zealand and Vodafone flags around me and fell asleep despite the freezing cold.

I got up at 6am and started walking back to Pangboche. It was a spectacular day, with Ama Dablam towering into the clear blue sky above me. It was so good to be alive. About halfway back, a friend of Gyurme's met me and walked with me back to Pangboche. Gyurme was extremely happy to see me as he'd been very worried when I hadn't turned up the night before.

I had a shower and got into my Skins compression clothing then I rang home to tell everyone I was ok. They'd been a little worried. The data from the Spot tracker wasn't good enough to prove I'd broken the world record, but Wendy told me that the Spot tracker showed that I'd done the necessary 42 kilometres so I was very happy. I'd given it everything I had and that was good enough for me. It was more about the adventure than any official record for me. And I sure found the place I was looking for – I knew that I had 'it', I was strong!

My body felt good. I was sore but I felt ok. I didn't seem to have any injuries but the two-day walk out the next day would be the real test. The rest of the team arrived and were really happy to see me. Apparently, poor Ang Nuru had returned the previous night to be with the team. He and Nawang had been extremely worried that I hadn't shown up at Pangboche the night before. They had every reason to be worried and, in hindsight, I was probably a little naïve to do what I did. But, hey, no one ever achieved anything exceptional without taking some risks.

Before we left Pangboche, the team stopped to help paint the stupa that we'd funded the cement for. The Lama was so grateful for our help. It was great to be able to do something for the village in such a visible fashion. There were two other stupas that looked quite rundown. Some of the locals told me that these stupas were over 1000 years old. I offered to help repair them but was told that they were happy with them as they were. 'They are our heritage. But thank you.'

When we got back to Kathmandu, I had some important family business to attend to. Maya had turned seven so she was coming to see Everest with Dad. I met Maya and Wendy at the airport. I was excited but Maya was more excited. She loved the trip into Kathmandu from the airport. As I'd done with Ethan, we checked in to our hotel and then went straight out shopping. The Nepalese people just loved my girl and kept asking what her name was. When she said, 'Maya,' they'd say, 'No, no, your English name. Maya is a Nepalese name!' When she told them her real name was Maya, they loved it. In Nepalese, Maya means 'big love'.

That night the whole base camp team went out for a celebration dinner. Nawang, his wife Dolma, and their daughter came with us. Nawang's little girl Karsang was the same age as Maya and they hit it off instantly. They started drawing pictures of their homes for each other. It was really interesting hearing them explain their drawings. 'Here is my house. This is our yak. Here is my grandmother.' Then, 'This is my house. Here is my cat, these are my brothers and this is my pet turtle.' It was priceless.

Wendy only stayed for a day before returning home with the rest of the team. This was my time with Maya. We flew to Lukla the next day, and as usual we went straight to see Dawa at Paradise Lodge. Then we were off trekking. We walked along, chatting away until lunch time. Maya was doing so well. We had lunch and it started to rain, so we put on our raincoats and kept going, stopping for the night in a little village called Benka. The next day we made it all the way to Namchee. It was an amazing effort from Maya – she was so strong and determined, just like her mum!

We spent a lovely couple of days in and around Namchee, staying with Palden Sherpa at Namaste Lodge. We even went to a local school where Maya got to stand in front of all the kids and tell them about her life. Once again, her pet turtle was a source of great interest. Most of the children spoke English and the teacher would translate from time to time.

When one of my local friends, Nyima, came to visit us at Palden's he suggested that we go to the pub for a beer. I refused, saying I couldn't leave Maya. One of the things I found really important about travelling with the kids was that it was vital to make sure they felt secure. I would go to bed at the same time as them and get up at the same time as them. I'd never ever leave their side no matter what we were doing. I found this gave them the confidence to meet people and try things that they might find a bit scary. They could do it so long as they knew Dad was right there with them.

My friend said, 'It's ok. She's seen you drink a beer before. There's no legal age limit for going to the pub here, so let's go.' And off we went. As soon as we got there another Sherpa friend took Maya off to play foosball. She loved it, giggling away, high fiving the Sherpa. It was lovely to see her so comfortable in such a strange environment.

The next day we said our goodbyes and started down the valley. Soon after leaving Namchee, my lower back began to hurt. I had been carrying all the gear for both me and Maya so my pack weighed about 27 kilograms. It was a bit heavy but it was nice trekking with just the two of us and no guides or porters with us. It also helped me to slow down to the pace of a seven year old. As I readjusted the pack, a searing pain shot through my pelvis. It shocked me a little as I'd never felt pain like it. I thought about it for a second, and then told myself to harden up before doing the pack up and carrying on. But something wasn't right.

FALSE START

When I got back to New Zealand, there were just six weeks to go before the start of the 777 Project on 5 July 2012.

I continued training and planned to do two 30-kilometre runs back-to-back, and then taper for three weeks. Something had changed in my running and I didn't feel 100 per cent. As I increased the distance I was running, I developed a sciatic nerve pain in my left glute but I pushed on thinking I could manage it.

As a key sponsor, Air New Zealand supported me by managing all the media and PR for the project. They even made a very tongue in cheek *Catch Me if You Can* style video with me all dressed up in my pilot's uniform walking through the terminal with a beautiful flight attendant on each arm. The attendants then tearily waved me off as I was a man on a mission of my own. They even had me spinning around in front of a green screen in my uniform then again in my running gear, as if I was turning into super running man. I was a bit nervous about it all because I didn't want to look silly but a friend of mine said, 'You're either all in or all out.' I was all in.

Once the video came out, it was fantastic. It went absolutely viral and the project gained heaps of attention because of it. Before long, the project caught the eye of journalists in both television and radio, both in New Zealand and overseas. I even did radio interviews in the Falkland Islands!

Everything was coming together beautifully until I went out for a 21-kilometre run with a few of the pilots from work. A journalist from the *New Zealand Herald* was there to see us off so it was great publicity for the project. I managed to complete the run in just over two hours but it was a real struggle. The sciatic pain was back and it was bad. I pushed through it but there was no doubt in my mind that this whole project was going to hurt … a lot.

The next day I went out for a slow 10-kilometre recovery run just to get thing flowing again. Before I'd even made it to three kilometres, there was a deep grinding pain shooting from my pelvis towards my lower back. I was in agony. I've pushed through the pain barrier many times before but this was different. This was serious. I was scared.

I called my osteopath, Royden McWha, and he suggested I get an ultrasound to find out what was going on. Wendy took it up a notch and called a friend of hers, Stewart Walsh, who is one of New Zealand's top orthopaedic surgeons. He referred me to see one of his friends, Graham Paterson, who is a sports medicine specialist who has worked with all sorts of world champs from the All Blacks to Valerie Adams.

There was no mucking around. I went along to his rooms that evening and he sent me for an x-ray at 9pm. He promised he'd look at them first thing in the morning and let me know what he thought was happening. I really hoped that whatever it was could be easily fixed with a cortisone injection or something. That night I didn't really sleep. So many people were counting on me to make this project happen. I was out there in the media talking about what I was going to do. KidsCan had launched a big campaign … the pressure was very intense.

The next morning the doctor called. He couldn't see anything from the x-rays but wanted me to have an MRI scan – at 9am that morning. There's no time like the present, I guess. After the MRI was done, I headed home to do a couple of media interviews. As soon as I got off the phone, Wendy came into the room looking really upset. Oh god. What was it? What had happened? I could feel the panic rising in me.

'The specialist just called. Mike, I'm so sorry,' she sobbed. 'The MRI has shown up a stress fracture in your lower spine …'

I couldn't believe it. A million things went through my head. What was I going to tell my sponsors? They had put so much into the project. They believed in me. How could I let them down? Oh god, what about KidsCan? I'd convinced them that I could do this for them. I really wanted to be able to help them. And then there was me. I'd been in the paper, in magazines, on the radio talking about this huge challenge and now I'd have to tell them that, actually, I couldn't do it. I felt like I was in a nightmare.

I sat down for a bit and gathered my thoughts. After about five minutes, I pulled myself together and rang Julie at Kidscan, she was really nice and totally supportive. I then called my contacts at Air New Zealand, Vodafone and USANA with the bad news. Every single one of them was supportive and told me not to worry about it. They all committed to supporting me no matter how long it took for my back to heal.

I went back to see Graham Paterson and asked if I could push through the pain and still run the marathons. He said I could. I was delighted. And then came the inevitable 'but'...

'But at some stage, it could completely fracture and you would grind to a complete halt.' The thought of being flown home lying flat on my back in total agony halfway through the project wasn't at all appealing. Thankfully, he assured me that as the fracture wasn't in one of my vertebrae, but in my sacrum there was little chance of any permanent damage. That was a relief.

His advice was that I should rest and recover from the injury. I felt terrible. I had let so many people down, and even though everyone was really supportive, I still felt bad. I cancelled all the flights and hotels. It was a logistical nightmare and it also cost me a lot of money but I had no choice.

I took another team to Everest base camp in October and thankfully didn't have any trouble with my back while I was trekking with them. When I got back I decided to lock in the new date for the 777 Project.

I wanted to do it before the autumn fog set in on the Falkland Islands. There's only one flight a week to and from the Islands and the whole project depended on me making that flight. The earlier I could schedule the run, the better, so I decided 16 February 2013 was the go date. I was happy to finally have a date to focus on but slightly stressed that it only gave me three months to train.

I called Lisa Tamati and she assured me that a three-month build-up would be fine. I was doubtful but she told me that she reckoned the key to my success was mental toughness and that I had heaps of that. I wasn't so sure.

I drew up a training program that consisted of a month's fitness conditioning, a month of four short runs and one long run a week, then a month with four short runs then two back-to-back long runs each week. Lisa looked at my program and agreed that it was ok.

To get my body in peak form for the project, I also took up Pilates. I was assessed by an instructor, and found that my body was completely out of balance. My left side was quite weak so my right glute, quad and hamstring had all been overcompensating. Within a few weeks of working with my Pilates instructor, I was feeling stronger. More importantly, I found my love of running again.

While I was the only one who could sort my physical problems out, the logistics master that was Torran got back into rebuilding my itinerary. Where he could he changed the tickets he'd already booked for me and where necessary he booked new ones.

The months leading up to the start of the 777 Project were really hectic. Trying to balance all of the logistics, media and training was difficult for me and began to take their toll. Luckily USANA stepped up and provided me with public relations support in the form of a fantastic PR person, Nic Carter. It was a huge relief for me to be able to hand over all the media management to her. Nic organised all of my interviews with print media, radio and TV as well as looking after the project's social media presence. One of my friends at work, flight attendant Ashleigh Henwood was studying PR at university, and offered to help out by writing my media releases.

Vodafone kitted me out with everything I needed to stay in touch with home while I was away – a waterproof Samsung phone that would work as a back-up GPS to record my distance, as well as a Samsung Galaxy Note tablet that would allow me to update my website and Facebook wherever I was in the world. I would also be running with a Spot tracker, which would make the whole project more interactive as it would upload my location to the website and people could watch me all over the world. I knew that the more interest there was in what I was doing, the more money we'd make for KidsCan.

There was a USANA conference in Auckland just before the 777 Project started and I was invited to speak. When I got on stage USANAS's True Health Foundation gave me a $2000 cheque for KidsCan and pledged another $1000 for each marathon I completed, rounding it up to $10,000 when I crossed the finish line. I was so stoked. By this stage, donations were rolling in – each time someone made a donation on my website I'd get sent an email causing my phone to beep. It was beeping all the time … All I had to do now was run.

I went to see my osteopath Royden for one final check and he gave me a clean bill of health. Funnily enough, he even commented on how good my knees were. I'd never had any knee issues in the past so I remember thinking it was a bit odd.

Then came my last day of work before taking off for the Falklands. When I got home, the kids were bouncing off the walls waiting for me. 'Dad, Dad, you were on TV! You were really funny.' The sports magazine show *The Crowd Goes Wild* had interviewed me and their take on the project was, as usual for the guys, irreverent. I was comfortable with the report, until I heard the reporter say, 'And he's got a day job, he's a pilot and a damn sexy one ...' Crank up the embarrassment factor to ten! But then, I remembered, I had to be either all in or all out.

There were more New Zealand radio and television interviews and then came my big overseas break. USANA who had employed a top public relations company in Australia asked me to block out a few hours on the day before I was due to leave for the Falklands. Then they sent me a spreadsheet listing 19 – NINETEEN! – radio interviews booked over three hours. It was brilliant exposure for the project, for my sponsors and, of course, for KidsCan.

When I finally got to the airport the next day, all my family were there to see me off. It was wonderful. But I was nervous. As I sat in the departure lounge worrying about flights, delays, injuries, money, and everything else that could possibly go wrong, I had a call from Lisa Tamati. She has a knack of saying the right thing at the right time. 'Mike, there's no doubt you can do this. The only thing that is going to stop you now is if you get hit by a car and break your leg, so relax.' This made all the difference to me. I was off on a great adventure – I was excited.

FALKLANDS

My route to the Falkland Islands was anything but direct. First I flew Air New Zealand to Los Angeles, where I spent a day working through route logistics for my run there. The LA marathon was the one with the tightest turnaround. I planned to be on the ground for less than seven hours so I put that extra day to good use.

The following day, I flew LAN Airlines to Lima in Peru, then on to the Chilean capital, Santiago. When I boarded the flight, I was introduced to the captain. He greeted me warmly, and said in a thick Chilean accent, 'My friend, what you are doing is fantastic. I have a small gift for you – business class.' I was stoked. The more rest I could get now, the better.

With a night in Santiago, I booked a running tour. It's a great service – a personal trainer takes you on a tour of the city but instead of walking or driving, you run. It was a great way to see the city, and for me it was a great way to organise my marathon route. We covered about 12 kilometres of the route that I was planning to run in a few days' time.

The next day I was off to the Falklands on a two-stop service, with stops in the Chilean city of Punta Arenas and Rio Gallegos in Argentina. The whole flight took nine hours. There was only one flight a week to the Falkland Islands so I had to spend a week there before running my marathon on the day the next flight was due to depart.

Landing at Mt Pleasant airport was an unusual experience. The airport is a functioning military base, with plenty of associated activity going on. Clearing Customs was very quick and then it was into the main town, Port Stanley, on a shuttle. I had absolutely no idea what to expect of such an isolated place. I arrived at my accommodation, Lafone House, where I was greeted by the owner, Arlette Betts. When I walked into my room, it was huge with an amazing view. 'Cool,' I thought, 'I can spend a week relaxing here!'

Arlette was a fantastic host, nothing was a hassle for her. She arranged for me to rent a bike and she gave me great advice on island life. That evening I went into town – well, there isn't really much of a town as Port Stanley is very small. I had dinner at a restaurant called Malvina House then I went to the local pub. The locals were very friendly and it would have been really easy to spend too long in the pub. But a hangover was the last thing I needed so I went back to Lafone at a sensible time.

The next morning was spectacular. I hopped on my bike and rode out to see a colony of Magellanic penguins at Gypsy

Cove. The weather was beautiful, not a cloud in the sky, so I rode and rode, seeing only a few vehicles, all British Land Rovers proudly flying the Union Jack from their aerials. I came to the top of a hill looking down on Palm Beach, which had to be one of the most spectacular beaches I've seen anywhere in the world. I could see hundreds of penguins on the sand, so I rode down a small dirt road hoping to walk along the deserted, white, sandy beach. When I got to the end of the beach, there was a fence blocking access to the beach. The fence was covered in signs that all warned of the same thing – mines!

During the Falklands conflict in 1982, which saw the United Kingdom and Argentina go to war over the Islands' sovereignty, the Argentineans planted landmines on various parts of the island. Many of these have since been removed by the British army but unfortunately this beach was too dangerous to demine because the mines can sink and shift in the sand. I did wonder if any of the little penguins ever got blown up but I never found out the answer.

One morning I was at the hotel and Arlette was talking to an Argentinean lady in her 80s who was visiting the island with her two grandchildren, who were aged 12 and 14. She explained to Arlette that she wanted to visit an Argentinean war grave. Arlette explained to her that it was probably over at Goose Green, where there was an Argentinean war cemetery containing the remains of 237 combatants. It was about an hour and a half's drive away from Port Stanley. Arlette offered the lady her car but the Argentinean woman was too scared to drive on the island. I had nothing much planned that day so I offered to drive them on the three-hour round trip.

Situated in East Falkland, Goose Green was occupied by some 1200 Argentinean troops and it was the site of one of the main land battles of the war. It took place on 28–29 May 1982 and saw the deaths of 47 Argentinean and 17 British troops.

We talked the whole way to Goose Green in broken English and Spanish. When we arrived at the Argentinean cemetery, it was very sad seeing all those graves. Surrounding the graves were a whole lot of glass plaques. On these plaques were written the names of the 649 Argentineans killed in the conflict. What a waste of life. I could see the old lady was upset and I just gave her and her grandchildren some space.

As we got ready to leave, she had tears in her eyes as she asked me if I thought it would be ok if she took some earth with her. It was for her best friend whose son was buried in the cemetery. I put my hand on her shoulder and told her I thought it would be fine. I then helped her to scrape some earth into a small plastic bag. She said it was the soil of the Malvinas Argentinas – the Argentinean name for the Islands – and that it would be very special to her friend.

From the cemetery we drove to the Goose Green battlefield before heading back to Port Stanley. She was very quiet on the way home. After a while she turned to me and said, 'I'm 86 and all my life I have believed these islands belong to Argentina. I sang songs about them as a child at school. But it is only now I have been here that I understand they are not. These people are not Argentine, they are British. Everyone in my country should come and see this.'

During my time on the island, I was invited to have a cup of tea with the Governor of the Falkland Islands, Nigel Haywood. It was a real honour so I got dressed up in my best shirt and pants. It turned out the Governor was a bit of a runner himself so I invited him to run with me. Unfortunately, he'd committed to do a half marathon race the day after my run so he couldn't. But he did offer me some help for my run – he offered to leave the front door of Government House open on the morning of my marathon so I could use the toilet and grab some fresh water and food if I needed it.

Before I left I asked him if I could have a photo taken with him. He was very obliging and said, 'Ok, let's do a squeeze and grin.' I was a bit confused, so he explained, 'It's easy, squeeze my hand and grin at the camera!'

I got some incredible insights into what it was like to fight on the Islands one night in the pub. I met a group of guys who had been in the 3rd Battalion of the parachute regiment fighting at Mt Longdon. Twenty-eight British and 31 Argentineans were killed in the battle, with 17 of the British soldiers coming from the same regiment as my new friends. This group of guys were here to climb the mountain before marching back to Port Stanley. Most of them had been shot, blown up or lost limbs during the battle of Mt Longdon. One of them, Jimmy, had been shot in the head and was missing an eye. Their approach to adversity was incredibly inspiring.

Apart from the first two days, the weather had been overcast with drizzle and a cold 4°C. I wasn't worried about the cold but I prayed it wouldn't rain – I knew running in the rain would mean I'd end up with blisters that I would then have to manage for the next six marathons.

When the night before the first marathon finally came around, I set out all my gear. Then I consulted my timetable. I was going to start at 5am Saturday Falklands time, which was 9pm Saturday New Zealand time, which meant I had to be back in New Zealand and finished the last marathon before 9pm Sunday, technically the end of the seventh day.

I woke with my alarm at 3am, ate a USANA Nutrimeal, took some supplements then went back to sleep for a while before getting up at 4.30am. I put on my running gear, GPS watch and my Spot tracker, and then I packed my food for the run, which was a mixture of gels and bars. I cut the first two centimetres down the front of my brand new Icebreaker socks a trick Lisa Tamati taught me to lessen the swelling in my feet. Then I did my shoes up loosely. I stretched for about 15 minutes then plugged in my headphones and listened to some music while I visualised myself finishing, uninjured and smiling. I pictured this over and over in my head as I walked down the hotel driveway to my start line.

Given all the sponsorship, all the work and all the media attention the project had had, the start was very low key. There was no one else there, no starting gun or big roar, just me and my GPS watch. I started my watch then I'm not sure why but I crossed myself and then just started running. It was a very crisp morning. I had two layers of Icebreaker clothing on plus a wind shell jacket but I still felt cold so I pulled out my beanie and put that on as well.

After so many months of planning, it felt great to be actually running around Port Stanley at 5am with no one around. I ran out towards Wireless Ridge to the point where the road stopped then I turned around and headed back towards town. As promised the Governor had left Government House open so I snuck in, used the bathroom and had a drink of water. Then I ran out towards the Stanley airfield. All up this made about 21 kilometres so I planned to do the loop twice. The road out to the airfield was long and straight and the sun was just rising. The colours were breathtaking and I couldn't have asked for a better day.

As I ran, I worked out the distances in my head. I thought I was going to end up back at the lodge a little short of the necessary 42.2 kilometres so I doubled back a kilometre – only to find my GPS clocked over the 42.2 k mark about two kilometres out of town! I had hoped to finish in about 5 hours and I finished in 4 hours and 59 minutes – perfect. I walked the rest of the way back to the lodge to find Arlette and her family out on the deck cheering me in.

I was stoked to have the first run down but I didn't have time to stop and celebrate. I had half an hour to be in the car on my way to the airport. I ate a Nutrimeal, took some more supplements, and then drank plenty of water. There was no bath at the lodge so Arlette had arranged for her daughter to collect me and drive me around to her house so I could have a bath.

I ran the bath, chucked in some ice and hopped in. Whoa! It was cold, Antarctic cold. I hadn't really figured that the water out of the tap would be ice cold anyway. Normally,

I try and stay in the ice bath for 10–15 minutes but after four minutes in the Falklands' bath water my whole body was numb. I couldn't feel my toes so I hopped out and got my Skins compression gear on. The combination of the ice bath and the Skins was perfect for flushing out the lactic acid that had built up during my run.

Then I hooked up my secret weapon, a device called the firefly. Basically, it's a little piece of kit that you stick on the side of your knee and it electronically stimulates the nerves in your leg, causing them to mimic the movement you'd make if you were doing a warm-down exercise like having a light run. The firefly helped to boost my blood circulation while I was sitting down, which I would be doing for the next nine hours back to Santiago.

SANTIAGO

The first sector to Rio Gallegos was short so I only got 20 minutes' sleep and woke up with really painful legs. Thankfully, we didn't have to get off the plane so I could stay seated throughout the stopover. In Punta Arenas, however, we had to disembark, clear Customs then get back on the plane. This meant standing around queuing for an hour with my legs feeling like concrete the whole time.

By the time I finally got to Santiago it was late. I checked in to my hotel at 11pm and the forecast was for a scorching 32°C the next day so I was going to have to start running early. I set about six alarms – on my watch, my tablet and my phone – and I ordered a wake-up call from reception. After a massive two hours' sleep, I woke at 2am to eat a Nutrimeal and top up on supplements before going back to sleep for 90 minutes.

When the 3.30am alarm went off, I was fired up. I got all my gear on and swung into action. When I started stretching, my right knee was a bit sore. It wasn't anything major, it just felt a bit different. I figured it was just a bit of a niggle and off I went.

It was nice and cool as I started running. I'd agreed to do a live interview with Mark Richardson on Radio Sport back in New Zealand while I was running. My phone rang at about the 12-kilometre mark and I chatted away as I ran. I was feeling good and the interview went well, although I think Mark thought I was totally mad.

Running around Santiago super early in the morning was lovely as it was still reasonably cool. I ran a 12-kilometre route that my running guide had shown me the week before. Part of it took me through a park where there were wild pink flamingos standing asleep in a pond. Beautiful.

As I was running I turned to see a very large, jet black American bulldog right on my heels. I just about jumped out of my skin in fright, letting out a little shriek as I did. I must have given the dog a fright as he jumped too. Despite my original fear, he was friendly and stayed beside me for a few kilometres before getting bored. Along the way I saw a few other packs of stray dogs that, thankfully, took little interest in me.

At about the 25-kilometre mark everything started to go a little pear shaped. My right knee really started to throb. It was very painful when I bent my knee even a little. Despondent, I stopped and sat on a rock beside the road. What the hell was I going to do? I was only one and a half marathons in and I felt dreadful.

Everything piled in on top of me – the media, work, my Facebook page, the project sponsors – all these expectations that I'd brought on myself and now it looked like I wasn't even going to finish two marathons. The next three, LA, London and Casablanca, were always going to be the hardest – how on earth was I going to do it?

I put my head into my hands and just sat there. Then my phone beeped. I had left it on after I did the radio interview. It was a woman who posted a note on my 777 Project Facebook page. She said how I had inspired her to start running again after 20 years. Then my phone beeped again and it was another guy from the US thanking me for what I was doing. Instantly, I got to my feet; my throbbing knee was not going to stop me. I kept running, altering my stride, taking smaller steps, searching for a rhythm that didn't hurt, but unfortunately there wasn't one. But I didn't care if I had to use crutches for the last marathons, I was doing this. Pain is only temporary, quitting is forever.

As the temperature rose, I would take an electrolyte tablet and an L-Glutamine pill every hour. I was concerned about the electrolytes as every doctor I had spoken to had told me to be very careful with my potassium levels, as they can affect your heart if they are too high or too low.

I was getting very good at guessing my heart rate within a few beats, even taking into account the pace I was doing and the terrain. I thought my heart rate would be around 135–137 beats per minute but when I looked at my watch, it was 100 bpm. I knew something wasn't right. Could it be the electrolyte pills? Were my potassium levels too high or too low? I just didn't know. Thankfully, there were only a few kilometres to go and eventually my heart started beating normally. Then my GPS watch ticked over 42.2 kilometres and I threw both hands in the air and shouted a loud, 'YES!', gaining me a few funny looks from people in the now-crowded street.

I went up to my room and did my usual post-run ritual – food, drink, ice bath, compression gear. Then I lay on the bed with my feet up on my bags and pillows. I picked up Lisa Tamati's book *Running to Extremes* and it had some great running tips in it. I started thumbing through it to see if there was anything about potassium and heart rates in there when I realised it would be easier to just call the woman herself.

I caught her up on the first two runs then asked her about the whole electrolyte thing. I told her I'd been taking one electrolyte pill each hour and mentioned that my heart rate had been a bit strange. She said she thought I was probably overdoing the electrolytes and to take one every two hours. We agreed that so long as I took some sort of electrolyte and made sure I peed at least a couple of times during each marathon, I would be ok.

I had five hours before I needed to depart for LA so I booked a massage in the hotel's beauty clinic and took my chances. I wasn't sure whether a beautician would be able to give me the kind of sports massage I needed but thankfully the hotel's masseuse was fantastic. She really worked on my knee and sent me off with some medicated cream for it.

I tried to sleep a little before departing for the airport but was too wound up so I decided to get up and pack my gear. I decided that to be safe I needed to pack everything I needed to run a marathon in my hand luggage just in case my baggage went missing. My food was easy, I had USANA Nutrimeals and nutrition bars. Then it was a case of fitting my shoes, orthotic insoles, shorts, Icebreaker running shirt, hat, GPS watch, Spot tracker, iPod, chafing cream, Vaseline, water, sunscreen and running gels into the allowed seven-kilogram bag.

When I got to the airport, the check-in queue was massive. The lovely LAN staff in Los Angeles had told me to ask for assistance if the queues were really long at Santiago. I found a staff member and explained what I was doing and asked if there was any possibility of helping me avoid standing up for the long wait to get to check-in. Unfortunately, the answer was a firm 'NO!' so it was to the back of the line for me.

I queued for about an hour and my legs were absolutely throbbing. Thankfully, the lady at check-in took pity on me and gave me an exit row seat, which meant I could stretch out with a bit of extra leg room. One of the stewards on the flight was an ultrarunner himself so he kept me supplied with bottled water throughout the 13 hours it took us to get to Los Angeles.

Two hours before arriving in Los Angeles, I started eating my USANA food, and then I got changed into my running gear just before we landed. I got some really funny looks from the other passengers. I told my new buddy, the steward, about how tight my turnaround in Los Angeles was going to be. I had just seven hours between landing and taking off again and in that time I had to run a marathon. To help me out he moved me up to the front row of business class so I could get off the plane quickly as soon as we landed. Little gestures like this made all the difference to me as I raced around the world on this crazy adventure.

LOS ANGELES

The plane landed about 30 minutes late, which made my tight turnaround even tighter. As soon as the door opened, someone called out my name and then I was whisked out through Customs. I dreaded having to clear US Immigration and Customs as my travel plans were more than a little unusual. Thanks to my colleagues at Air New Zealand, the Customs officers knew all about me and they cleared me really quickly. A couple of minutes later I grabbed my bag and I was off.

When I got out into the arrivals hall, I was met by our Air New Zealand Los Angeles Airport Manager Sheila, and Thierry, one of our lounge concierges. Thierry was already in his running gear and was ready to run half the marathon with me. Sheila grabbed my bags and we were off upstairs to get a satellite signal for my GPS devices. I did a few quick stretches even though stretching seemed pointless as I was so stiff, and that was it. I pushed the start buttons on my watch, Spot tracker and my phone and then we began running.

For some reason, I've always felt a bit funny about running with other people so I'd always run on my own. But within a couple of minutes, I was really comfortable running with Thierry. Having been on my own so much over the past few days, it was nice to have someone there to talk to. We ran out of the airport and down to the beach, chatting as we went. Before long, Sheridan who works for Air New Zealand in the LA office, turned up with water, sports bars and fruit. It was great to see her. I grabbed a bottle of water off her and kept running. Then a chap called Brian came along and surprised me by saying, 'Hey, Mike, is it ok if I run with you?' I had no idea who he was or how he knew who I was but as we ran he explained that he was from the LA Marathon Club and he'd been following the project on the internet. This really brought home to me that people were actually tracking my progress and knew what I was doing.

A little further down the road, I saw a man I recognised – none other than New Zealand's champion distance athlete, Rod Dixon. Rod had won many races, including a bronze medal at the 1972 Munich Olympic Games, but I remembered him for winning the 1983 New York marathon. As a kid, I'd got up early and watched that whole marathon on television. I'd screamed and cheered as Rod took the lead right at the end.

Dixon lived in Los Angeles and someone on the Air New Zealand team had told him what I was doing and arranged for him to meet me. I couldn't believe my eyes. I ran over and shook his hand. I was like a little kid meeting his hero. I chatted away to Rod saying how I had watched him win the New York marathon on telly, and how much I loved the famous photograph of him crossing the finish line that day. He walked over to his car and brought out a large wrapped flat object and handed it to me. I opened it up and it was a painting of the famous New York marathon photograph. Rod explained that NYC Marathon own the rights to the photo and Rod could not use it so a friend painted a version of the famous photograph. He gave me one of only 50 copies in the entire world.

Rod and I talked for a little while, but I had to keep running. I almost fell over when he asked if he could run with me for a little bit. Now there were four of us running. Rod told me about his Kids Marathon Foundation, which encourages children to take up running by getting them to run the distance of a full marathon but bit by bit over a period of about eight weeks.

I pulled out my camera and filmed myself running along with Rod, I couldn't resist. The hurt and pain seemed to disappear for a while. Once we got down to the beach, almostly directly in front of Los Angeles airport. Rod and Brian both left us so it was just me and Thierry for a while. Then another Air New Zealand staff member called Erica turned up on a bike. Her timing was impeccable as just as she arrived my right knee had really started to hurt.

I told her what was happening and she took off to meet Sheridan. The pair of them went to a sports shop and when Thierry and I stopped for a water break at the 16-kilometre mark, Erica was there with two brand new knee braces.

I slipped one on over my right knee. It was like putting on a very thick tight sock and it felt amazing. Having support for my ailing knee made it so much easier to run. It was starting to get a little hot, but I was feeling good.

The route took us from the airport to the waterfront where we ran along the boardwalk of some of California's most famous beaches – Manhattan, Hermosa, Redondo and Palos Verdes. It was a beautiful coastline and we even saw orcas playing in the waves offshore. It was hard to believe that we were running in one of the biggest cities in the world. The other form of entertainment along the way was the people. I was never sure what I'd see next, from gorgeous women skating past in tiny bikinis, to a slightly overweight hairy man wearing a mankini, which is basically a pair of tiny yellow underpants attached to straps pulled up over his shoulders.

Along the way, Thierry chatted to lots of people, telling anyone who would listen about the 777 Project. They would then clap and cheer in amazement, and getting that bit of support really helped me to keep running. I'm not sure how I would have done it without Thierry. He had only planned to do half the marathon with me but he stuck with me the whole way.

The last eight kilometres seemed to really drag, until I spotted a guy called Michael Callejas along the way. Michael is one of USANA's top associates. With him he had a big bunch of what looked like cheerleaders. They all went mad, cheering and clapping, as I ran along. A few hundred metres down the road there was another group of USANA people cheering me on. Some of them ran with me for a while, patting me on the back, and offering words of encouragement. Those last kilometres were hard but great. As my GPS watch clicked over 42.2 kilometres, Sheridan was right there cheering loud.

Then it was straight off to Sheridan's car. She opened up the trunk and I undid my gear bag, got something to eat then grabbed my razor and started shaving. Sheridan cracked up. 'Why are you shaving?' All I could say was, 'No time – have to go.'

Sheridan dropped me off at the Radisson Hotel at the airport. I checked in at 3.13pm, and my flight to London was leaving at 4pm. I had a quick ice bath and then checked out at 3.29pm. That 16 minutes cost me US$200 and it was worth every penny! I ran outside and there was Sheridan waiting for me. She drove me to terminal 2 where there was an Air New Zealand staff member waiting with my passport and boarding pass. They escorted me through security, where Sheila the Air New Zealand manager for LAX met me. She grabbed my hand and led me towards the plane. At this stage, I was fighting back the tears. It felt like my body was going into shock and my hands and legs were shaking badly. To be honest, if I'd stopped and actually thought about what I was doing, I would have crumbled into a heap on the floor.

Sheila put me on the plane at 3.54pm, the door was shut and we were off. It was a very close call and I am so grateful for all the help my colleagues in Los Angeles gave me to make that tight turnaround work for me.

Settling into my seat, I felt like I was home. My friends

and workmates on the flight were tremendously supportive. They couldn't have done more for me on that flight. A couple of the flight attendants even offered me a leg massage!

Truth be told, I was a mess. My knees hurt really badly but then so did everything else. I thought about taking some painkillers but I was worried about the possible side effects. As soon as I started worrying about my body, my emotions seemed to take over and doubts started to flood in. To stop this from happening, I narrowed my focus and began asking myself good questions. 'What do I need to do now to move forward, to help me heal, to get ready for marathon four?' The more I focused on keeping busy, the better I felt mentally, asking myself good questions was the key.

I felt a little bad for the other customers in business class who had to put up with a train of people coming to say hello to me. I introduced myself to a few of the other passengers and they suddenly understood why I was so popular. They couldn't believe what I was doing and one of them even promised to donate $1000 to my charity. Sure enough, when I arrived in London there was a $1000 donation. I was blown away.

LONDON

After 12 hours, we landed in London at 11am and once again it was my Air New Zealand colleagues to the rescue. I was met by Chris, who had been to Everest base camp with me the year before. He whisked me through Customs and out into the London winter. It was the first nice day they had had for a while, beautiful clear skys but very cold −1°C.

My knees were both swollen and really sore. Thankfully, Chris had arranged for a physiotherapist to meet me at Air New Zealand's head office in London. In typical Kiwi fashion, the physio Brad was married to our London marketing manager, Claire.

As Brad manipulated my knees, he could clearly tell I needed some reassurance. When he stepped back to tell me what he thought, I held my breath. I dreaded him telling me that I couldn't go on.

'Well, Mike, all your tendons and ligaments are fine, they feel strong.' I breathed out and waited for the inevitable 'but'.

'But you have a lot of swelling, Mike. If that fluid gets into your joints you are going to be in a lot of pain.' A lot of pain? What was I in now? I didn't like the sound of that but there was a bigger question playing on my mind.

'Am I doing any permanent damage?'

'I don't think so. There's nothing catching under your knee cap and this swelling will go down when you stop.'

I was happy, very, very happy. If I'd been risking permanent damage, I would have had to reconsider the rest of the challenge. But even though I was in lots of pain, I was stoked that I could keep running. No amount of pain would have stopped me, but a torn ligament or tendon would have … maybe. I still had the back-up plan of using a pair of crutches, even if it took me 10 hours to do the marathon. I didn't mention this plan to Brad as he strapped my knees.

The atmosphere in the office was electric. All of the staff were cheering me on as I readied myself to start running. Just like in Los Angeles, I was going to have company along the way. Running with me were three of the Everest base camp gang, Chris, Jo and Hamish and many other Air New Zealand staff. I hit all the start buttons on my various GPS gadgets and we were off. Chris had organised a fantastic route, starting at head office in Hammersmith then we headed along the banks of the Thames River before crossing over and running back down the other side. I had been really worried about the weather as rain in February is almost guaranteed but London put on a spectacular day. Running around the streets and along the Thames was fantastic. Even though I'd spent plenty of time there before, I was surprised at just how pretty London could be. I guess I'd never spent so long just taking in my surroundings. Along with all the parks and historic buildings along the way, it was the pubs that really intrigued me. There was a pub about every 200 metres along the way and Jo seemed to know a bit about all of them. We gave her heaps about having such a good knowledge of local drinking establishments.

Also with us was my old mate Mikey Davey. We kept in touch and Wendy and I flew to England for his wedding a few years back. It was brilliant to see Mike again, albeit with one fewer toe than he'd had last time we'd met. After he got back from Everest, the frostbite meant he'd had to have a toe amputated. That didn't stop him from running and biking the whole marathon with us though.

The amount of support I had in London was fantastic and it made a huge difference to my mental state. The going was starting to get really tough for me. I felt a bit like I was on a train that wasn't stopping for a week. I kept telling myself over and over again that I was strong and I could do it.

While the scenery was great, running in London was hard as some of the streets were paved with uneven cobblestones, others were made of cracked concrete, and then there were the gravel pathways we took through some of the parks. The changing conditions underfoot made it a bit difficult to get a decent rhythm and I was worried that in my exhausted state I would injure myself by tripping on a cobblestone or a tree root.

At about the 35-kilometre mark, we crossed a really pretty

bridge over the Thames. I'm amazed that I noticed it because by that stage, I had my head down and was really plodding along just keeping myself together. I thought about taking a photo and texting it to Wendy but I was just too stuffed. But then I thought, 'Come on, Mike, harden up. Just take a photo while you're running. Wendy will really appreciate it.' So I fumbled around with my phone, though even that tiny extra effort seemed so hard. I stopped for a couple of seconds, took the photo and sent it off to Wendy. She sent me a wonderful text back that gave me exactly the little boost I needed. It was now getting tough, really tough. Marathon number four, day four, it was cold, I was cold.

My phone beeped and I thought it was Wendy so I looked at the message. It was another friend asking me to 'just take a photo wherever I was and upload it to Facebook'. What might seem like a harmless request that I could easily ignore really rattled me. I got annoyed thinking that if they'd known the state I was in, they would never have asked me to do that. And at that moment, I realised just how exhausted I really was. Because minor things don't normally rattle me.

Whenever I'd spoken to media or updated my Facebook page, I never mentioned how tired I was or how difficult I'd been finding things. I chose to keep it to myself because I felt like if I talked about it, I might just fall apart. The other reason I kept quiet about the tough times was that I had decided to run these marathons for myself, for adventure and to raise money and awareness for KidsCan. No one had made me do it so it would be rich for me to bleat on about how hard it was.

On a quiet London street, 5 hours and 56 minutes after starting, my GPS watch clicked over another 42.2 kilometres. Chris, Hamish and Mike were the ones left with me. We hugged and celebrated briefly before I was on to thinking about the next marathon. Chris Myers, Air New Zealand's then General Manager, UK and Europe, drove me back to Kirsty's house (another cool Air New Zealander) where I went through my usual post-run ritual. Chris then took me to Claire and Brad's place for some serious physiotherapy. And I mean serious – it was 11pm and Brad spent an hour and a half working on my legs before taping my knees and putting on compression bandages. In hindsight, I don't know how I would have survived the rest of the week if it hadn't been for Brad.

CASABLANCA

After three hours' sleep, I was up at 4am to get ready for my flight to Casablanca. Before I left Auckland I thought that one of the hardest parts of the challenge would be having to get up in the morning. Boy, was I wrong. Each morning I would wake up and the switch was ON! No motivation required. This morning I checked Facebook and was really surprised to see a YouTube clip from USANA's CEO Dave Wentz. In it he wished me well and called me an inspiration then said that every USANA staff member and associate around the world was right behind me. This took my spirit to new heights.

This morning was a bit different, because I was going to have company all the way through the next leg. Mikey was coming with me to Casablanca. Our flight transited through the Spanish capital of Madrid, where we had a few hours before carrying on to Morocco. At Madrid airport, I found

Mike Allsop

the nearest wall and lay down with my feet up on the wall, trying to reduce the swelling. As I lay there, I updated my Facebook, caught up on my emails and texted Wendy and the family to let them know how I was getting on. I was so grateful for Vodafone backing the project as it made it so much easier for me to stay connected with the world.

Flying south across the Straits of Gibraltar was really spectacular. I'd never seen this part of the world before and I was excited to be setting foot in Africa. When we arrived in Casablanca, we managed to get into the slowest moving Customs queue ever. When we were finally cleared to enter the country our next mission was to change some money. Unfortunately, that took ages too as ahead of us there were two Saudi guys who seemed to be buying all the cash in the country!

When we arrived at our hotel, we were greeted with typical Moroccan hospitality – one of the hotel stewards in traditional dress served us sweet mint tea. It was really refreshing and the perfect start to our brief stay in Casablanca. Having Mike with me was great as I got to leave all the logistical details to him. While he was dealing with hotel check-in, I went up to the room to get ready to run.

It was already quite late – almost 4pm – but I still made time to lie down for a bit of meditation. It gave me a chance to try to calm down and focus on the run. Unfortunately, all I wanted to do was sleep and I must have nodded off as I woke feeling groggy. As soon as I realised where I was, I flew out of bed and seconds later I was totally in the zone.

One of my favourite sayings is, 'Do or do not, there is NO try.' Yeah, the great philosopher, Yoda from *Star Wars*, is an inspiration! In my head, my voice was yelling, 'This is the time to DO IT, JUST DO IT!'

I ran my checklist, Vaselined all the bits that needed Vaselining and used my anti-chafing cream on some other bits. It must have worked as so far I had had no chafing or blistering at all. I had been running in Icebreaker socks and I'm sure that made all the difference to my feet. Once I was completely organised, I went downstairs to meet Mike. We headed out of the hotel to get a GPS signal then I turned on my Spot tracker. Mike had planned to ride alongside me on a bike but he'd had no luck finding a bike in Casablanca. Instead he decided he would run with me for about 10 kilometres then wait while I ran out and back, then meet up with me to run the last 10 kilometres with me.

The streets of Casablanca were gridlocked with traffic and we weaved our way through the cars as best we could. The car fumes and smog combined with the stopping and starting to get through the traffic made it quite hard to get a rhythm. After about a kilometre, my left leg felt a bit strange, a bit numb. This was not a good sign. A short time later, I had slowed to a walk when all of a sudden my left calf just seized up. A wave of fear came over me. I'd never felt like this before.

I stopped and stretched out my leg. Then I tried to walk a little. It was no good. I stopped again and stretched a bit more. It still really hurt but I managed to start running again … well, hobble would be more like it. In the distance, I could see the Hassan II mosque. This was the biggest mosque in the country and I was really looking forward to running past it.

When I reached the mosque, there was a security guard standing at the entrance to the huge courtyard. As the mosque was a place of worship, the last thing I wanted to do was offend anyone by running through the courtyard. I stopped and asked the security guard if it was ok. He smiled and said, 'Of course, please …' and pointed us on our way.

I forgot about my leg for a few minutes. The courtyard was so beautiful, with its intricate paving. It seemed to stretch for hundreds of metres. The huge mosque building looked like nothing I'd ever seen before – massive and majestic with its tower climbing into the sky. There were so many people around and no one seemed to mind me running along.

As I got to the end of the courtyard my phone rang. I wasn't expecting anyone to call but I answered it anyway. It was Tony Veitch, the sportscaster from Radio Sport. I'd spoken to him a few times and liked his style and questions. He was always positive and upbeat so I agreed to talk to him. It was pretty surreal to be doing an interview with an Auckland radio station from the courtyard of Morocco's biggest mosque.

'So how are you feeling, Mike?' was his first question. 'You must be absolutely shattered?'

I couldn't admit how I was really feeling. 'I'm only talking about the good stuff, ok? I'm moving along and that is the main thing.'

Veitch wasn't having it. 'Come on! You must be stuffed. Tell us how you are really feeling, Mike.'

'It's all good,' I said again. 'I'm moving and that's all that matters.'

Most of the conversation was a blur but just talking to

Tony took my mind off the pain and how uncomfortable I was feeling. When I finished the interview, I seemed to have passed through the little wall I'd been experiencing.

A few kilometres past the mosque was a shanty town of tin houses. There were kids playing outside, so I waved and smiled and shouted, 'Bonjour, ça va?' They spoke back to me in French and I tried my best to answer in French and bits of English. A few of them started running with me, smiling away. They were so curious and friendly – kids are the same all over the world, rich or poor.

It was getting dark and I had only just passed the 10-kilometre mark. My guts were playing up really badly and I had watery diarrhoea – watery explosive diarrhoea. When you're running your fifth marathon in five days, it's not ideal if you can't decide whether you're about to let out a tiny little fart or you're going to completely shit your pants.

It was then we saw the golden arches of McDonald's up in the distance. I knew that a clean toilet and fresh water would be waiting there so I sped up slightly. I popped inside and used the bathroom then left Mike behind. It was the perfect spot for Mike to wait for me while I ran my out-and-backs before picking him up for the last 12 kilometres. Although Mike was very fit, he hadn't trained to run two marathons with me. The previous day he had biked 21 kilometres and then run 21 kilometres with me and today he would probably run another 25 kilometres as well. It was a bloody impressive achievement but then only people with strong mental determination can summit Everest and Mike had it in spades.

I ran along the waterfront and it was lovely. The sun was setting and there were people out and about heading out for dinner. I clocked up another six kilometres and then turned around. There was another McDonald's in the distance, which I figured would be a good place for Mike to wait for me while I ran another loop.

I went back and collected Mike and we headed towards the second McDonald's. I'd run about 22 kilometres by this time and it was starting to get dark and it was getting colder. The mood of the people around us was changing. They seemed to stare at us a bit more, which made me a bit uncomfortable.

We came to a big shopping complex and we started running through the car park to get to the other side of it. Then came the high-pitched screech of a whistle. A security guard was chasing us and calling out to us to stop. Mike was talking to some locals and they reckoned we would be in big trouble for having shorts on. I was nervous.

I stopped and the security guard walked over to me. He was very big, about six foot six, and armed. He was not happy. He said gruffly in English, 'You want to speak English or French?'

'Umm, English please,' was my reply.

'Right, there is NO running in the mall!'

'Oh, ok,' I said. I was nervous so I decided to explain what we were doing. 'My name is Mike, I'm from New Zealand. I'm running seven marathons in seven days on seven continents for charity. Only five other people have ever done it before ...'

He looked like he was going to explode. 'You can run marathons in any other place, I don't care. But there is NO running in the mall!'

'Ok, sir, very sorry.'

Mike came over and we both walked off. Then we got around the corner and started running again. It probably wasn't the best idea but we felt like naughty teenagers getting told off by mall security. The only issue was that this security was armed with an AK-47.

We ran to the second McDonald's and Mike stayed there while I continued running. It was not long after I left him there that my world came crashing down. I went from feeling average to feeling unbelievably terrible. My feet were so painful they felt like they had been pounded by a thousand hammers; every step I winced with pain. I couldn't run anymore so I walked. I drank some water, and ate some energy gels, but nothing made me feel any better.

I called Wendy. She had been watching me on my website via the Spot tracker so she knew I'd slowed down a bit. It was great to hear her voice. I told her how bad I was feeling and she was a great help. She encouraged me saying, 'You can do this, Mike. I know you can. I'll call Monica Lewis and ask her about your supplements and I'll call Lisa and let her know you're going to call her. It's not far now, Mike. Hang in there.'

Dr Monica Lewis, a friend of ours in Auckland, is a doctor and also works for USANA. While Wendy was getting some medical advice for me, I called Lisa. I knew she'd understand what I was going through as she'd been through it many times on her ultramarathons.

'My feet, Lisa, my feet are so painful every step,' I stammered.

'Mate, I know what you're going through – trust me. How far have you got to go?'

'Eight kilometres,' I said.

'Ok, so first things first, you ARE going to make this one, ok? And once you do, you need to rest and get your feet up as much as possible. I'll get Wendy to organise some walking poles for Hong Kong, ok? They will help reduce the load off your feet.'

Just hearing Wendy and Lisa's belief in me really helped me to get going again. I started narrowing my focus to just running another 100 metres, then another, then another. Just like I had done on Everest, I narrowed my focus to a single step.

Eventually, I met up with Mike and he started running with me again. The great thing about Mike was that he would just keep chatting away to me about whatever came into his mind. He didn't care whether I answered him or not and this helped. I tried to talk sometimes but it was mostly an incomprehensible mumbling that he got in response.

We were running through an unlit part of the waterfront that had a motorway alongside it. Both Mike and I kept looking around and, probably typical of any city at night, we felt a bit unsafe. We ran a little and walked a little.

At one point, I stopped to go to the toilet and I stopped my GPS watch at the same time as I wasn't actually running. I was absolutely devastated when I realised that I'd run another 1.5 kilometres without switching it back on. I told Mike that I would stop when my watch said 40.7 kilometres since I'd already done another unrecorded 1.5 kilometres.

He wasn't having a bar of it. 'Yeah, mate, just suck it up and stop when your watch says 42.2 kilometres. If you don't, Mike, you'll really regret it.'

He was right. Of course he was right. This was the worst marathon of the week and the worst run of my life.

When my watch hit 42.2 kilometres – with an actual distance of 43.8 kilometres – Mike and I hugged then flagged down a taxi to take us back to the hotel. It was hell but I'd done it. It was around midnight by the time we got back to the hotel.

Back at the hotel, I ate straight away then got into an ice bath. I had about five hours to rest before I needed to be up for the flight to London. While I was in the bath, Wendy called. She'd spoken to Monica who had told her that I probably needed more calcium and magnesium. She suggested that I took two pills every two hours. I was a bit concerned about overdoing it but she reckoned the main side effect would be diarrhoea, luckily my diarrhoea had cleared up so I could tell if I was overdoing it.

I slept for a few hours but it didn't make a lot of difference. When the alarm went off, I felt as if I hadn't slept at all. Mike and I packed and hopped into a cab to the airport. On the way, I thought about how I would love to come back to Morocco and see the real country, not just 42.2 kilometres of pavement, two McDonald's and the inside of a hotel! The people we met there were so friendly and there is just so much to explore in the country.

HONG KONG

I was booked on a Virgin Atlantic flight to Hong Kong as Air New Zealand didn't fly that route every day. I walked up to the check-in counter and said, 'I have a little story to tell you ...' before launching into my well-rehearsed explanation of the 777 Project. She smiled and the next thing I knew she'd blocked out a whole row at the back of economy, just in case I couldn't get upgraded. She then wished me luck and gave me a pass to the airline's lounge.

When I walked in I was mesmerised. I've been in plenty of airline lounges around the world but I'd never seen anything like this. It felt like something out of *Thunderbirds*. I sat down in the bar area, and was handed the longest bar menu I've ever seen – there was even a separate menu for whiskey! It all felt like a bit of a waste as all I wanted was water. The very thought of alcohol made my stomach churn.

Getting on the plane, I was offered either a premium economy seat or a whole row of economy seats. It was a no-brainer. I took the whole row in economy. It meant that I'd be able to stretch out completely and sleep during the 12-hour flight to Asia. The crew on the flight were absolutely fantastic. I told them about the 777 Project and they made sure I had whatever I needed – food, water, earplugs, you name it.

Once I landed in Hong Kong, I collected my bags and Felix and Viola from USANA were there to meet me. They whisked me into a van and had everything sorted. They'd even worked out that a route I'd chosen to run purely from looking at Google Maps wasn't going to work so they'd put together a new route for me.

As they dropped me at the hotel that night, we agreed to a four o'clock start time the next morning so I could avoid the heat and the smog. I felt like I was finally on the homeward stretch so I slept like a log that night.

The alarm went at 2.30am and I rolled out of bed, ate my usual breakfast of a Nutrimeal and two nutrition bars, then went back to bed for an hour. I set six alarms and they all went off at 3:30am. It's hard to describe the feeling of waking to six alarms knowing you have to run a marathon, the sixth in six days. I was a bit nervous about what the day might hold as the Casablanca run had been so terrible.

I got ready and went downstairs where Felix and Viola were waiting as we'd agreed. Just as I got there, I realised I'd forgotten to do something so I went back up to my room. It will probably sound a bit strange, but I'd forgotten to power pose.

An American social psychologist, Amy Cuddy, developed the idea of power posing. According to her, if you stand in front of a mirror with your arm outstretched like you're a winner and believe that you're a true champion, then this posing has an amazing impact on your brain and, in turn, your hormone levels. Your testosterone spikes and your cortisol decreases. Cortisol is a stress hormone. For power posing to work, you need to hold the pose for at least two minutes. At first I felt a bit silly doing this but I quickly got used to it. I didn't care how daft it looked, I needed all the help I could get.

Felix and Viola dropped me off where I was going to start. Basically I was going to run out and back along a motorway, so I arranged to meet them back at the start after I had run 20 kilometres. Then off I went with a huge smile on my face. I felt fresh and strong. Amazingly my feet didn't hurt My knees were beyond hurt but I just put up with that pain, blocking it out as best I could.

I banged out the first 20 kilometres singing to myself as I ran. The route was a bit of a nightmare as it was along the side of a motorway and there were large buses speeding past me. As they came towards me, I would have to jump off the roadway and onto the berm, which was sometimes covered in thorny bushes.

Running back to the start line, Felix and Viola had arranged to have a team of USANA Hong Kong supporters waiting for me. They were pumped up, cheering and shouting and clapping me in. It was magic to see them. I stopped for a minute and took some photos with them. I had asked for some water and Gu energy gels and sure enough they had them there waiting for me. It was great to have a support team again.

When I started running again, heaps of them started running with me and as they slowly drifted off they had a support van along the way to collect them. When the last person dropped off, I put my head down and banged out the last 15 kilometres on my own. To my surprise my feet didn't even hurt. Monica's calcium and magnesium suggestion had worked a treat. I crossed the finish line and the support team were there waiting. My feet might've been ok but the rest of me was absolutely shot! The second I stopped, it hit me. I felt pretty bad.

I had hoped to get a lift in the van back to my hotel but it was being used to take some of the team home. My hotel was about a kilometre away and rather than wait to be driven back, I staggered back through a collection of shopping malls and walkways. When I got there, the USANA team wanted to do a post-run interview with me. I was happy to do it but I explained that I needed to do my usual post-race rituals – food, drink, supplements and an ice bath. They were happy to wait while I got myself organised.

It took me about 30 minutes to get everything done and head back downstairs. By then, all I wanted to do was collapse on the ground. The cameraman and I went outside for the interview and it was only then that he started setting up his filming gear. I couldn't believe he hadn't done it already but he obviously didn't realise what a bad state I was in.

I did my best to keep it together but the ache in my legs was more intense than I had ever experienced before.

It made me feel like I was going to vomit. All I knew was that I needed to lie down and get my feet elevated. There was nothing else for it, I just lay down on the spot outside the hotel. This really got the film crew's attention. They were really concerned for me. I guess I should have warned them about how bad I was feeling. They quickly got the camera ready and I put on a brave face for the interview. I hate to think how I came across in it.

With the interview over, I had a two-hour nap before going for a massage. Waking up was horrendous as I just wanted to keep sleeping. But the thought of a massage was enough to get me to drag my weary body out of bed and walk 15 minutes to find this massage place.

When I got there, it was actually a beauty salon. I must have looked like a pretty unlikely sort of customer! I explained to the masseuse what I was doing and she couldn't believe it. She was so concerned for me. Thankfully, she was a skilled sports masseuse and she worked on my knees a lot. They were a mess. Fluid from the swelling had got into the joints, which was what was causing the hideous new ache in them. It was incredibly painful to bend my knee even a few degrees.

I couldn't think about running another marathon. I was just focused on whatever I needed to do next. Walk back to the hotel. Pack my bags. Fulfil my media commitments. Call Wendy. Just the thought of coming home brought tears to my eyes.

HOME AGAIN

I got into my running gear just before my flight landed in Auckland. Flying back from Hong Kong was really special as the Air New Zealand crew were all people I knew and they were really excited about the project. More than that though, I knew I was on my way home.

After landing in Auckland, I stopped at the duty free shop and bought some Moët to drink at the final celebrations. As I was shopping, Wendy called and told me to hurry up because there was a lot of media waiting to see me come through. It was all a bit surreal but I managed to think clearly enough to hide the bottles of champagne in my luggage. I figured it probably wouldn't be a good look for a marathon runner to greet the waiting media lugging a couple of bottles of wine!

As I came out into the arrivals hall, I was so thrilled to see Wendy and my family. I was transfixed by Wendy – she looked so beautiful in a long flowing dress. We hugged and I didn't want to let go. But I had a job to do, I still had a marathon to run.

There were three camera crews waiting and I gave them footage from all around the world and then I was interviewed by each one. They were all really nice. But the pressure was on, TVNZ wanted to cut live to me crossing the finish line during their news broadcast at 6.30pm. To meet their deadline, I'd have to run a 5 hour 20 minute marathon – given the week I'd had, that was going to be a hard ask!

The idea was to run straight from the airport into the city, where a welcome home party was waiting. Geared up and ready to run with me was none other than Lisa Tamati. Having such expert company – and a very good friend – to run with me gave me another boost of confidence. I was going to finish this thing, there was no doubt in my mind.

We were straight out of the airport and off running through Auckland's suburban streets. I felt really good – running on adrenalin is the best! My brother Bob couldn't make it because he was working – well, one of us had to be flying Air New Zealand's planes, didn't we? I was stoked to see his wife Jess and their kids Benson and Elsie ready to join us a few kilometres into the run. The kids were on their bikes and Jess ran with me and Lisa.

Around the 15-kilometre mark I started feeling terrible, I felt so low on energy and tired. This was going to be my wall. I walked a bit and then started running again. I would simply have to push through the pain, I had no choice.

At the 20-kilometre mark, I got a call from one of New

Zealand's top sports radio hosts, Murray Deaker. Deaks has a reputation for calling a spade a spade and I was a little nervous about what he'd think of the 777 Project. If he thought it was a stupid idea, he'd surely tell me and I didn't know how I'd deal with it.

Thankfully, he was great. He said he could relate to what I was doing as my marathon times had been about the same as what he'd run single ones in. 'And I had trouble walking the next day, let alone running another six marathons. I take my hat off to you.' I was delighted. The interview carried on for a while and I kept running the whole time. It really took my mind off the pain and it got me through my little wall.

At the 21-kilometre mark, a group of friends were waiting to run with me. I started to get a little emotional just seeing them. Matt, Liza, Carlie, David and Diane joined Lisa and me for the run into town, along with Diane's son Jordan, who was only eight years old.

We all ran through town and along the way other friends would pop out and say hi. Our good friend Pia was driving a support car full of ice and other goodies. At one point, I stopped and bent over with my hands on my knees struggling a little bit. Over came Pia and she rubbed my back for a while. 'Hey, Mike, I don't know much about running but I wore this dress just for you!' She giggled and shook her, how shall I say it, well-endowed chest almost in my face. I saw this flash of flesh in front of me and just absolutely cracked up laughing. It was just this kind of small gesture that really made me appreciate my friends. It put a smile on my face and a little spring in my step.

Running with Lisa was great. Her running resumé is impressive. She's run all over the planet clocking up enough miles to have run around the world almost two and a half times. We get on really well and seem to have a similar mental toughness. At one point, my left calf muscle started to seize up a bit. I tried to stretch it out on a wall. Seeing what was happening, Lisa knelt down and punched it to get it to release. It must have looked absolutely hilarious to anyone going past.

With 10 kilometres to go, Wendy was waiting to run the rest of the marathon with me. She had been training towards doing it and this would be the furthest she had ever run. I was so proud of her. We hugged and kept running another good friend Marie joined us as well Shortly after, a little voice came from behind me, 'Mike, slow down!' It was Wendy. We both laughed. Me? Slow down? I was going really slowly as it was.

Eventually, Wendy got into the groove of it and we ran down Ponsonby Road then down College Hill. Going down the hill with about six kilometres to go my calf finally went into a full cramp and no amount of stretching helped. Pia pulled up in the support car and not even her dress was going to fix this. Wendy went over to the car and pulled out some chewable calcium and magnesium tablets. I munched away on them and slowly hobbled on down the hill. Five minutes later, at the bottom of the hill, my calf released and I started running really freely again.

We ran down to Victoria Park and did a few laps of the park until my GPS clocked over the 37-kilometre mark.

The plan was then to head over to the Vodafone Hub before running the last four kilometres with anyone that wanted to join me.

As I lapped the park, I got a glimpse of all the people waiting for me and I started to cry. A stranger on the side of the road started cheering for me, shouting, 'Unbelievable, Mike, unbelievable. Go, go, go!' I started running as fast as I could. I guess I wanted to blow off all the emotion now so I was ok when I met up with all the people waiting for me. I really didn't want to be a mess in front of them. I just put my head down and ran. Wendy knew what I was doing and kept everyone behind me as I did the last few laps. They were the fastest two kilometres of the whole 777 Project!

After my little blowout I felt heaps better. The emotion had gone and I could simply enjoy the final few kilometres with my friends and supporters. As I ran around the corner of the Vodafone building, I was absolutely staggered. There were hundreds of people waiting there for me. A huge roar went up and everyone was cheering and clapping. Ethan, Maya and Dylan were there giving me high fives. I ran up the stairs and turned around to face the crowd. I'll never forget the look on everyone's faces. I think they were all shocked to see me still actually running. It was magic.

I stood there for a split second, trying to work out what to say. I hadn't even thought about speaking at all. Eventually, I realised there wasn't anything to say except, 'Ok – let's go before I seize up!' and then I started running again.

Together, we all ran through the viaduct area past its trendy bars. I was out the front and there were about 200 people running behind me all whooping and hollering. One of my friends, Ian, was egging everyone on shouting, 'Seven marathons in seven days on seven continents! Let's hear it for Mike!'

There were heaps of kids there, and Ethan was right at my side. I was so proud. I'd missed my kids so much while I was away. Diane was still there with Jordan; he'd completed his first half marathon at eight years old – amazing!

Running towards the finish I looked at my watch. I could still make the deadline for the live news feed but it would mean not running with my three kids for the last kilometre. It was a no-brainer. My kids are the most important thing in the world to me so I flagged the live feed and stood on a park bench and waved everyone past while I waited for Maya and Dylan to meet me. All the other runners would get in first and then line the course to the finish line while I ran across it with my family.

I took off with Ethan, Maya and Dylan knowing that Wendy would catch us up. A few hundred metres later there was the Boeing sales director, Christie, with a heap of 777 hats which the kids put on and kept running. Then along came Nic, the amazing USANA PR person. She quickly explained that the sun was all wrong and that I should run into the finish in a slightly different direction to get the best shots for the media. I took her word for it but all I cared about right then was just finishing.

Wendy caught up and the five of us ran along holding hands and laughing. Then I looked at my watch. It said 42.2 kilometres. I had done it! I stopped and said, 'Guess what? That's it, kids! I've done it – 42.2 kilometres ... it's all over.'

We had a family group hug, and then Maya took off ahead and looked around the corner. 'Wow, Dad, there are HEAPS of people waiting for you!'

'Ok, let's go, let's finish it.' I ran the final few metres down towards the finish line with Wendy, Ethan, Maya and Dylan. The route was lined with people cheering and clapping. When I crossed the finish line, it was a very special moment. I couldn't believe it was actually over. I had done it. All those flights, countries, miles upon miles of running, all the planning, logistics, sponsors, meetings, emails and Facebook updates. Wow. It was over.

I had done it in 7 days 21 hours and 30 minutes. I could barely believe it. But it wasn't just me by myself. Taking on a massive challenge like this project really made me realise how fantastic my friends are – and just how many great friends I have. And it was brilliant to see so many of them there waiting at the finish line.

Two of the first people I saw were Julie and Jan from KidsCan New Zealand. The run had raised $25,000, which would go directly to helping Kiwi kids. In hindsight, I'm probably more proud of the fact that I helped those kids in some small way, than I am about actually crossing the finish line. (This figure was soon to be $75,000 in total after Hyundai New Zealand and their dealer network donated $50,000 after I had made a speech at a dinner for them a few weeks later.)

Straight after I finished the run, I managed to get up in front of everyone and say a few words. But I barely remember it – I couldn't think straight. All I wanted to do was spend time with the family but I knew I needed to ice my muscles. Thankfully, the kids managed to find a way to combine the two things. Along with their friends, they took great delight in taking it in turn to rip off the strapping tape that was holding my knees together while I lay in a paddling pool full of ice. Before the project started, I'd refused to shave my legs – I just couldn't bring myself to do it. And boy did I pay the price. At least with the kids ripping the tape off I had to act tough when really it hurt like hell!

While I was still in the pool, my wonder PR person Nic Carter handed me a phone. I'd agreed to do an interview. I have no idea who it was with and I'm pretty sure I was completely incoherent throughout the talk but I hope they got what they needed.

Once I managed to climb out of the paddling pool, I wandered off to the men's bathroom to get changed. I was so stiff and sore that I could hardly move so my eldest son Ethan had to help me get dressed. I could see in his eyes how proud he was of his dad and that made me so proud. We must have hugged each other a dozen times – I was so happy to have made it back to my family in one piece.

The finish line was at Jack Tar Bar on the waterfront, and there was a bit of a prize-giving do. Paula, who'd introduced me to USANA all those months ago was the MC and she did a great job. It was a real pleasure to have the chance to thank all my friends and my sponsors. One of the things

I learned along the way with this project is that life is made up of moments and we build our lives with these moments. Ultimately, I will not remember most of the marathons, but I will remember the people that supported me, it was the people that made this project so very special to me.

But while I was speaking that afternoon, I made a huge mistake – one that I still can't believe. I forgot to thank Wendy. Throughout the project, and our lives together, Wendy has been my rock. The support she gave me in thousands of ways made the whole thing possible.

After a few more interviews and my first normal meal in ages, it was finally time for me to sleep. Wendy had booked us all into a suite at a five-star hotel in the city. Weirdly, even though I was exhausted I felt quite scared to sleep. I didn't know what sort of state I'd be in when I woke up, if indeed I woke up at all. My brain was just so wiped out I couldn't think straight.

The jetlag did its thing and I slept for a few hours before waking at 3am. I lay there for a while but my mind was wide awake so I got up and went off to answer a whole lot of emails. When the kids got up a few hours later, I took them with me to do an interview at TVNZ at 7am. This time, there was no forgetting – I made sure I thanked Wendy in front of the entire country!

The next day, I went to see Gerald Lewis, a cardiologist who'd offered to give me a check-up. As we were chatting he hooked me up to a cardiogram. When I asked him what he was doing, I wasn't really prepared for the answer.

'Looking to see if you have done any permanent damage to your heart.'

Permanent damage? The thought had never occurred to me. Thankfully my heart was fine. But then he looked at me and asked, 'How are you really, Mike?'

Completely unexpectedly, I started choking up with tears welling up in my eyes. I think I underestimated the emotional toll the project would have on me. While Everest was a lot bigger and harder in many ways, the 777 Project really took it out of me – the mental determination required to keep running, catching the flights and then running over and over again was in a word simply … epic.

After a few days recovery, I went back to work and life started to get back to normal. It was fantastic to be back in my usual routine and my friends and colleagues at Air New Zealand made me feel really special. A lot of our passengers recognised me from the TV coverage and would stop me and have a chat. I loved that it gave me another way to engage with our passengers.

I guess it took about three months for me to feel completely normal again. Both mentally and physically, I needed that time to recuperate so I tried not to put too much pressure on myself. I went for a few runs but nothing major.

I knew I was fully recovered when I started to think about my next challenge. It had to be the one that got away – the world's highest marathon record, the run that broke my back. So slowly I got back into training, back into organising and back into thinking about putting my body and mind through the seemingly impossible. To be honest, my motivation comes and goes but I've learnt that when I'm in the zone I do exactly what I need to do when I need to do it. The most important thing for me was feeling right mentally and not starting to train until I felt good and ready.

Looking back over the last few years, I've achieved a lot of things I'm really proud of. Adventures like climbing Mt Cook and Alpamayo in South America were private feats but they were just as epic and special as my more public achievements of climbing Everest or completing the 777 project.

There's been a lot of publicity lately about climbing Everest becoming easier and that it's not what it used to be. To that I say, Everest is Everest and no amount of money can buy you the summit, no one can drag you up there. The more expensive, fully-guided expeditions in some ways give you a higher degree of safety but they can't carry you to the summit. Every single person who stands on the summit of Everest is strong, both physically but even more mentally strong. And I like to think that I'm like that.

Having done some of the things I've done, some people seem to think I'm some kind of superman. But the truth is I'm just Mike, Wendy's husband and Ethan, Maya and Dylan's dad. As for being a superman? I cry in sad movies, I make mistakes and I'm scared of heights. I reckon all of those things make me pretty normal.

I reckon I've been able to achieve some great things because I want to sit in my rocking chair at 90 years old and look back on my life with happy memories knowing I made the most out of it for myself, for my family and for other people. I want to be able to tell my grandchildren some crazy stories and encourage them to live their lives well and do what they want to do.

Making things happen for me is about three key factors: dreaming big, planning a long way in advance and never ever giving up. Once I'm really sure about something I want to do, I put the plan into action by refining it into smaller goals to work towards the end goal – achieving each of those smaller goals keeps me motivated and gets me closer to my dream destination. The more detailed the plan the better. Sometimes I get it down to steps as small as 'research climbing boots or running shoes on the internet'. Just doing those small things every day means I'm always moving forward towards my goal. For me, committing my thinking to paper (well, to my iPad) works best because that way I can easily keep track of what needs doing and I can also make sure that the forward movement continues.

Telling people I trust about my goals is important too as it means I get help and encouragement along the way, and it also means I'm committed to staying on track towards achieving those goals. This is probably because fear of failure is always a big hurdle. Getting my head around it took me a while as I just hated the idea of letting myself and other people down. But then I realised that if I was scared to even attempt something because failure was a possibility, then I'd never achieve anything. Everyone fails at something, it's just a fact of life and once I came to terms with that, I think it made me a much stronger person. I've failed. When I broke my back before the first planned 777 Project, I saw that as a complete failure. And it was incredibly difficult to come back from (excuse the pun!) but I dug deep, really deep and focused on my goal. Was I scared of failing again? Absolutely. I didn't know how I was going to pull it off, all I knew was that I was going to give it my absolutely best shot. I ignored the odd naysayer and the fear of failure, trusted myself and went for it.

For every negative person, there are usually 99 positive people. They're the ones you want to listen to, they're the ones I drew strength from.

I've learned some good lessons in life along the way: believe in yourself, think outside the square and, most important of all, don't be afraid to fail.

I guess if I had to sum up my story, it's this – work hard, focus on your goals and *never* give up. If you don't give up, you'll always be working towards your goals. We all have challenges to overcome, but everyone can have a life filled with adventure – we can all have our own Everests.

Think about how you want to build your life and ask yourself questions like 'Who do I want to be?' 'How do I want to look back on my life and remember it?'

Get out there, be willing to give it a go and push your limits. We are only limited by the limitations we set upon ourselves.

Thank you for sharing some of my adventures and challenges with me. If you're up for more adventures check out my website <mikeallsop.co.nz> or email me at mike@mikeallsop.co.nz

You'll have a front row view of what I'm up to. See you there!